Dictionary of Occupational Terms

A Guide to the Special Language & Jargon of Hundreds of Careers

Nancy E. Shields

Project Director: Spring Dawn Reader
Developmental Editor: David F. Noble
Production Editor: Sara Adams
Cover Design: Robert Steven Pawlak
Interior Design: Spring Dawn Reader
Composition/Layout: Carolyn J. Newland

Dictionary of Occupational Terms----*A Guide to the Special Language & Jargon of Hundreds of Careers*

Printed in the United States

99 98 97 96 95 94 93 9 8 7 6 5 4 3 2 1

Disclaimer of liability: The author and publisher have been careful to obtain reliable and accurate information in this work but can accept no responsibility for any omissions or errors in fact nor for any decisions made or actions taken as a result of the information provided. As in all things, we humbly suggest that you accept your own judgment as the ultimate human authority.

Send all Inquiries to:

JIST Works, Inc.
720 North Park Ave. • Indianapolis, IN 46202-3431
Phone: **(317) 264-3720** • FAX: **(317) 264-3709**

Library of Congress Cataloging-In-Publication Data
Shields, Nancy E., 1928-
Dictionary of Occupational Terms : A Guide to the Special Language & Jargon of Hundreds of Careers / Nancy E. Shields.
p. cm.
Includes index.
ISBN: 1-56370-054-9 : $12.95
1. Occupations----Dictionaries. 2. Professions----Dictionaries.
3. Vocational guidance----Dictionaries. I. Title.
HF5382.S524 1993
331.7'003----dc20 93-32323
CIP

ISBN: 1-56370-054-9

For my children
Erin and Tom,
and the other hardworking individuals
who have built this great country

Table of Contents

Introduction

What is a COLA and ADA? What does a podiatrist do? What is a thanatologist? The answers to these and many other questions are provided in this book. Many of the words and terms contained in this dictionary are not listed in standard dictionaries, and simple definitions are not easily obtainable from any single source. With the increasing specialization of our labor market, more and more work-related words and terms need to be understood or used. In some cases, the need to do so may come from reading a news article or hearing someone use a term that is new to you. In other cases, you may simply want to learn more about an occupation or the words and terms used in it.

The main purpose of this unique *Dictionary of Occupational Terms* is to bring together words and phrases that deal with occupations in general, as well as related terms from business, trade unions, the Federal civil service, the Armed Forces, labor laws, Federal Government agencies and departments, education, Social Security, and other areas. Knowledge of these terms can have a positive impact on the occupational decisions individuals must make about jobs and careers throughout a lifetime.

Who This Book Is For

The *Dictionary of Occupational Terms* is useful for anyone who needs information on occupations. It is a storehouse of words related to specific jobs, careers, and the broad world of work. One use is for those looking up a specific unfamiliar word or phrase. Others, such as writers and various professionals, may want to become more savvy with the language of different occupations. The index, which cross-references definitions by occupation or topic, will allow you to quickly locate occupation-specific language and definitions.

But there is another use that we think makes this *Dictionary of Occupational Terms* particularly useful for those who are deciding on career directions or conducting a job search. Call it work, a job, an occupation, a career, or a profession. Whatever it is called, the occupation an individual chooses is one of the most important decisions a person can make. The choice of a career dictates not only how, where, and with whom you spend at least a third of your most productive years, but also to a great extent how you will spend your retirement years. Advance familiarity with the language and concepts of particular occupations will help you make sound decisions in the selection of a career.

Long gone are the days when boys simply followed their fathers into farming or mining, and girls stayed home to help their mothers and work on items for a hope chest. Gradually over the years new occupations and new ideas have expanded occupational horizons. Today many families are not surprised if a son wants to become a nurse or if his sister plans to be a physician. Knowledge of the terms in this *Dictionary* will help broaden your awareness of new career opportunities for both men and women.

More recently, rapid technological advances have resulted in rapid changes in many occupations, and drastic changes in our society have complicated the choosing of a career. More women are in the work force. Fewer jobs require manual labor, and more require advanced education or technical training. Jobs have become more specialized, and more people----whether by choice, corporate takeover, or company downsizing----are retiring at an earlier age. The *Dictionary of Occupational Terms* will help you learn some of the new language of today's fast-changing world of work.

This book is also for people who are *changing careers or looking for a job.* Experts say that people entering the work force should expect to change jobs or careers several times during their lifetime as technology, international competition, and changing needs affect their jobs. If you, by choice or of necessity, are thinking of changing careers or looking for a new job, this new book might acquaint you with the language of an alternative career you might be considering.

How This Dictionary Is Arranged

In this *Dictionary of Occupational Terms*, words are alphabetized word by word rather than letter by letter. Numerals are alphabetized as if spelled out. A word in boldface type in a *See* or *See also* reference means that the word is itself a term listed and defined in the *Dictionary*. An occupation or term is followed by the word *military* in parentheses if the relation of the term to one or more of the Armed Forces is not self-evident. The designation is omitted if the term is obviously a military term. **Note:** the *military* designation in parentheses is not considered in the alphabetical arrangement of the terms.

For More Information

This dictionary defines terms related to the world of work from the preparation stage to retirement. Although hundreds of occupations, many of them new and not found in other books dealing with occupations, are briefly described, serious research on a specific occupation should be done in one of the many books that deal exclusively with the distinguishing features of a particular job. The *Occupational Outlook Handbook*,[1] developed by the U.S. Department of Labor, Bureau of Labor Statistics, provides additional information on the nature of the job, employment, working conditions, earnings, job outlook, training or education needed, related occupations, and sources of additional information. For military jobs, additional information about the nature of the job, helpful attributes, work environment, physical demands, training provided, civilian counterparts, and opportunities can be found in *Military Careers: A Guide to Military Occupations and Selected Military Career Paths,*[1] available at most recruiting offices. Many definitions in the *Dictionary of Occupational Terms* contain cross-references to these two resources when further research in them would seem worth while.

1 The *Occupational Outlook Handbook* and *Military Careers: A Guide to Military Occupations and Selected Military Career Paths* are available also from JIST Works, Inc., or through most libraries and bookstores. The books' ISBN numbers are 1-56370-044-1 and 1-56370-124-3 respectively.

◆Aa◆

AARP An abbreviation of *American Association of Retired Persons*. *See* **minorities.**

abandonment of position In the Federal civil service system, the action of an employee who fails to report for duty or return from leave or furlough of 30 days or less and does not submit a resignation.

ability Natural talent or acquired skill. *Examples:* absolute (perfect) pitch as a natural ability; accurate typing as an acquired skill.

able seaman *See* **deckhand.**

absence (or absent) without leave (AWOL) The absence of an individual from duty without prior approval and therefore without pay. An individual who is "AWOL" may be subject to disciplinary action. *See also* **leave without pay.**

absenteeism rate The percentage of people absent from their workplace, school, or other institution.

abstractor An individual who summarizes pertinent legal or insurance details from reference books for the purpose of examination, proof, or ready reference; or searches titles to determine whether a title deed is correct.

academic Pertaining to a college, university, or other educational institution.

academic librarian An individual who works closely with faculty and students in colleges and universities to ensure that the library has reference materials required for courses; helps students and faculty search databases; and maintains research collections.

acceptable level of competence In the Federal civil service system, a level of Federal employee performance acceptable for advancement under the General Schedule. *See also* **General Schedule.**

accession In the Federal civil service system, a personnel action that results in the addition of an employee to the rolls (staff) of an agency.

accidental death and dismemberment (AD&D) A type of insurance, provided by some employers or benefit funds, that pays a benefit in the event of an accident or injury resulting in death or dismemberment.

accompanist An individual who plays a musical instrument for another performer, such as a singer.

account collector An individual who ensures that customers pay their overdue accounts. *See also* the OOH.

account executive **1)** An individual who acts as a liaison between an advertising agency and an advertiser. Responsibilities may include the planning of an advertising campaign, selection of media, research, copywriting, and sales promotion. **2)** An individual who acts as a sales representative for nonfinancial products, such as books and printing. **3)** An individual who buys and sells stocks, bonds, mutual funds, and other financial products for a client. *See also* **securities sales representative.**

accountant An individual who prepares, analyzes, and verifies financial information. *See also* the OOH.

accountant/auditor (military) An Army, Navy, Air Force, Marine Corps, or Coast Guard officer who develops ways to track financial transactions, directs and helps in the collection and analysis of financial data, and examines records of financial transactions to make sure they are recorded correctly. *See also* the *Military Careers* guide.

accounting The practice and theory for setting up and maintaining systems to record and analyze business records.

accounting auditor An individual who evaluates the procedures used by businesses for bookkeeping purposes.

accounting clerk *See* **accounting, auditing clerks,** and **bookkeeping.**

accounting specialist (military) In the Army, Navy, Air Force, Marine Corps, or Coast Guard, an individual who records details of financial transactions on accounting forms, prepares forms for entering payment information into computers, and audits financial records. *See also* the *Military Careers* guide.

accreditation The process of certifying that certain standards or requirements have been met.

Accrediting Commission for Trade and Technical Schools An organization which certifies that private trade and technical schools have met certain standards and requirements. *See also* the *Handbook of Accredited Private Trade and Technical Schools.*

accrue To accumulate through periodic additions or growth. *Example:* interest that accrues daily on a savings account.

accuracy The quality of being exact, correct, precise, or free from error.

acquisitions librarian An individual who selects and orders books, periodicals, films, and other materials and deals with publishers and wholesalers of books, records, and films.

acronym A word usually formed from the beginning letter of words in a phrase or compound term. *Example:* AIDS, which stands for acquired immune deficiency syndrome.

active duty In the Federal civil service system, full-time duty.

active duty (military) In the Armed Forces, full-time duty with military pay and allowances, except for training, determining physical fitness, or serving in the Reserve or National Guard. Active duty includes "annual" active duty for training but excludes weekend Reserve meetings.

actor An individual who entertains by playing a part in the theater or on film, television or radio. *See also* the OOH.

actuary An individual who designs insurance and pension plans after assembling and analyzing statistics to calculate probabilities of death, sickness, injury, and disability, or to calculate probable property loss from accident, theft, fire, or other hazards. *See also* the OOH.

acupuncturist An individual who practices the medical treatment of acupuncture, which attempts to cure conditions and illnesses by the insertion of needles at specific points in various parts of the body.

ad A magazine or newspaper advertisement that an employer can use to solicit applications for an available job (help wanted ad) or that a job seeker can place to notify a prospective employer that the individual is available for particular types of jobs (situations wanted ad). *See also* **help wanted ad, situations wanted ad,** and **blind ad.**

ad hoc arbitrator An individual selected to act in a specific case, or a limited group of cases, requiring arbitration. *See also* **arbitrator** and **permanent arbitrator.**

ADA An abbreviation of *Americans with Disabilities Act. See* **Americans with Disabilities Act.**

AD&D An abbreviation of *accidental death and dismemberment* insurance. *See* **accidental death and dismemberment.**

addiction counselor An individual who assists and advises people who are addicted to drugs, alcohol, or other habit-forming substances.

adjusted basic pay In the Federal civil service system, an employee's rate of basic pay plus any interim geographic adjustment, locality comparability payment, or special pay adjustment (for law enforcement officers) to which the employee is entitled.

adjuster An individual who investigates claims for insurance companies, department stores, and banks; inspects property damage to determine the extent of a company's liability; and negotiates with claimants.

adjustment clerk An individual who investigates and resolves customers' complaints about merchandise, service, billing, or credit ratings.

administration The process of managing an office or institution.

administrative assistant An individual who serves as an aide and performs various duties for an executive or manager.

administrative law judge An individual employed by government agencies to rule on appeals of agency administrative decisions regarding eligibility for benefits, enforcement of health and safety regulations, and compliance with economic regulatory requirements.

administrative occupations *See* **general manager/top executive; hotel manager/assistant;** and **administrator, education.**

Administrative Occupations (military) One of the twelve broad categories used by the Armed Forces to group occupations for enlisted personnel.

administrative secretary An individual who usually works in an office that has a word processing center and whose duties can include filing, routing mail, answering phones, doing research, or preparing statistical reports. Because of the word processing center, the work of an administrative secretary does not usually include dictation and typing.

administrative services manager An individual who coordinates and directs various supportive services for private industry or government agencies. *See also* the OOH.

administrative support specialist (military) In the Army, Navy, Air Force, Marine Corps, or Coast Guard, an individual who types letters, reports, requisition forms, and official orders; proofreads written material for spelling, punctuation, and grammatical errors; and organizes and maintains files and publications. *See also* the *Military Careers* guide.

administrative workweek In the Federal civil service system, a period of seven consecutive calendar days designated in advance by the head of a Federal agency. Usually an administrative workweek coincides with a calendar week.

administratively uncontrolled overtime (AUO) In the Federal civil service system, an increment of up to 25 percent of basic pay paid on an annual basis for substantial amounts of overtime work that cannot be controlled administratively and are required irregularly.

administrator, education An individual who provides direction, leadership, and day-to-day management of an educational institution. *See also* the OOH.

administrator, health services An individual whose responsibilities can include the management of services, facilities, programs, staff, and budgets for a health care facility. *See also* the OOH.

admission A statement, action, or omission that is inconsistent with a party's interest, defense, or allegation, and which may be offered against that party to prove or disprove a material fact.

admissions interview An interview usually conducted by an educational institution, medical/mental health facility, or special housing authority to determine whether an applicant is acceptable for admittance.

admissions officer An individual whose primary responsibilities are managing the process of application to an educational institution and deciding which students will be admitted. Other duties may include preparing catalogs and recruiting students.

admissions requirements The conditions, such as test scores, age, experience, sponsorship, references, and financial assets, necessary for admittance to an institution, program, or facility.

admitting clerk An individual who works in a hospital or clinic and gathers all of the preliminary information required for admission.

admonishment In the Federal civil service system, a supervisor's informal reproval of an employee for improper behavior. An admonishment is usually oral and is viewed as a disciplinary action.

ADP An abbreviation of *automatic data processing*. *See* **automatic data processing.**

adult education teacher A teacher who performs the usual duties associated with teaching but who works with adults instead of children or adolescents. Adult education classes range from basic educational subjects, such as reading or writing, to preparation for a new occupation or courses taken for personal pleasure, such as cooking, dancing, and photography. *See also* the OOH.

adult services librarian An individual who handles materials suited for adults and conducts educational programs.

advance Money or wages paid before goods are delivered or services are rendered. *See also* **draw.**

advance man An individual who precedes entertainers or politicians to make arrangements for their future appearance.

advanced degree program (military) A Marine Corps program in which a master's degree is partially funded for selected officers.

advanced formal school (military) One of the schools operated by the Marine Corps to teach specific job skills to enlisted personnel after they have completed their recruit training.

advanced individual training (military) After basic training, further training to prepare Army personnel for specific Army jobs.

advanced training (military) Courses developed to improve the technical skills of the enlisted work force. Advanced training includes courses covering new or additional job-related equipment or management and supervisory skills. Self-study correspondence courses also are available to enlisted personnel as part of the advanced training program.

advancement A promotion or upgrading in some job area.

adverse action In the Federal civil service system, the removal, suspension, or furloughing of an employee without pay for 30 days or less, or the reduction of an employee in grade or pay.

advertising clerk An individual who takes orders for classified ads from customers for a newspaper or magazine.

advertising copywriter An individual who writes advertising copy for use by publications or broadcast media to promote the sale of goods and services.

advertising manager An individual who is in charge of the advertising department of a company and whose duties may involve the managing of an advertising campaign, or who sometimes acts just as a liaison between the company and its advertising agency. *See also* the OOH.

aerobics instructor A person who teaches individuals or groups to improve physical fitness by exercises for elevating oxygen consumption through increased respiration and circulation.

aeronautical drafter An individual who prepares engineering drawings for the manufacture of aircraft and missiles.

aeronautical engineer *See* **aerospace engineer.**

aerospace engineer An individual who applies engineering skills to the design and development of aircraft. *See also* the OOH.

aerospace engineer (military) A Navy, Air Force, Marine Corps, or Coast Guard officer who plans and conducts research on aircraft guidance, propulsion, and weapons systems; studies new designs for aircraft, missiles, and spacecraft; and helps select private companies to build military aircraft, missiles, and spacecraft. *See also* the *Military Careers* guide.

aesthetic *See* **esthetic.**

aesthetician *See* **esthetician.**

affidavit A written statement made or taken under oath before an officer of the court, a notary public, or other authorized person.

affirmative action A Federal Government policy that requires businesses and colleges to give special assistance to minority groups who have been discriminated against in the past. Affirmative actions can include efforts to recruit minorities, special incentives, and hiring quotas.

affirmative action coordinator An individual who resolves problems, keeps records, and implements programs to ensure that a company or organization is in compliance with affirmative action and equal employment opportunity requirements.

AFL-CIO An abbreviation of *American Federation of Labor* and the *Congress of Industrial Organizations*. *See* **American Federation of Labor and Congress of Industrial Organizations.**

AFSCME An abbreviation of *American Federation of State, County, and Municipal Employees.*

after-tax income Money left after Federal income taxes have been deducted.

age bias *See* **ageism.**

age discrimination The illegal practice of treating employees unfairly because of their age.

ageism Bias or discrimination against older people. *See also* **age discrimination** and **older workers.**

agency **1)** A unit of an organization, business, or government that provides a specific service. **2)** In the Federal civil service system, any department or independent establishment of the Federal Government, including any Government-owned or -controlled corporation that has the authority to hire employees in the Competitive, Excepted, and Senior Executive Service.

agent An individual who acts for or does the actual work of some other person. *See also* various types of agents.

agent, insurance *See* **insurance sales worker.**

agent, purchasing *See* **purchasing agent and manager.**

agent, real estate An individual who sells land or property and acts as an intermediary between the prospective buyer and seller. *See also* the OOH.

agent, reservation An individual responsible for making reservations for people who want to travel by airplane, train, or ship.

agribusiness Large agricultural enterprises that employ modern business methods and techniques to maximize productivity and profit.

agricultural commodity grader An individual who applies quality standards to aid the buying and selling of commodities and to ensure that retailers and consumers receive wholesome and reliable products.

agricultural commodity inspector An individual who enforces rules and regulations designed to protect the public from harmful or substandard agricultural products.

agricultural equipment mechanic An individual who maintains and repairs the various kinds of specialized equipment used on farms.

Agricultural, Fishery, Forestry, and Related Occupations One of the nine primary categories for grouping occupations in the Dictionary of Occupational Titles. Examples: **animal breeder, farm worker,** and **lawn service worker.**

agricultural quarantine inspector An individual who inspects ships, planes, trains, and automobiles entering the United States from a foreign country to prevent the importation of diseased animals or pest-infested plants.

agricultural scientist An individual who develops techniques to improve the quantity and quality of farm crops and animals. *See also* the OOH.

agricultural technician An individual who works with agricultural scientists in food and fiber research, production, and processing.

agriculturist *See* **agricultural scientist.**

agronomist An individual who develops techniques to improve the quantity and quality of field crops, such as corn, cotton, and wheat.

AIDS *See* **acronym** and **AIDS counselor.**

AIDS counselor An individual who assists and advises persons suffering from acquired immune deficiency syndrome (AIDS). *See also* **acronym.**

air-conditioning mechanic *See* **heating, air-conditioning, and refrigeration mechanic.**

air-conditioning mechanic, automotive An individual who installs and maintains automobile air-conditioning units and other equipment, such as compressors and condensers.

air crew member (military) In the Army, Navy, Air Force, Marine Corps, and Coast Guard, an individual who operates aircraft communication and radar equipment, operates and maintains aircraft defensive gunnery systems, and operates helicopter hoists to lift equipment and personnel from land and sea. *See also* the Military Careers guide.

Air Force Under the direction of the Department of the Air Force, whose broad responsibility is to provide an Air Force that is capable, in conjunction with the other Armed Forces, of preserving the peace and security of the United States.

Air Force Reserve Flying and support units of the Air Force.

Air National Guard Flying units and mission support units, based in every state and during peacetime help with disaster relief, maintain peace and order, and provide civilian defense.

air safety inspector An individual who enforces the rules and regulations of the Federal Aviation Administration (FAA). This agency is responsible for the safety of aircraft and the training and certification of pilots.

air traffic control manager (military) An Army, Navy, Air Force, or Marine Corps officer who plans work schedules for air traffic controllers, evaluates job performance of controllers, and manages air traffic control center operations to ensure safe and efficient flights. *See also* the *Military Careers* guide.

air traffic controller An individual who directs aircraft to ensure an orderly and safe flow of air traffic as planes take off and land. *See also* the OOH.

air traffic controller (military) In the Army, Navy, Air Force, or Marine Corps, an individual who operates radio equipment to issue takeoff, flight, and landing instructions to pilots; relays weather reports, airfield conditions, and safety information to pilots; and uses radar equipment to track aircraft in flight. *See also* the *Military Careers* guide.

airbrush artist An individual who uses special art tools, compressed air, and spray paint for painting and restoration. Such an artist may paint advertisements; restore damaged and faded photographs; or color drawings to simulate photographs.

aircraft electrician (military) In the Army, Navy, Air Force, Marine Corps, or Coast Guard, an individual who uses test equipment to troubleshoot aircraft electrical systems; repairs or replaces defective generators and electric motors; and inspects and maintains electrical systems. *See also* the *Military Careers* guide.

aircraft launch and recovery specialist (military) In the Navy or Marine Corps, an individual who operates consoles to control launch and recovery equipment, including catapults and arresting gear; operates elevators to transfer aircraft between flight and storage decks; and installs and maintains visual landing aids. *See also* the *Military Careers* guide.

aircraft mechanic (military) In the Army, Navy, Air Force, Marine Corps, or Coast Guard, an individual who services and repairs helicopter, jet, and propeller aircraft engines; inspects and repairs aircraft wings, fuselages, and tail assemblies; and services and repairs aircraft landing gear. *See also* the *Military Careers* guide.

aircraft mechanic and engine specialist An individual who specializes in the maintenance and repair of aircraft. *See also* the OOH.

aircraft pilot An individual who has met licensing requirements to fly planes or helicopters. *See also* the OOH.

aircraft technician *See* **aircraft mechanic and engine specialist**.

airline reservation and ticket agent An individual who makes reservations and issues tickets for people who want to travel by plane.

airplane navigator (military) A Navy, Air Force, Marine Corps, or Coast Guard officer who uses radar, sight, and other navigation methods to direct the course of aircraft; operates radios and other communication equipment to send and receive messages; and uses radar equipment to locate other aircraft. *See also* the Military Careers guide.

airplane pilot (military) An Army, Navy, Air Force, Marine Corps, or Coast Guard officer who flies airplanes, checks weather reports to learn about flying conditions, and develops flight plans showing air routes and schedules. *See also* the *Military Careers* guide.

alcohol, tobacco, and firearms agent An individual who enforces laws under the jurisdiction of the Bureau of Alcohol, Tobacco, and Firearms.

alcohol, tobacco, and firearms inspector An individual who inspects companies that produce alcoholic beverages, tobacco products, or firearms.

alderman In some areas of the country, an elected official who makes laws or modifies existing laws to improve conditions for those who elected the official.

alderwoman Since the 18th century, a woman who, as an elected official, makes laws or modifies existing laws to improve conditions for those who elected the official.

alien A person from a foreign country who is not a naturalized citizen and, if seeking employment, must present documents that establish identity and employment eligibility. *See also* **employment eligibility documents** and **undocumented alien**.

allegation An assertion made by a party in a legal or administrative proceeding.

allowance (military) Benefits consisting of quarters (housing) allowance and subsistence (food) allowance for military personnel who live off base.

alternative career A career that usually requires similar skills, has similar responsibilities and status, and is a possibility for consideration when an individual wants to change careers.

alternative patterns of work New and nontraditional work patterns, such as a four-day week, flextime, and job sharing. *See also* **flextime** and **job sharing**.

alumni Literally, male graduates of a school, college, or university. As Latin distinctions become less maintained in American culture, the term is being used more and more to describe graduates of both sexes. *See also* **alumnae.**

alumnae Women who are graduates of a school, college, or university. *See also* **alumni.**

ambience The atmosphere, mood, or quality that characterizes an environment. *Example:* a restaurant that has a peaceful ambience.

ambulance driver/attendant An individual who drives an ambulance or assists ambulance drivers in transporting sick, injured, or convalescent persons.

American Federation of Labor and Congress of Industrial Organizations (AFL-CIO) A federation of two large trade union organizations. The Congress of Industrial Organizations broke away from the American Federation of Labor in 1935, and the two became reunited in 1955.

Americans with Disabilities Act (ADA) A law that went into effect in 1992 and prohibits discrimination against disabled individuals in transportation, public accommodations, employment.

amnesty discharge (military) A termination from a continuous period of active duty in the Armed Forces under conditions that are not honorable. An amnesty discharge is not considered to be an honorable discharge.

amusement/recreation attendant An individual who schedules the use of recreation facilities, allocates equipment, and collects fees.

analytical chemist An individual who determines the structure, composition, and nature of substances and develops analytical techniques.

analyze To separate something into parts and to study the parts and their relationship to each other in order to understand a particular problem, situation, or condition.

anchorman The preferred unisex term is news anchor. *See* **news anchor.**

animal attendant *See* **animal caretaker, except farm.**

animal breeder An individual who selects and breeds animals to improve their quality.

animal caretaker, except farm An individual who feeds, waters, and exercises animals; cleans cages; and monitors animals for symptoms of illness. *See also* the OOH, **veterinary assistant, zookeeper, laboratory animal technologist,** and **pet store caretaker.**

animal control officer An individual who works for a governmental unit and is usually responsible for removing dead animals from streets and roads, and for confining and caring for abandoned or unlicensed animals.

animal health technician *See* **animal caretaker, except farm.**

animal scientist An individual who does research on the selection, breeding, feeding, management, and health of domestic farm animals.

animal technician An individual who works under the supervision of a veterinarian and whose duties may include assisting with surgery, doing laboratory work, and performing clinical tasks for animals.

animal trainer An individual who teaches animals to perform in the entertainment industry, work for security companies, or help the handicapped.

animator An artist who draws a large number of pictures that are transferred to film and become the animated cartoons seen in movies or on television.

announcer An individual employed by a radio or television station to report news, sports, or weather. Depending on the type and size of the station, other duties may include playing recorded music, reading commercials, or hosting special types of programs, such as interviews, call-in shows, or swap programs. *See also* the OOH.

annual leave In the Federal civil service system, the number of days per year that an employee may be absent from duties without loss of pay.

annual report A statement issued yearly by a company and can be used as a valuable source of information about a prospective employer. An annual report usually includes statistics about profits or losses, new products, future prospects, and employee relations.

annuitant In the Federal civil service system, a retired Federal civil service employee or a survivor (spouse or child) being paid an annuity.

annuity The annual sum payable to a retired Federal employee.

answering service A service that receives telephone calls and messages for its clients. This type of service is used especially by doctors, entertainers, and small-business persons.

anthropologist A social scientist who specializes in the study of the cultures of people all over the world. An anthropologist is especially interested in the origins, physical characteristics, social customs, language, and beliefs of a particular people.

antiques dealer An individual who buys and sells items from an earlier period. Items at least 100 years old are considered antiques.

apartment manager An individual who leases apartments, arranges for necessary repairs, and enforces rules and regulations.

apiculturist An individual who studies the culture and breeding of bees.

APL An abbreviation of *a programming language*, used mainly for mathematical and scientific computer applications.

apparel worker An individual who transforms cloth, leather, or fur into clothing and other consumer products. *See also* the OOH, **custom tailor, hand sewer,** and **garment sewing machine operator.**

appeal A request by an employee for review of a decision.

appliance repairer An individual who repairs and maintains household items, such as washers, dryers, ranges, and refrigerators.

applicant **1)** An individual who has asked to be considered for a job. **2)** In the Federal civil service system, an individual who has requested consideration for a job with an agency and may be a current employee of the agency, an employee of another agency, or a person who is not currently employed by any agency.

application A written form for gathering information about an individual applying for a job. *See also* **job application** and **Standard Form 171-Application for Federal Employment.**

application essay A short composition required by some educational institutions and businesses for evaluating how well an applicant can express thoughts, interpretations, and information in writing.

application forms In the Federal civil service system, documents such as Standard Form 171 and supplementary forms, completed by persons seeking Federal employment. The forms require information about the applicants' qualifications for the positions for which they are applying and about their suitability for Federal Service. *See also* **Standard Form 171- Application for Federal Employment.**

applications programmer An individual who writes the step-by-step instructions or programs that enable a computer to process information. The work of the applications programmer usually involves business, engineering, or science. *See also* **systems programmer** and **computer programmer.**

applicator, drywall *See* **drywall installer.**

appointee An individual being hired for a position in a Federal agency.

appointing officer In the Federal civil service system, a person having power by law, or by duly delegated authority, to make appointments to a position.

appointment The formal action taken to fill a position with the selected candidate.

appointment, noncompetitive In the Federal civil service system, employment with the Federal Government without competing with others.

appointment, provisional *See* **provisional appointment.**

appointment, superior qualifications In the Federal civil service system, an appointment to a Federal Government position in Grade 11 or above of the General Schedule because of the candidate's superior qualifications. *See also* **General Schedule.**

appointment, TAPER In the Federal civil service system, employment with the Federal Government that is a *t*emporary *a*ppointment *p*ending *e*stablishment of a *r*egister (TAPER), which occurs when there are insufficient eligibles on a register for a particular position. *See also* **register.**

appointment, temporary limited In the Federal civil service system, a nonpermanent Federal Government job appointment for a specified time (less than a year) or for a seasonal or intermittent period.

appointment, term In the Federal civil service system, a nonpermanent Federal Government position appointment to work on a project expected to last over one year, but less than four years.

appraisal interview A type of interview in which the employer attempts to estimate the worth or quality of a prospective employee. *See also* **interview.**

appraise To estimate the value or worth of something.

appraiser An individual who estimates the value of various types of goods, such as jewelry and antiques.

appraiser, real estate See **real estate appraiser.**

apprentice An individual who learns a trade by serving an apprenticeship, which involves working with an experienced, skilled craftsman. In many instances, some type of formal instruction is required in addition to on-the-job training. After a specified and satisfactory period of apprenticeship, the apprentice can advance to journeyman. *See also* **apprenticeship** and **journeyman.**

apprenticeship A combination of on-the-job training and related classroom instruction in which a worker learns the practical and theoretical aspects of a highly skilled occupation, such as carpentry, painting, plumbing, and welding. *See also* **apprentice** and **journeyman.**

approach letter A letter used to establish contact with a prospective employer and to seek advice or information.

approval Satisfaction or endorsement.

Aptitude Area Program (military) An Air Force program which guarantees that qualified applicants will be classified according to one of four aptitude areas: mechanical, administrative, general, or electronic.

aptitude testing Special testing to determine an individual's abilities or talents that can be used for a particular occupation or further training.

aptitudes Special abilities, talents, or qualities. Whereas an *ability* is often thought of a practical skill that has been tested and is ready to use, an *aptitude* is a capacity that is yet to be realized or fulfilled.

aquatic biologist An individual who studies plants and animals living in water.

arbitration A negotiated grievance procedure's final step, which may be invoked by an employer or a labor union if the grievance has not been resolved. Arbitration involves the use of an impartial arbitrator selected by the employer and union to render a binding award or decision to resolve the grievance. *See also* **arbitrator, ad hoc arbitrator, permanent arbitrator, conciliation,** and **mediation.**

arbitrator An individual with special training to act as a third person in a dispute and decide the issue. The arbitration process is used many times when labor unions and employers cannot agree on a contract. *See also* **arbitration, conciliator, ad hoc arbitrator, permanent arbitrator,** and **mediator.**

archaeologist A social scientist who gathers information about a particular culture by excavating and studying the remains of earlier civilizations.

archery instructor An individual who teaches the safe use and recommended techniques of using bows and arrows.

architect An individual who designs homes and other types of buildings and in many cases also supervises their construction. *See also* the OOH.

architect, landscape An individual who designs parks, golf courses, and the areas around homes and other buildings to make the land attractive and functional.

architectural drafter An individual who draws architectural and structural features of buildings.

archivist An individual who preserves historical documents or objects. The archivist's duties may include acquiring, restoring, maintaining, cataloging, and exhibiting the objects or documents. *See also* the OOH.

area of consideration In the Federal civil service system, a geographical area from which, in some cases, Federal agencies will consider job applicants.

area offices of the Office of Personnel Management Offices for administering and implementing all Office of Personnel Management (OPM) programs, except investigations. These area offices provide personnel management advice and assistance, supply leadership for recruiting and examining and special programs, and are the principal source of employment information for Federal agencies and the public. *See also* **Office of Personnel Management.**

Armed Forces The collective term for the Army, Navy, Air Force, and Marine Corps.

Armed Forces experience In the Federal civil service system, when veterans apply for a civil service position, they are given extra points for Armed Forces experience. Usually, an honorably discharged veteran receives five points, and a disabled veteran ten points. Extra points are given also to mothers and wives of disabled veterans, and to widows of those who died in military service. *See also* **preference.**

Armed Services Vocational Aptitude Battery (ASVAB) A test administered to prospective Armed Forces recruits to measure their chances of qualifying for entry and their abilities in four occupational areas: mechanical and crafts; business and clerical; electronics and electrical; and health, social, and technology. Minimum entry scores vary by service and occupation.

Army A division of the Armed Forces and under the administration of the Department of the Army, whose broad responsibility is to organize, train, and equip active duty and Reserve forces for the preservation of peace, security, and the defense of the nation.

Army Civilian Acquired Skills Program An Army enlistment program that recognizes skills acquired through civilian training or experience. This program allows enlisted members with previously acquired training to be promoted more quickly.

aromatherapist An individual who creates fragrances to alleviate some condition. *See also* **aromatherapy.**

aromatherapy The use of fragrances created to relieve a condition. *Example:* an airline that supplies business class passengers with oils that offset the effects of jet lag.

art careers *See* **illustrator, animator, visual artist, sculptor, painter, commercial artist, art director,** and **graphic artist.**

art director **1)** An individual responsible for the visual segments of a film or television program. The art director might be responsible for the sets, lighting, and costumes. **2)** An individual who supervises the design and production of a booklet or other type of graphics presentation.

artificial intelligence The capability of a machine to do some of the functions usually associated only with humans, such as thinking or reasoning.

artillery crew member In the Army, Navy, Marine Corps, or Coast Guard, an individual who uses computers or manual calculations to determine target locations; sets up and loads artillery weapons; and prepares ammunition, fuses, and powder for firing. *See also* the *Military Careers* guide.

artillery officer An Army, Navy, Marine Corps, or Coast Guard officer who directs training activities of artillery and gun crew members; directs fire control operations and firing procedures; and directs naval gunnery operations. *See also* the *Military Careers* guide.

artisan An individual skilled in a particular craft or applied art.

artist **1)** An individual who uses various types of media and techniques---for example, painting, sculpting, or graphics---to express an idea, give esthetic pleasure, or produce a product that serves some functional purpose. **2)** An individual skilled in one or more of the performing arts, such as singing or dancing.

ASAP An abbreviation of *as soon as possible.*

assembler, electrical and electronic An individual who performs work on electrical and electronic components at a level less than that required at the precision level. *See also* **assembler, precision.**

assembler, machine *See* **machine assembler.**

assembler, precision An individual who puts together a part of a manufactured item. The assembly jobs of a precision assembler require great skill, patience, judgment, and accuracy. These abilities are especially important with the increasing sophistication and miniaturization of electronic products. *See also* the OOH.

assemblyman In some areas of the country, an elected official---often a state official---who makes laws and modifies existing laws to improve conditions for the people the official represents.

assemblywoman In some areas of the country, a woman who, as an elected officia---often a state official, makes laws and modifies existing laws to improve conditions for the people the official represents.

assertiveness The quality of confident and assured behavior combined with the ability to present and maintain an opinion, right or claim. *See also* **assertiveness training.**

assertiveness training Special instruction, usually employing behavior modification techniques, to create a confident, assured individual who has overcome inhibitions about expressing feelings and opinions. *See also* **behavior modification.**

assess To determine the value of something for the purpose of taxation, insurance, damages, or fines. *Example:* a house assessed at $100,000.

assets Tangible items of value, such as houses, cars, money, and bonds, as well as intangible items of value, such as motivation, intelligence, patience, industriousness, and interpersonal skills.

assign To distribute work to a particular individual. *Example:* a manager who assigns to an employee the task of building a model.

assistant An individual who aids or works for someone of a higher rank or status.

assistant laboratory animal technician An individual who performs routine tasks associated with the care of small animals, such as sanitizing cages and feeding the animals.

assistant principal An individual who performs a variety of tasks to aid the principal in the overall administration of a school.

assistantship Financial aid given to a college or university graduate student as payment for the student's assistance to a faculty member or for work in a college laboratory.

astronaut An individual who is, or is training to become, a member of a spaceship crew.

astronomer An individual who uses scientific training to answer questions about the universe by studying and analyzing data about the sun, moon, planets, stars, galaxies, and other space phenomena. *See also* the OOH.

ASVAB An abbreviation of *Armed Services Vocational Aptitude Battery. See* **Armed Services Vocational Aptitude Battery.**

"at will" clause Sometimes included in a job application, a phrase which means that the employee may resign at any time and the employer may discharge the employee at any time.

athletic director In an educational institution, an individual who is in charge of the physical education program, the scheduling of athletic events, and the purchasing of athletic equipment and supplies.

attache (military) An Army, Navy, Air Force, or Marine Corps officer who collects and reports information about the military forces of foreign countries, holds meetings with foreign military and government officials, and advises commanders about situations in foreign countries. *See also* the *Military Careers* guide.

attendance officer An individual who investigates excessive unexcused absences of pupils from public schools.

attitude A mental position, emotional feeling, or physical position of an individual toward a situation, place, thing, idea, or some other person or group of persons.

attorney An individual who advises clients on legal matters and represents them in court if necessary. *See also* **lawyer.**

au pair An individual, usually a young woman from a foreign country, who is hired for domestic work and to care for small children as an occasion to improve knowledge of the local language and to experience a new culture. *See also* **nanny.**

auctioneer An individual who conducts a sale by describing items and then accepting bids from interested participants until the highest possible price is attained.

audio control engineer An individual who works in the radio or television industry and regulates the pickup, transmission, and switching of sound.

audiologist An individual who identifies, assesses, and treats hearing problems. *See also* the OOH.

audiovisual production director (military) An Army, Navy, Air Force, or Marine Corps officer who plans and organizes audiovisual projects, including films, videotapes, TV and radio broadcasts, and artwork displays; determines the staff and equipment needed for productions; and directs actors and technical staff during performances. *See also* the *Military Careers* guide.

audiovisual production specialist (military) In the Army, Navy, Air Force, Marine Corps, or Coast Guard, an individual who assists producers and directors in selecting and interpreting scripts, works with writers in preparing and revising scripts, and operates media equipment and special effects devices. *See also* the *Military Careers* guide.

audit supervisor An individual who supervises a staff involved in auditing the books of a large business. The audit supervisor also acts as a liaison with the client and reviews the finished product.

auditing **1)** The process of examining and verifying financial records. **2)** Attending a class in which the student listens to the lectures without any obligation to do work or take tests and for which no credit is given.

auditing clerk *See* **bookkeeping, accounting, and auditing clerks.**

auditor **1)** An individual who examines and verifies financial records. *See also* the OOH. **2)** An individual who listens to a teacher or lecturer but has no obligation to take tests or earn credit. *See also* **auditing.**

auditor (military) *See* **accountant/auditor (military).**

authority The power to make decisions, judgments, and expert opinions.

authorize To establish or sanction officially, give authority to, or empower.

auto body repairer *See* **automotive body repairer.**

auto mechanic *See* **automotive mechanic.**

automatic data processing (ADP) The processing of information by using electronic machinery with a minimum of human intervention.

automatic equipment technician An individual who installs, maintains, and repairs a variety of transmitting and receiving equipment in telegraph company offices and on customers' premises.

automatic indexed increases *See* **automatic pay increases.**

automatic mounter An individual who tends the automatic mounting presses that cut slide film into individual transparencies and seal them in mounting frames.

automatic pay increases Automatic increases in wages when there is a change in some official statistical report, such as the consumer price index, known also as the cost-of-living index. *See* **consumer price index** and **cost-of-living index.**

automatic print developer An individual who operates a machine that develops strips of exposed photographic paper.

automatic transmission mechanic An individual who works on gear trains, couplings, hydraulic pumps, and other parts of automatic transmissions.

automation The development of equipment and processes to make an operation automatic or self-controlling so that human labor is kept to a minimum.

automobile mechanic (military) In the Army, Navy, Air Force, or Marine Corps, an individual who troubleshoots problems in vehicle engines, electrical systems, steering, brakes, and suspensions; uses test equipment to tune and repair engines; and replaces clutches, brakes, transmissions, and steering assemblies. *See also* the *Military Careers* guide.

automotive air-conditioning mechanic An individual who installs and repairs air conditioners and service components, such as compressors and condensers.

automotive body repairer An individual who repairs or replaces the damaged body sections or frames of motor vehicles. *See also* the OOH.

automotive body repairer (military) In the Army, Navy, Air Force, or Marine Corps, an individual who uses pry bars, mallets, and hammers to pound out dented panels and fenders; welds damaged body parts and frames; and replaces damaged body parts. *See also* the Military Careers guide.

automotive mechanic An individual who services, maintains, and repairs motor vehicles. *See also* the OOH.

automotive painter An individual who sands and prepares a motor vehicle for painting and then uses a spray gun to apply several coats of special lacquer. *See also* the OOH.

automotive-radiator mechanic An individual who cleans radiators with caustic solutions, locates and solders leaks, and installs new radiator cores or complete replacement radiators.

automotive service technician *See* **automotive mechanic.**

AUO An abbreviation of *administratively uncontrolled overtime. See* **administratively uncontrolled overtime.**

aviation safety inspector An individual who is employed by the Federal Aviation Administration (FAA) and inspects aircraft to see whether they are in compliance with FAA rules and regulations. Aviation safety inspectors also examine and certify pilots and pilot training schools.

avionics technician An individual who inspects, maintains, and repairs the flight control, communication, and navigation systems on aircraft.

avocation A hobby or a job done occasionally.

AWOL An acronym for *a*bsence (or *a*bsent) *w*ith*o*ut *l*eave. *See* **absence (or absent) without leave.**

♦Bb♦

baby boomers Individuals born between 1946 and 1964, who, because of their large number, cause major economic, cultural, and social changes.

baby-sitter An individual who cares for infants or children at their home on an irregular basis. *See also* **au pair, governess, infant nurse,** and **nanny.**

bachelor's degree A degree awarded by a college or university after the successful completion of four years of study. The degree may be a Bachelor of Arts or a Bachelor of Science.

back burner *Informal:* a program or project that has been given less priority or temporarily postponed.

back pay Money that was not paid when due, usually because of a contract dispute or contract negotiations that were concluded at a later time and which established a higher rate of pay. *See also* **retroactive pay.**

background check/investigation In the Federal civil service, the act of gathering information on a job applicant especially when the job involves sensitive information or requires a security clearance.

baggage porter An individual who carries baggage for travelers at transportation terminals or hotels.

bagger An individual who works in a grocery store or supermarket and bags groceries, carries packages to customers' cars, and returns shopping carts to designated areas.

bailiff An individual who maintains order in a court room, serves writs, and may perform other duties similar to those of a deputy sheriff.

baker An individual who prepares breads, cakes, pies, pastries, or other baked products. *See also* the OOH.

baker, manufacturing An individual who mixes and bakes ingredients to produce breads, pastries and other baked goods in large quantities for sale through grocery stores and supermarkets.

Bakke case A U.S. Supreme Court case in which a white applicant to a medical school charged that his rights had been violated because of an affirmative action policy. *See also* **affirmative action, Equal Employment Opportunity Commission, minorities,** and **reverse discrimination.**

ballpark figure *Informal:* an approximate amount or estimate. *Example:* a company president who gives a ballpark figure for the number of new people to be hired next year.

band manager (military) An Army, Navy, Air Force, or Marine Corps officer who plans musical programs, leads bands and choirs in performances, and supervises training and rehearsals for musicians and choirs. *See also* the *Military Careers* guide.

bank manager An individual responsible for the daily operation of a bank and its employees. *See also* the OOH.

bank teller An individual who processes deposits, withdrawals of funds, and other routine bank transactions for bank customers. *See also* the OOH.

banquet chef An individual responsible for the ordering, preparation, and serving of food to large groups of people, usually at a hotel, conference center, or private club.

bar code A series of vertical bars and half bars that can be read by optical character reader equipment and is used to automate various operations, such as supermarket checkout, library circulation, car rental check-in, and ZIP code reading.

barber An individual who is trained to shampoo, cut, and style hair. *See also* the OOH.

bargaining agent The status conferred on a labor organization receiving a majority of votes cast in a representation election and which entitles the organization to act for, and negotiate agreements covering, all employees included in an appropriate bargaining unit.

bargaining chip *Informal:* a condition or situation that gives an individual or a group a special advantage, especially when bargaining or negotiating. *Example:* a union that uses a serious labor shortage as a bargaining chip in negotiations with management.

bargaining, collective *See* **collective bargaining.**

bargaining, industrywide Bargaining by a labor organization with a whole industry rather than just one business. *Example:* industrywide bargaining with the automotive, mining, or steel industries.

bargaining rights A legally recognized right of the labor organization to represent employees in negotiations with employers.

bargaining unit A group of employees who are represented by a union in the collective bargaining process. *See also* **collective bargaining** and **union.**

barrister *England:* a lawyer who tries cases in higher courts.

bartender An individual who is trained to prepare and serve various kinds of alcoholic and nonalcoholic beverages. *See also* the OOH.

bartender helper An individual who assists a bartender by doing such tasks as keeping the serving area stocked with supplies and removing dirty serving items.

base (military) A locality or installation that a military force relies on for supplies or from which it initiates operations.

base rate The established rate of pay by the hour, piece, or some other measure. Additions to the base rate may be made for overtime work, holiday pay, or a production bonus.

basic formal school (military) A type of school operated by the Marine Corps to give advanced training to individuals who have finished recruit training.

basic pay (military) The amount of pay a military member receives, as determined by pay grade and length of service. Basic pay does not include other benefits, such as allowances and bonuses.

basic rate *See* **base rate.**

basic skills Acquired abilities essential for employment. Examples: reading, writing, and arithmetic.

basic training (military) A rigorous orientation to the military, lasting from six to ten weeks and providing a transition from civilian to military life.

basic workweek Usually consists of five 8-hour days, Monday through Friday.

beautician *See* **cosmetologist.**

beauty operator *See* **cosmetologist.**

before-tax income Money earned from which no deduction for Federal income taxes has been made.

behavior modification A system aimed at changing the behavior of an individual by rewarding desirable behavior and punishing undesirable behavior.

bellhop An individual who carries luggage for hotel patrons and may perform other services, such as unlocking doors or turning on lights.

bench technician An individual who works in a central facility in order to maintain and repair computers and office machines.

benchmark Formerly, a mark made on something (a workbench) from which other things were measured; currently, a standard of achievement or merit by which other things are judged.

Benchwork Occupations One of the nine primary categories for grouping occupations in the *Dictionary of Occupational Titles. Examples:* balloon maker, patternmaker, and sequins stringer.

benefit Something advantageous, used especially for employee compensation given in addition to wages. *Examples:* paid health insurance, pension fund contributions, and vacation time with pay.

benefits, Social Security *See* **Social Security benefits.**

bibliographer An individual who compiles lists of books, periodicals, articles, and audiovisual materials on a particular subject for library patrons.

bicycle repairer An individual who repairs and services bicycles.

bill collector An individual who works for a collection agency and attempts to secure payments from individuals who have overdue accounts. *See also* the OOH.

billing clerk An individual who computes fees and costs; records data; and produces statements, bills, and invoices for businesses and organizations. *See also* the OOH.

bindery worker An individual who performs various operations, such as folding, gluing, stitching, trimming, and sewing, to bind book or magazines. *See also* the OOH.

binding award A decision or an award by an impartial arbitrator to solve a dispute between a union and an employer. *See also* **arbitration** and **arbitrator.**

biochemist An individual who uses scientific training to study the chemistry of living matter. *See also* the OOH.

biographer An individual who collects detailed information about a person's life and may use this information to write an article, research paper, or biography.

biological scientist An individual who uses scientific training to study living organisms and their relationship to the environment. *See also* the OOH.

biological technician An individual who works with biological scientists to solve problems related to living organisms. A biological technician sometimes analyzes blood, food, or drugs or examines evidence in police investigations.

biologist *See* **biological scientist.**

biomedical equipment repairer An individual

who tests, adjusts, and repairs biomedical equipment.

biomedical equipment technician An individual who maintains sophisticated biomedical equipment.

bionic-medical technician An individual who creates bionic body parts for the disabled.

biotech *See* **biotechnology.**

biotechnology **1)** The production of scientific and medical products as a result of research with living organisms. **2)** The industries that produce such products.

bite the bullet *Informal:* to decide to do some unpleasant task. *Example:* a person who bites the bullet and starts figuring his income tax.

black economy *Informal, England:* wages paid to an individual that are not entered in the company's books and on which taxes are not paid. *Informal, U.S.:* underground economy. *See also* **underground economy** and **off-the-books.**

blankbook binding worker An individual who binds blank pages to produce notebooks, checkbooks, address books, diaries, calendars, and note pads.

blasting specialist (military) In the Army, Navy, Air Force, or Marine Corps, and individual who determines the amount of explosives required for each job; transfers explosives from magazines to blasting areas; selects explosives; and assembles charges, fuses, and blasting caps. *See also* the *Military Careers* guide.

bleaching and dyeing machine operator, textile An individual who operates the equipment that dyes and finishes textiles.

blind ad A job advertisement that does not include the name or address of the prospective employer. The applicant is usually instructed to write to a post office box.

blindness Individuals are considered vocationally blind if their condition results in the loss of employment at their present job. For an organization that provides information on career planning, training, or public policy support for blind individuals, contact Job Opportunities for the Blind Program, National Federation for the Blind, 1800 Johnson St., Baltimore, MD 21230. Phone: toll-free, (800) 638-7518.

blood bank technologist An individual who collects, types, and prepares blood and its components for transfusion.

blower An individual who works in a steel mill and is responsible for the quality and quantity of the iron produced.

BLS An abbreviation of *Bureau of Labor Statistics. See* **Bureau of Labor Statistics**

blue-collar worker *Informal:* a skilled or semiskilled factory worker. *Britain:* a cloth cap.

blue-collar worker supervisor An individual who directs the duties of factory or semiskilled workers to ensure that work is done correctly and in an efficient manner. *See also* the OOH.

blue flu *Informal:* a protest or unofficial strike usually by police or firefighters. Individuals in these uniformed services stay away from their jobs by claiming illness.

blueprint A mechanical drawing, architect's plan, or map made by a photographic process which produces the blue background responsible for the name.

board of directors A group elected or chosen to make policy and decisions for a business, institution, or organization.

board of governors A group elected or appointed to direct or control an organization, governmental unit, or institution.

boat engine mechanic An individual who services, repairs, and maintains the various types of gasoline engines used to power boats. *See also* the OOH.

boatswain An individual who works on a boat and supervises the deckhands who carry out sailing/fishing operations. *See also* **mate, deckhand,** and **captain.**

body language Posture, movements, or gestures that communicate feelings, attitudes, or emotions in a nonverbal way. *Examples:* tapping a foot impatiently or raising eyebrows to show surprise or disapproval.

body repairer, automotive *See* **automotive body repairer.**

bodyguard An individual who is hired to escort people and protect them from injury or invasion of privacy.

boiler operator/tender, low pressure An individual who operates or tends low-pressure stationary steam boilers and auxiliary steam equipment.

boiler technician (military) In the Navy or Coast Guard, an individual who operates main and auxiliary boilers; operates the steam turbines that generate power for the ship; and repairs valves, pumps, and forced-air blowers. *See also* the *Military Careers* guide.

boilermaker An individual who constructs boilers by cutting the necessary parts and assembling them according to specifications. Boilermakers also repair boilers and other large metal items. *See also* the OOH.

bonus Something given to an employee, usually money, which is over and above the regular salary.

bonus plan A system that pays employees for superior performance, such as exceeding a production quota, in addition to regular wages.

bookbinder An individual who operates machinery designed to cut and assemble single sheets into units through a process of sewing, cutting, trimming, and gluing. These units are then assembled into bound books. *See also* the OOH.

bookbinding worker An individual who may be involved in a variety of tasks associated with the binding of business forms, catalogs, directories, ledgers, and receipt books. Some of these tasks might include gathering, folding, trimming, and wrapping. *See also* the OOH.

bookkeeper An individual who keeps financial ledgers and journals, prepares fiscal statements, and records money transactions. See also the OOH.

bookkeeping, accounting, and auditing clerks Individuals who compute, classify, and record numerical data in order to develop and maintain financial records. *See also* the OOH.

bookmobile driver An individual who drives a van stocked with library books to specific places on a regular schedule.

bookmobile librarian An individual who operates from a bookmobile to provide library services to members of the community.

border patrol officer An individual employed by the Federal Government to patrol areas near the Canadian and Mexican borders to prevent illegal immigration into the U.S.

bordereau clerk An individual who works as a typist for an insurance company, compiles data, and types applications.

botanist A scientist who specializes in the branch of science that deals with plants and their environment. *See also* the OOH.

bottom line *Informal:* the end or final result of something. *Example:* an impatient shopper who tells a salesperson to get to the bottom line (final price).

brain drain *Informal:* the emigration of large numbers of highly educated individuals from one country to another to earn higher salaries or to enjoy better living or working conditions. *Examples:* scientists, doctors, and other professionals who move from England to the United States.

brainstorming The technique of gathering together a group of individuals for the purpose of generating ideas or suggesting solutions to a particular problem or situation.

brake operator An individual who does the physical work involved in adding and removing railway cars at railroad stations and assembling and disassembling trains in railroad yards.

brake repairer An individual who adjusts brakes, replaces brake linings and pads, and repairs hydraulic cylinders on automobiles.

brazer *See* **solderer and brazer.**

bread baker An individual who produces bread and rolls for restaurants, institutions, and retail bakery shops.

breadwinner *Informal:* the family member who is employed and provides the money for household expenses.

break A brief period of paid time granted to an employee for relaxation during the day.

break in service In the Federal civil service system, the period of time between separation from a job and reemployment, which may cause a loss of rights or privileges.

brewmaster An individual who is an expert in the process of preparing fermented (brewed) beverages, such as beer or ale.

bricklayer An individual who builds walls, partitions, fireplaces, and floors from masonry materials, such as bricks, concrete blocks, and cinder blocks. *See also* the OOH.

bricklayer and concrete mason (military) In the Army, Navy, Air Force, or Marine Corps, an individual who builds foundations and walls with bricks, cement blocks, or stones; uses mortar to set masonry in correct position; and mixes and pours concrete to form footings, foundations, and floor slabs. *See also* the *Military Careers* guide.

brickmason *See* **bricklayer.**

broadcast and recording technician (military) In the Army, Air Force, or Marine Corps, an individual who sets up and adjusts microphones and tape recorders; records sound effects and background music for film, radio, and television; and sets up and operates public address systems. *See also* the *Military Careers* guide.

broadcast field supervisor An individual who supervises the technicians who operate and maintain broadcasting equipment.

broadcast news analyst An individual employed by a radio or television station to analyze, interpret, and comment on news events.

broadcast standards editor An individual who edits scripts for television productions to ensure that they do not violate the moral or ethical standards of the network. An earlier term for this occupation was censor. *See also* **censor.**

broadcast technician An individual who maintains and operates the electronic equipment used by radio and television stations to record and transmit signals. *See also* the OOH, **transmitter engineer/operator, maintenance technician, audio control engineer,** and **recording engineer.**

broker An individual who brings together buyers and sellers of goods and services to produce a sale or an exchange. The broker is paid a commission for this service. *See also* **brokerage; commission; broker, insurance; broker, real estate;** and **broker, securities and financial services.**

broker, insurance An individual who represents many insurance companies instead of a single company. The insurance broker searches various insurance firms for the best insurance policy to suit the needs of a client.

broker, real estate An individual who may work alone as an independent business person, acting as a middleman in the buying and selling of property/land, or may manage a realty office and employ real estate agents who also list and sell property. *See also* the OOH.

broker, securities and financial services An individual who buys and sells financial products, such as bonds, stocks, and mutual funds, for a client. *See also* the OOH.

brokerage The business of an individual (broker) who arranges sales of goods and services. *See also* **broker.**

brokerage clerk An individual who performs various duties to facilitate the sale and purchase of stocks, bonds, commodities, and other kinds of investments. *See also* the OOH.

brokers' floor representative An individual who buys and sells securities on the floor of the New York Stock Exchange. *See also* **securities sales representative, account executive,** and **broker.**

brown bagging *Informal:* the practice of carrying lunch from home to the workplace. *Example:* an employee who economizes by brown bagging her lunch.

brown drain *Informal:* the emigration of unskilled workers from underdeveloped countries to countries where jobs are available and salaries and benefits are better.

brownie points *Informal:* recognition or credit obtained by doing favors for a boss or superior. *Example:* brownie points received from baby-sitting the manager's daughter. *See also* **brownnose.**

brownnose *Informal:* to try to obtain favors, especially from a boss or superior, by using excessive flattery or insincere statements or gestures. *Example:* an employee whose efforts to brownnose the boss were so outrageous that the other members of the department became angry. *See also* **brownie points.**

brush cleaning laborer An individual who clears areas of brush and other growth to prepare for logging activities and to promote the growth of desirable species of trees.

bucker An individual who trims off the tops and branches of trees and cuts (bucks) the resulting logs into specified lengths.

buddy system *Informal:* the practice of hiring or promoting a friend or buddy instead of choosing the best qualified applicant or employee. *See also* **nepotism** and **cronyism.**

budget The sum of money set aside in various categories by a business, organization, or individual for a specified period of time. *Example:* a company's budget approved by the board of directors for the next fiscal year.

budget analyst An individual who examines and analyzes budgets to improve efficiency, increase profits, and distribute funds and resources. *See also* the OOH.

building custodian An individual who cleans and takes care of routine maintenance in buildings, such as apartment houses, schools, stores, or office buildings. *See also* the OOH.

building electrician (military) In the Army, Navy, Air Force, Marine Corps, or Coast Guard, an individual who installs and wires transformers, junction boxes, and circuit breakers; reads blueprints, wiring plans, and repair orders to determine wiring layouts or repair needs; and inspects power distribution systems, shorts in wires, and faulty equipment. *See also* the *Military Careers* guide.

building inspector An individual who checks new buildings or the repairs or alterations of existing buildings to determine whether they meet code requirements and construction specifications. *See also* the OOH.

bulldozer operator An individual who uses a bulldozer to move heavy materials, such as earth or trees at a construction site, or goods, such as coal or grain. *See also* the OOH.

bump *Informal:* a promotion or demotion.

bumping *Informal:* a practice used when the number of workers is being reduced and an employee with greater seniority takes the job of another employee with less seniority.

Bureau of Apprenticeship and Training A U.S. Department of Labor agency that encourages and promotes the establishment of apprenticeship programs and provides technical assistance to program sponsors. Regional offices are located in ten major cities. The main office is the Bureau of Apprenticeship and Training, U.S. Department of Labor, 200 Constitution Ave. NW., Washington, DC 20210. Phone: (202) 535-0545. *See also* **apprenticeship, apprentice,** and **journeyman.**

Bureau of Labor Statistics A U.S. Department of Labor agency that gathers and publishes statistical data on labor-related subjects.

burnout *Informal:* a condition that affects the attitude and job performance of individuals because they are suffering from exhaustion and emotional stress. *Example:* the high rate of burnout experienced by air traffic controllers who have immense responsibility and must concentrate intensely over long stretches of work.

bus driver An individual who picks up and discharges passengers on a prearranged route. School bus drivers are responsible for the welfare of the students who ride their buses. Bus drivers who work for commercial enterprises also collect fares, sell tickets, and give directions. *See also* the OOH.

bus mechanic An individual who repairs and maintains the engines of buses.

busboy An individual who removes dishes and wipes tables. A nonsexist term for this occupation is *dining room attendant.*

business agent An individual in a trade union who negotiates labor agreements with contractors, assigns jobs to union members, and handles grievances. *See also* **union** and **union hiring hall.**

business education A group of educational courses in various business subjects, such as accounting, bookkeeping, and data processing.

business license A document, usually issued by

agovernmentagency,whichindicatesthatcertain requirements have been met or a fee has been paid.

business machine repairer An individual who repairs and maintains office and business equipment, such as typewriters, copiers, and cash registers. *See also* the OOH.

butcher and meat, poultry, and fish cutter An individual who cuts animals, poultry, and fish into smaller pieces, sold to consumers or restaurants. *See also* the OOH.

butler An individual who performs for wealthy people a number of personal services, such as receiving and delivering messages, announcing guests, and supervising other members of the household staff.

buyer, wholesale and retail trade An individual who selects and purchases merchandise from a wholesaler for resale to consumers in a store or shop. *See also* the OOH.

buyout An offer, usually a cash payment, by an employer to persuade employees to leave their jobs. Unlike an early retirement incentive, a buyout is not limited to a certain age group.

by-the-piece A method of payment by which an individual is paid according to the number of items produced. *See also* **wage, commission, salary,** and **tip.**

cabinetmaker An individual who is highly skilled in making items, such as furniture, from wood.

cable equipment technician, submarine *See* **line installer** and **cable splicer.**

cable splicer An individual who repairs, maintains, or completes the connection of electric, telephone, or fiber optic lines to provide power, telephone, or cable service. *See also* the OOH.

cable TV line installer and repairer An individual who places, maintains, and repairs the lines that connect cable customers with the central office or transmission point. *See also* the OOH.

CAD An acronym for *c*omputer-*a*ided *d*esign. *See* **computer-aided design.**

CAD/CAM drafting technician An individual who works with CAD (*c*omputer-*a*ided *d*esign) and CAM (*c*omputer-*a*ided *m*anufacturing) software programs.

CAE An abbreviation of *computer-aided engineering*. *See* **computer-aided engineering.**

cafeteria plan A plan that permits employees to choose benefits from a number of benefits to form a package to suit their individual needs. *Example:* choosing more money and extra vacation time rather than health insurance and tuition reimbursement.

CAI An acronym for *c*omputer-*a*ided *i*nstruction or *c*omputer-*a*ssisted *i*nstruction. *See* **computer-aided instruction.**

call the shots *Informal:* to take on the responsibility of making decisions. *Example:* a person who acquires a new company and calls the shots by making all the decisions about the company's products and marketing strategy.

CAM An acronym for computer-aided manufacturing.

camera operator *See* **photographer.**

camera operator, offset printing An individual who makes a lithographic plate for printing by photographing and developing negatives of the material to be printed.

camera operator, television, video, and mo-

tion pictures An individual who uses various kinds of camera equipment to photograph individuals and events in staged or spontaneous situations. *See also* the OOH.

camera repairer An individual who repairs and adjusts cameras and photographic equipment.

cameraman A preferred nonsexist term is *photographer* or *camera operator*.

camp counselor An individual who leads and instructs campers in recreational and educational activities.

can of worms *Informal:* a troublesome or unpleasant problem or situation. *Example:* an employee who decides not to open a can of worms by filing a sexual harassment charge.

candidate list In the Federal civil service system, a list of eligibles ranked, according to regulations, for appointment or promotion consideration.

candy striper *Informal:* a hospital volunteer who performs clerical or small personal services for patients. The term originated from the striped uniforms that were worn to distinguish volunteers from regular hospital personnel.

canned *Informal:* dismissed from a job.

cannery worker An individual who performs a variety of routine tasks in canning, freezing, preserving, or packing food products.

canon An individual who, in some religious denominations, acts as an assistant to a bishop or cathedral dean.

canvass An inquiry to an individual on an eligible list for a civil service job to determine whether the person is willing to accept an appointment. A canvass inquiry is not a job offer.

captain An individual who plans and oversees the operation of a ship. *See also* the OOH.

card-carrying *Informal:* being a full or an official member of an organization. *Example:* a person who was once a card-carrying Communist.

cardiopulmonary/EEG technician (military) In the Army, Navy, or Air Force, an individual who takes patients' blood pressure readings; operates electrocardiographs (EKGs), electroencephalographs (EEGs), and other test equipment; and helps doctors revive heart attack victims. *See also* the *Military Careers* guide.

career A job or profession requiring some type of training.

career appointment In the Federal civil service system, a competitive service permanent appointment given to an employee who has completed three substantially continuous, creditable years of Federal service. In special cases, career appointments may be given to an individual at the time the person is hired from a civil service register. *See also* **temporary appointment, term appointment,** and **career-conditional appointment.**

career assessment A procedure intended to allow an individual to consider skills, interests, and abilities to determine possible career choices.

career blueprint A step-by-step plan to achieve a certain career or to advance to a higher level in a career.

career center A facility, usually in a school, college, or university, which aids persons seeking or preparing for a career.

career changer An individual who decides to pursue a different career. *See* **job hopper** and **career switching.**

Career College Association The organization that distributes the *Handbook of Accredited Private Trade and Technical Schools*, which lists schools accredited by the Accrediting Commission for Trade and Technical Schools. Copies are available from Career College Association, 750 1st St. NE., Washington, DC 20002. Phone: (202) 659-2460.

career-conditional appointment One of the four types of Federal appointments. This type of appointment is for the three years prior to a career appointment, with the first year of the three being a probationary period.

career counseling Services to help individuals assess their skills, abilities, interests, and aptitudes; determine qualifications required for potential occupations and how the requirements relate to their individual capabilities; define career goals and develop plans for reaching the goals; identify and assess education and training opportunities; identify factors that may impair career development; and learn about resources where additional help is available.

career day A day set aside by some schools to give students access to speakers representing a variety of occupations and to information and representatives from businesses.

career development Programs to enhance an employee's performance on the current job, to teach a new procedure, or to develop an employee's potential for advancement.

career enhancement *See* **career development.**

career exploration Researching various aspects of a career, such as required education, duties, working conditions, and outlook.

career goals The objectives that an individual hopes to achieve in a job or profession.

career guidance specialist A person who counsels and advises individuals on career and education choices. *See also* **career counseling.**

career hop A move from one career to another. Career counselors expect that individuals will change careers from three to five times during their lifetime. *See also* **career switching, job hopper,** and **career changer.**

career information delivery system (CIDS) A system available in many states that permits job seekers to use computers, printed materials, microfiche, and toll-free hot lines to obtain information on occupations, educational opportunities, student financial aid, apprenticeships, and military careers. CIDS can be found in some high schools, colleges, universities, vocational schools, libraries, vocational rehabilitation centers, and employment offices.

career ladder A series of developmental positions of increasing difficulty in the same line of work through which an employee may progress. *Example:* a school paraprofessional who becomes a fully licensed teacher.

career path A defined course of jobs that can lead to better pay and increased responsibility. *See also* **career ladder.**

career planning An organized system of deciding the various steps needed to attain a chosen career.

career planning counselor A specially trained professional who advises and assists students and other persons in all phases of career planning. *See also* the OOH.

career plateau A stage in an individual's career when it appears that no progress is being made toward a better job or increased pay.

career research The process of gathering career information usually found in libraries and guidance departments or from career counselors.

career reserved position In the Federal civil service system and within the Senior Executive Service of the Federal Government, a position that has a specific requirement for impartiality and may be filled only by career appointment.

career strategies Various techniques or methods that can be used to achieve or advance a career. *Examples:* resume writing, interview techniques, and networking.

career switching Changing from one career to another. *See also* **career hop, job hopper,** and **career changer.**

career values Beliefs, customs, or ideals that an individual may take into consideration when choosing a career. *Examples:* beliefs or ideals relating to conservation, ecology, or health care.

careerism The practice of seeking one's professional advancement by all means possible.

careerist An individual who has a career.

caretaker An individual who is paid by the owner of a home to oversee the general care and maintenance of the house.

cargo specialist (military) In the Army, Navy, Air Force, Marine Corps, or Coast Guard, an individual who loads supplies or equipment into trucks, transport planes, or railway cars. *See also* the *Military Careers* guide.

caricaturist An artist who draws portraits that exaggerate or distort some feature of a person to satirize or ridicule the individual.

carpenter An individual who performs a variety of tasks associated with building with wood, such as constructing a framework, building partitions, and installing paneling or flooring. *See also* the OOH.

carpenter (military) In the Army, Navy, Air

Force, Marine Corps, or Coast Guard, an individual who erects wood frames, lays roofing materials, installs plasterboard, and lays floors. *See also* the *Military Careers* guide.

carpet cleaner An individual who cleans rugs and carpets. Work on wall-to-wall carpeting is done at the home or business, but rugs are sometimes removed to a shop for cleaning.

carpet installer An individual who specializes in laying rugs and carpets in homes and public buildings. *See also* the OOH.

carry the can *Informal, Britain:* to hold responsible or accountable.

cartographer An individual who uses aerial photographs, satellite data, and information from geodetic surveys to prepare maps.

cartoonist An artist who specializes in drawing comic strips or political cartoons.

case aides An individual who works with human services workers and may provide information and transport or accompany clients to medical facilities or meal sites.

caseworker *See* **social worker.**

caseworker and counselor (military) In the Army, Navy, Air Force, Marine Corps, or Coast Guard, an individual who interviews personnel who request help or are referred by their commanders; identifies personal problems and determines the need for professional help; and counsels personnel and their families. *See also* the *Military Careers* guide.

cash register servicer An individual who repairs and maintains cash registers used in business establishments.

cashier An individual who adds up bills, receives money, and makes change in supermarkets, restaurants, stores, theaters, and other types of businesses. *See also* the OOH.

casual worker In the United States Postal Service, a noncareer employee with a limited-term appointment.

casualty insurance agent/broker An individual who sells insurance policies that protect individuals and businesses from financial loss as a result of automobile accidents, fire, theft, or other catastrophes. *See also* **insurance sales worker.**

cataloger An individual who prepares the information that enables a library patron to find needed materials. This information may be on catalog cards or a computer. *See also* **classifier, librarian,** and **media specialist.**

caterer An individual who is hired to provide a service, such as supplying food and beverages for a party or meeting.

catering A business that provides a needed service for a fee.

Catholic priest *See* **Roman Catholic priest.**

ceiling, glass *See* **glass ceiling.**

ceiling, personnel The maximum number of employees authorized at a given time.

cellular technician An individual who repairs portable, transportable, and mobile cellular telephones.

cement mason and terrazzo worker A cement mason is an individual involved with the placing and finishing of concrete usually at construction sites. The tasks of a terrazzo worker are similar because they involve making patios, walkways, and floors of concrete decorated with marble chips or stones. *See also* the OOH and **concrete mason.**

cementing and gluing machine operator and tender An individual who operates and tends cementing and gluing machines used to join various materials.

cemetery worker An individual who prepares graves and maintains the cemetery grounds.

censor An individual who examines scripts, articles, films, and books to ensure that they do not violate the moral or ethical standards of the organization. *See also* **broadcast standards editor.**

Central Intelligence Agency (CIA) The Central Intelligence Agency collects, evaluates, and disseminates vital information on political, military, economic, scientific, and other developments abroad needed to safeguard national security.

central office equipment installer An individual who sets up, rearranges, or removes switching and dialing equipment used in central telephone offices. *See also* the OOH.

central office operator An individual who

works in a central telephone office and assists customers with calls that cannot be dialed directly, calls from mobile phones, and collect calls. *See also* the OOH.

central office repairer An individual who tests, repairs, and maintains various kinds of switching equipment. *See also* the OOH.

central office technician *See* **central office repairer.**

centralization The consolidation of business functions into a single authority that makes decisions for the various company units in other areas. *See also* **decentralization.**

CEO An abbreviation of *chief executive officer*. *See* **chief executive officer.**

ceramic engineer An individual who specializes in the development of ceramic materials, as well as the methods for using ceramic materials to make various products. *See also* the OOH.

certificate In the Federal civil service system, a list of eligibles taken from a register and submitted to an appointing officer for appointment or promotion consideration. *See also* **candidate list** and **eligible list.**

certification **1)** The act of confirming that certain acts or statements are true. Certain occupations are described as certified (for example, a CPA-certified public accountant). **2)** The process by which eligible individuals for Federal Government jobs are ranked for appointment or promotion consideration. *See also* **certification requirements, candidate list,** and **certificate.**

certification requirements Items needed for receiving a document or certificate stating that a certain level or status has been achieved. Requirements may include education, experience, and written examination. *See also* **certification.**

certification, selective In the Federal civil service system, the act of certifying only the names of eligible individuals for Federal Government jobs who have special qualifications required to fill particular vacant positions.

certification, top of the register The act of certifying in regular order, beginning at the top of the register for the names of individuals most eligible for a Federal Government job. *See also* **certification** and **selective.**

certified arbitrator An individual who has fulfilled the certification requirements for arbitrators. *See also* **arbitrator, arbitration, mediator,** and **conciliator.**

certified public accountant (CPA) An accountant who has fulfilled the certification requirements of an examining board.

chair A unisex term for chairman. *See* **chairman.**

chairman **1)** The presiding officer for a meeting, committee, or board. **2)** The person in charge of a department in an educational institution. A nonsexist term is *chairperson* or *chair*.

chairperson A unisex term for chairman. *See* **chairman.**

chamber of commerce An organization of businesses and organizations whose main purpose is the promotion of the businesses and the community and can be used as a source of information about employers in the area.

change in duty station A personnel action by the Federal Government that changes an employee from one geographical location to another in the same agency.

change of appointing office In the Federal civil service system, the movement of an employee from the jurisdiction of one appointing officer in an agency to that of another appointing officer in the same agency. This move usually involves a change from a position for which one personnel office provides service and maintains records to a position for which another personnel office in the same agency provides service and maintains records.

change to lower grade In the Federal civil service system, the act of downgrading a Federal position or reducing an employee's grade. *See also* **demotion.**

chaplain A member of the clergy who ministers to people in institutions, such as colleges, universities, hospitals, or prisons, or to members of the Armed Forces.

chaplain (military) In the Army, Navy, or Air

Force, an individual who conducts worship services, religious rites, and ceremonies and provides spiritual guidance to military personnel and their families. *See also* the *Military Careers* guide.

character evidence Information about a person's traits or qualities, usually offered through opinion testimony or testimony as to reputation. *See also* **background check/investigation.**

charge account clerk An individual who interviews applicants for credit cards and helps them fill out the application. *See also* the OOH.

chaser An individual who directs the placement of logs at landings and disengages their chokers (chains or steel cables).

chauffeur An individual who drives an automobile or limousine for a business or private employer.

checker 1) An individual who totals the charges for purchases in a supermarket, receives money, makes change, and bags items. *See also* the OOH. 2) An individual who checks materials, supplies, and equipment.

checkout clerk *See* **checker.**

chef An individual who is highly skilled in the preparation and presentation of food and has graduated from a culinary school or has served an apprenticeship under another chef. *See also* the OOH.

chef de garde manger An individual who preserves and produces cold food items for a restaurant.

chemical engineer An engineer who specializes in manufacturing or production processes that use or produce chemicals or chemical products. *See also* the OOH.

chemical equipment controller and operator An individual who controls or operates equipment to regulate chemical changes or reactions in the processing of industrial or consumer products.

chemical equipment tender An individual who tends equipment such as fermenting tanks, devulcanizers, and reactor vessels, in which a chemical change or reaction takes place.

chemical plant and system operator An individual who controls and operates an entire chemical process or system of machines, such as reduction pots and heated air towers, through the use of panelboards, control boards, or semiautomatic equipment.

chemical technician A skilled individual who works with chemical engineers and scientists in the development and use of chemical products. Chemical technicians specialize in the practical aspects of the process by doing tests and collecting and analyzing research information. *See also* the OOH.

chemist A scientist who uses knowledge of chemicals and chemistry to research and develop new chemical products and processes. *See also* the OOH.

chemist (military) An Army, Navy, Air Force, Marine Corps, or Coast Guard officer who conducts experiments in chemical synthesis, structure, and interactions; tests materials; and directs research for military and medical purposes. *See also* the *Military Careers* guide.

chief engineer An individual who supervises the technicians who operate and maintain broadcasting equipment.

chief executive, government *See* **government chief executive and legislator.**

chief executive officer (CEO) An individual who is in charge of the operation of a large corporation or organization and with the board of directors develops the policies that govern the company. *See also* the OOH.

child abuse worker *See* **human services worker.**

child health associate *See* **physician assistant.**

child welfare worker *See* **social worker.**

childcare A benefit provided by some employers to accommodate increasing numbers of working mothers. *See also* **fringe benefits.**

childcare worker An individual who provides care for infants and children during the day, usually for single or married working parents. *See also* the OOH, **nanny,** and **au pair.**

children's librarian An individual who specializes in finding materials that children will enjoy and showing children how to use the library.

chimney sweep An individual who cleans out chimneys.

chiropractor A health professional who treats patients for various medical problems by using nondrug and nonsurgical techniques designed to relieve interference with the nervous system. *See also* the OOH.

choke setter An individual who fastens steel cables or chains (chokers) around logs to be dragged by tractors or some other system to a landing.

choral director A musician who specializes in working with singing groups. A choral director usually selects the individual performers and then rehearses and directs the group.

choreographer An individual who creates dances for individual dancers or groups. In addition, the choreographer will usually teach the dances and direct the performance of them. *See also* the OOH.

choreologist An individual who records dance steps.

Christmas casual A temporary United States Postal Service employee appointed during the holiday season.

church careers *See* **minister, protestant; rabbi; Roman Catholic priest;** and **choir director.**

CIA An abbreviation of *Central Intelligence Agency*. *See* **Central Intelligence Agency.**

CIDS An acronym for *c*areer *i*nformation *d*elivery *s*ystem. *See* **career information delivery system.**

CIM An acronym for *c*omputer-*i*ntegrated *m*anufacturing. See **computer-integrated manufacturing.**

cinematographer An individual who uses a motion picture camera to record actions and individuals usually for the motion picture industry.

city manager An individual hired by the elected officials of a city to oversee day-to-day operations.

city planner An individual with special training who works with local or regional officials to develop programs to improve existing urban, suburban, or rural areas or to plan for their future growth. *See also* the OOH.

civil drafter An individual who prepares drawings and topographical and relief maps used in civil engineering projects, such as highways, bridges, and flood control projects.

civil engineer An individual who designs and supervises the construction of roads, bridges, and buildings. *See also* the OOH.

civil engineer (military) An Army, Navy, Air Force, or Coast Guard officer who studies the need for various types of roads or buildings, designs construction projects, and selects contractors. *See also* the *Military Careers* guide.

civil engineering technician A skilled individual who helps engineers plan and build highways, buildings, and bridges. *See also* the OOH.

civil service A system of appointing and promoting nonmilitary Government employees by a merit system in which employees are hired and promoted on the basis of their qualifications instead of political patronage or favoritism. *See also* **merit system, Merit Systems Protection Board, cronyism, Civil Service Commission, Office of Personnel Management,** and **spoils system.**

civil service announcements Public notices that a civil service job is available or a list of qualified applicants is being prepared. The announcement usually gives the job title, description of duties, salary range, last day to apply, and agency to contact.

Civil Service Commission A former agency of the Federal Government that acted as a personnel management bureau. This agency has been replaced by the Office of Personnel Management and the Merit Systems Protection Board. *See also* **Office of Personnel Management, Merit Systems Protection Board,** and **Civil Service Reform Act.**

Civil Service Commission Classification Standards A guide used to outline the duties of jobs at different grade levels.

Civil Service Commission Handbook X-118 — Qualifications Standards for Positions A publication that describes the knowledge, skills, and abilities needed to perform the duties of a position and is intended to ensure the recruitment of a competent, stable work force on the basis of merit and fitness for the work to be done. These standards are arranged by series code number in numerical order.

civil service eligibility A Federal grade-level rating awarded after the applicant's qualifications have been reviewed.

Civil Service Reform Act A law passed in 1978, which abolished the Civil Service Commission and established the Office of Personnel Management and the Merit Systems Protection Board. The Office of Personnel Management is responsible for the civil service employment rules. The Merit Systems Protection Board is responsible for overseeing employee appeals, violations of merit system rules, and disciplinary actions.

civilian Anyone not on active duty in the military.

civilian retiree In the Federal civil service system, a person who has retired from Federal Government civilian employment under a retirement system administered by the Federal Government.

claim adjuster An individual in the insurance industry who investigates claims by talking with the claimant or witnesses, reviewing claim applications, and inspecting damage. See also the OOH.

claim clerk An individual who obtains information from insurance policyholders regarding claims, prepares reports, and reviews insurance claim forms for completeness.

claim examiner An individual whose work with a life and health insurance company involves investigating questionable claims or those that exceed designated limits. The claims examiner may review applications or talk with medical professionals before deciding on a claim. *See also* the OOH.

claim interviewer *See* **claim clerk.**

claim representative An individual who investigates insurance claims, negotiates settlements, and authorizes payments to claimants. *See also* the OOH.

class A school (military) A term used by the Navy to designate its technical schools.

class action A legal/administrative action brought by a representative member or members of a group on behalf of all members of that group.

class B school A term used by the Coast Guard to designate a school for advanced petty officer training.

class C school A term used by the Coast Guard to designate special schools.

class of positions In the Federal civil service system, all positions sufficiently similar in the kind of subject matter of work, level of difficulty and responsibility, and qualification requirements, so as to warrant similar treatment in personnel and pay administration.

classification appeal *See* **classification review.**

classification review In the Federal civil service system, an official written request for reclassification of a position.

classified ad An advertisement that appears in a special section of a newspaper or magazine and is grouped under a category, such as help wanted, situations wanted, jobs wanted, and jobs offered. *See also* **help wanted ad, situations wanted ad, jobs wanted, jobs offered,** and **blind ad.**

classified service *See* **competitive service.**

classifier An individual who determines the subject matter of library materials and then assigns classification numbers and descriptive headings. *See also* **cataloger, librarian,** and **media specialist.**

classify In the Federal civil service system, to evaluate the duties and responsibilities of a position and assign to it a title, occupation series, and grade.

cleaner An individual whose work involves the cleaning of homes, office buildings, and hospitals. *See also* the OOH.

cleaner, vehicles and equipment An individual who cleans machinery, vehicles, storage tanks, and similar items.

cleaning lady A preferred nonsexist term is *cleaner.*

cleaning services Businesses that clean office buildings, restaurants, and private homes.

clemency discharge (military) *See* **amnesty discharge.**

CLEP An acronym for *C*ollege *L*evel *E*xamination *P*rogram. *See* **College Level Examination Program.**

clergy A collective term used to designate religious leaders such as ministers, priests, and rabbis.

Clerical and Sales Occupations One of the nine primary categories for grouping occupations in the *Dictionary of Occupational Titles. Examples:* **accounting clerk,** billing typist, and cryptographic-machine operator.

clerical supervisor/manager An individual who oversees the work of the clerical staff of an organization. Duties may include the hiring of clerical personnel, teaching office routines to new workers, and allocating work. *See also* the OOH.

clerk An individual who works with records in an office or organization. *See* specific type of clerk.

clerk-typist An individual whose work may involve filing, distributing mail, answering phones, and other office duties in addition to typing responsibilities. *See also* the OOH.

climatologist A scientist who analyzes records of rainfall, sunshine, wind, and temperature to provide information necessary for projects such as the designing of better heating and cooling systems.

clinical chemistry technologist An individual who prepares specimens and analyzes the chemical and hormonal contents of body fluids.

clinical dietician An individual who provides nutritional services for patients in hospitals, nursing homes, clinics, or doctors' offices.

clinical laboratory technician An individual who works under the supervision of a laboratory supervisor or a clinical laboratory technologist and performs some of the routine tests required by physicians.

clinical laboratory technologist A highly skilled individual with the necessary training to perform the many complex laboratory tests required by the medical professions. *See also* the OOH, **cytotechnologist, phlebotomist, microbiology technologist,** and **immunology technologist.**

clinical nurse specialist A nurse with expertise in some clinical area, such as pediatrics or gerontology/geriatrics.

clinical perfusionist an individual who operates a heart-lung machine, the intra-aortic balloon pump, or blood transfusion machines.

clinical psychologist A psychologist who generally works in a hospital, clinic, or university or for a community mental health program.

close of business The end of the official work day.

close to the vest *Informal:* keeping to oneself; used to describe the behavior of an individual who does not usually discuss personal matters or plans. *Example:* a person whose promotion came as a surprise to everyone because he had played his cards close to the vest.

closed shop A policy or trade union contract provision, now illegal, requiring employees to become members of the union before they could be hired, and to continue their membership in the union for as long as they were employed.

cloth cap *Informal, Britain:* a factory worker. *U.S.*: a blue-collar worker.

clothing and fabric repairer (military) In the Army, Navy, Air Force, or Marine Corps, an individual who inspects and marks items received for repair; repairs tents, covers, and other canvas equipment; and alters and repairs uniforms. *See also* the *Military Careers* guide.

coach An individual who trains or instructs athletes or performers.

Coast Guard The United States Coast Guard, which operates as a part of the Department of Transportation and maintains a system of rescue vessels, aircraft, and communications facilities to save lives and property on the high seas and navigable waters of the United States. In time of war or at the direction of the President, the Coast Guard operates as part of the Navy.

COBOL An acronym for *co*mmon *b*usiness *o*riented *l*anguage. *See* **common business oriented language.**

COBRA An acronym for *C*omprehensive *O*mnibus *B*udget *R*econciliation Act. *See* **Comprehensive**

Omnibus Budget Reconciliation Act.

COD An abbreviation of *collect on delivery*. *See* **collect on delivery.**

coffee break *See* **break.**

cognitive psychologist A psychologist who deals with the brain's role in memory, thinking, and perception or with research related to computer programming and artificial intelligence.

coil winder, taper, and finisher Individuals who use coil winding machines to wind wire coils used in the manufacturing of electrical components and equipment.

coin dealer An individual who buys, sells, and appraises coins.

coin machine servicer and repairer An individual who installs, services, and maintains the various types of vending machines that dispense food or beverages or provide a service, such as jukeboxes or game machines.

coinsurance The percentage of covered health insurance that the insured person is required to pay. *Example:* health insurance for which the insurance company may pay 80 percent of a claim, and the employee pays 20 percent.

COLA An acronym for *c*ost-*o*f-*l*iving *a*djustment/allowance. *See* **cost-of-living adjustment/allowance.**

cold calling The selling or job hunting technique of visiting or calling someone who has not expressed any interest in the service, product, or person.

cold contact An approach to a prospective employer either in person or by telephone without an appointment or any prior contact.

collateral lender An individual whose business is lending money to people who leave some item of value that can be redeemed when the money is returned. Another term for this occupation is pawnbroker.

collect on delivery (COD) A method of delivery in which the sender has not been paid for the item and the person to whom the item is addressed must pay the charges when the package is delivered.

collective bargaining The process by which the employer and the employee representative(s) meet at reasonable times to confer and negotiate in good faith and to execute a written agreement concerning conditions of employment and wages. *See also* **negotiations, arbitration**, and **collective bargaining agreement.**

collective bargaining agreement The contract that results from the collective bargaining process. *See also* **contract.**

collective bargaining unit A group of employees recognized as appropriate for representation by a labor organization for collective bargaining.

collector *See* **account collector.**

college career planning and placement counselor A specially trained individual who assists college and university students and alumni in planning their careers or finding employment. *See also* the OOH.

college career resource center Facilities established in colleges and universities to supply assistance and career information to students.

college catalog A publication issued by a college to provide information about the campus, facilities, faculty, majors and degrees offered, courses available, and financial aid.

college interview *See* **admissions interview.**

College Level Examination Program (CLEP) A standardized examination program for college credit.

college president *See* **general manager/top executive.**

college professor An individual who teaches and advises college students. *See also* the OOH.

college student development specialist *See* **counselor.**

college/university faculty A group of college-educated individuals who are organized into various departments or schools in a college or university and whose primary responsibilities are to teach and advise students. *See also* the OOH.

color film operator An individuai who uses specialized machinery to process color film in a professional photo processing lab.

color laboratory technician An individual who

produces color prints, negatives, and slides by hand or by automated machines.

color-printer operator An individual who controls the equipment used to produce color prints from negatives.

colorist An individual who applies oil colors to portrait photographs to create a natural, lifelike appearance.

columnist A writer who specializes in analyzing the news and writing columns or commentaries based on personal knowledge and experience.

combat engineer In the Army or Marine Corps, an individual who constructs trails, roads, and temporary shelters; constructs airfields and performs ground traffic control duties; and lays and clears mine fields and booby traps. *See also* the *Military Careers* guide.

Combat Specialty Occupations (military) One of the broad categories used by the Armed Forces to group occupations for enlisted and officer personnel.

commentator An individual who broadcasts for a radio or television station and specializes in interpreting and discussing news stories instead of just reporting them.

commerce An interchange of goods within a country or between different countries.

commercial and industrial electronic equipment repairer An individual who installs, maintains, and repairs electronic equipment used in various industries. *See also* the OOH.

commercial artist An individual who uses artistic talents for business purposes, such as illustrating newspaper ads and book covers. *See also* **visual artist.**

commercial electronics technician *See* **commercial and industrial electronic equipment repairer.**

commissary/exchange (military store) privilege A storelike facility operated as a benefit for Armed Forces members, who can purchase items at reduced cost.

commission A percentage of a purchase price paid to the salesman or broker. *Example:* after a $10,000 order for mutual fund shares, a 3 percent commission, or $300, paid to the registered representative who placed the order.

Commission on Civil Rights The commission holds public hearings and collects and studies information on discrimination because of race, color, religion, sex, age, handicap, or national origin. The recommendations of the commission are submitted to the President and Congress.

commissioned (military) The certification that an officer in the Armed Forces has met all of the qualification requirements.

commissioned officer (military) A member of the military holding the rank of second lieutenant or ensign or higher. The role of a commissioned officer is similar to that of a manager or executive.

committee A group of people who meet together to perform some service, find a solution to a problem, or investigate some situation.

common business oriented language (COBOL) A widely used, high-level business programming language.

communication The act of transmitting information or messages by various means, such as speaking, writing, nonverbal gestures, or telecommunication.

communication-center operator An individual who operates airport communication systems and monitors airport electronic equipment alarms.

communications equipment mechanic An individual who installs, repairs, and maintains various types of communications equipment. *See also* the OOH.

communications manager (military) An Army, Navy, Air Force, Marine Corps, or Coast Guard officer who develops rules or procedures for sending and receiving communications; directs personnel who operate computer systems and electronic telecommunications and satellite communications equipment; and directs personnel who maintain and repair communications equipment. *See also* the *Military Careers* guide.

communications specialist *See* **public relations specialist.**

communications, transportation, and utilities operations manager An individual who plans, organizes, directs, controls, or coordinates management activities related to communications, transportation facilities, and utility services.

community college A two-year college that primarily serves residents of the immediate area and usually offers degree programs for occupations which require less than a four-year college degree or preparatory courses which enable students to transfer to a four-year college.

community dietician An individual who counsels people in public health clinics, home health agencies, and health maintenance organizations on nutritional practices designed to prevent disease and to promote good health.

community health nurse A nurse who may work with patients in public health facilities such as clinics, schools, or retirement communities. Duties may include health education, immunizations, and testing and screening procedures for the general public. *See also* the OOH.

community outreach librarian An individual who develops library services to meet the needs of people in rural areas, migrant labor camps, inner-city housing projects, and nursing homes.

community outreach worker *See* **human services worker.**

community planner *See* **urban/regional planner.**

community resources Those agencies or institutions within a community that offer helpful services, such as employment counseling and job training.

commuter tax An income tax on the wages of workers who work but do not live in the taxing jurisdiction.

comp time *See* **compensatory time off.**

companion An individual who performs a variety of services for elderly or handicapped individuals. A companion may prepare food, do routine housekeeping chores, administer medicine, or shop.

company car A car owned and maintained by a business for use by an employee, such as a salesperson, who needs an automobile for work.

company man *Informal:* an individual who puts the interests of the company ahead of relationships with other employees, and, in extreme cases, even ahead of friends and family.

comparable worth The idea that jobs which require comparable skills, education, and qualifications should be paid similarly. Some companies have been accused of paying women employees less than men doing comparable work. *See also* **equal pay for equal work** and **glass ceiling.**

comparative psychologist A psychologist who studies the behavior of humans and animals.

compensation Something given as payment for goods or services. *See also* **wage, commission, salary,** and **piece rate.**

compensation manager An individual who determines and maintains a fair pay scale for the employees of a company or organization. *See also* the OOH.

compensation specialist *See* **compensation manager.**

compensatory time off Time off, hour for hour, granted instead of overtime pay to an employee.

competitive area In the Federal civil service system, that part of a Federal agency within which employees are in competition to be retained when the number of Federal employees is being reduced. Generally the area is restricted to what is considered a local commuting area.

competitive level In the Federal civil service system, a competitive level for reduction in force consists of all jobs in a competitive area which are so similar in all important respects that the agency can readily move an employee from one to another without significant training and without unduly interrupting the work program.

competitive medical plan A medical organization that provides health care in exchange for a monthly, fixed fee. *See also* **health maintenance organization.**

competitive position In the Federal civil service system, a position in the competitive service.

competitive service In the Federal civil service system, all civilian positions in the Federal Government that are not specifically excepted from the civil service laws and are not in the Senior Executive Service.

competitive status In the Federal civil service system, basic eligibility for noncompetitive assignment to a competitive position. A person on a career or career-conditional appointment acquires competitive status on satisfactory completion of a probationary period. Competitive status may also be granted by statute, Executive order, or civil service rules without competitive examination. A person with competitive status may be promoted, transferred, reassigned, reinstated, or demoted without taking an open competitive examination, subject to the conditions prescribed by the civil service rules and regulations.

compliance officer An individual who enforces policies, rules, regulations, and laws. A compliance officer may work for one of the many agencies that oversee immigration, wages, food, and interstate commerce. *See also* specific types of compliance officers.

composer An individual who writes the music for songs, symphonies, and operas. Many composers write also the words for their musical creations.

compositor An individual who works in the printing industry and places lines of metal type into the type frames used for the actual printing. *See also* the OOH.

Comprehensive Omnibus Budget Reconciliation Act (COBRA) A Federal law that permits qualified individuals who are losing coverage under a group health plan to continue coverage for limited periods of time at their own expense. In order to participate, a qualifying event, such as death of the covered member, divorce, or termination, must have occurred. *See also* **qualifying event, COBRA;** and **terminating event, COBRA.**

compressed gas technician (military) In the Navy, Air Force, or Marine Corps, an individual who operates valves to control the flow of air through machinery that compresses or liquefies gases, operates dry ice plants, and fills storage cylinders with compressed gas. *See also* the *Military Careers* guide.

computer-aided design (CAD) Computer software programs designed to create and alter computer designs.

computer-aided engineering (CAE) Computer software programs used to simulate the conditions to which a product may be exposed or to predict how it will perform.

computer-aided instruction (CAI) An instructional technique in which the student interacts with a computer program to learn a particular skill or concept.

computer and office machine repairer An individual who installs new machines, does preventive maintenance, or corrects emergency problems. *See also* the OOH.

computer and peripheral equipment operator An individual who is skilled in the use of computers, and computer-related equipment, such as printers, disk drives, and tape readers. *See also* the OOH.

computer-assisted instruction (CAI) *See* **computer-aided instruction.**

computer commuter *Informal:* an employee who can work at home on a computer electronically linked to the workplace. *See also* **remote work.**

computer data entry specialist (military) In the Army, Navy, Air Force, Marine Corps, or Coast Guard, an individual who operates keypunch machines to prepare computer punch cards; uses magnetic tape writers to code data onto data processing tape; and uses automatic typewriters to put data on computer paper tapes. *See also* the *Military Careers* guide.

computer equipment repairer (military) In the Army, Navy, Air Force, or Marine Corps, an individual who installs computers and other data processing equipment; inspects data processing equipment for defects in wiring, circuit boards, and other parts; and uses electrical voltage meters, circuit analyzers, and other special testing equipment to test and repair data processing equipment. *See also* the *Military Careers* guide.

computer-integrated manufacturing (CIM) A computer system that integrates the business functions with the manufacturing processes in a factory.

computer operator (military) In the Army, Navy, Air Force, Marine Corps, or Coast Guard, an individual who operates computers by entering commands through consoles; uses and maintains high speed printers; and operates specialized computers that calculate position, target weapons, and run machinery. *See also* the *Military Careers* guide.

computer programmer An individual who uses special training to write the detailed instructions or programs that direct a computer to perform a specific series of tasks. *See also* the OOH.

computer programmer (military) In the Army, Navy, Air Force, or Marine Corps, an individual who organizes and arranges computer programs into logical steps that direct computers to solve problems; codes programs into languages such as COBOL, FORTRAN, or BASIC that computers can read; and prepares detailed instruction sheets for computer operators who run programs. *See also* the *Military Careers* guide.

computer science The field of study that deals with the design, use, theory, and analysis of computers.

computer service technician An individual responsible for the installation, repair, and maintenance of computers and peripheral equipment, such as printers, disk drives, and networking equipment. *See also* the OOH.

computer systems analyst An individual who determines the needs of a computer customer, plans a system, and helps with the purchase of the computer equipment and software programs. *See also* the OOH.

computer systems analyst (military) In the Army, Navy, Air Force, or Marine Corps, an individual who helps military units determine their data processing needs; develops systems plans, including input, output, and processing steps, and information storage and access methods; and helps programmers program, test, and debug computer software. *See also* the *Military Careers* guide.

computer systems development officer (military) An Army, Navy, Air Force, Marine Corps, or Coast Guard officer who develops flow-chart diagrams or mathematical models of new computer systems, designs and maintains computer software and databases, and manages teams of systems analysts and programmers working on the designs of large systems. *See also* the *Military Careers* guide.

computer systems engineer (military) An Army, Navy, Air Force, Marine Corps, or Coast Guard officer who estimates memory and processing needs to determine the size of the computer needed, determines equipment and software needs for telecommunications linkages with remote equipment, and sets standards for and evaluates the performance of new computer systems. *See also* the *Military Careers* guide.

computer systems manager (military) An Army, Navy, Air Force, Marine Corps, or Coast Guard officer who prepares data processing plans and budgets; develops policies and procedures for computer facility operations; and directs teams of programmers, systems analysts, systems engineers, and computer operators. *See also* the *Military Careers* guide.

concierge An individual who works for a hotel or resort and welcomes guests, arranges for various services, and fulfills special requests.

conciliation The process of having a third party attempt to reconcile the differences between two deadlocked groups. *See also* **mediation; arbitration; conciliator;** and **conciliator, labor relations.**

conciliator An individual who attempts to settle a dispute and reconcile the participants.

conciliator, labor relations An individual who attempts to resolve differences between trade unions and management by offering advice, working out agreements, and providing counseling on disputed issues.

concrete mason An individual who makes sidewalks, floors, dams, and highways from concrete. *See also* the OOH and **terrazzo worker.**

concrete mason (military) In the Army, Navy, Air Force, or Marine Corps, an individual who mixes and pours concrete to form footings, foundations, and floor slabs; uses finishing tools such as floats, screeds, and edgers to finish surfaces of poured concrete; and uses mortar to set masonry in correct position. *See also* the *Military Careers* guide.

conductor, orchestra An individual who selects musicians and directs rehearsals and performances of an orchestra.

conflict of interest A situation that could interfere with the proper conduct of an individual's job. Example: a Federal Government employee owning stock in a company regulated by the employee's agency. *See also* **standards of conduct.**

conservation scientist *See* **soil conservationist** and **range manager.**

conservationist An individual who visits areas with erosion problems, finds the source of the problem, and helps landowners develop management practices to combat it. *See also* **soil conservationist.**

conservator An individual who coordinates the activities of workers engaged in the examination, repair, and conservation of art objects.

consolidation The bringing together of two or more things to form a new whole.

constituents The people who elect an individual, such as a Congressman, legislator, or the President, to represent them.

construction and building inspector An individual who examines the construction, alteration, or repair of highways, streets, sewer and water systems, dams, bridges, buildings, and other structures to ensure compliance with building codes and ordinances, zoning regulations, and contract specifications. *See also* specific types of inspectors.

construction equipment mechanic An individual who services and repairs various components of heavy construction equipment, such as backhoes, loading shovels, graders, and trenchers.

construction equipment operator Usually an operator of bulldozers, cranes, loaders, and similar equipment in the construction industry but also in the mining, logging, utilities, and other industries.

construction equipment operator (military) In the Army, Navy, Air Force, or Marine Corps, an individual who drives bulldozers, road graders, and other heavy equipment to cut and level earth for runways and roadbeds; uses winches, cranes, and hoists to lift and move steel and other heavy building materials; and operates scrapers and snow blowers to remove ice and snow from runways, roads, and other areas. *See also* the *Military Careers* guide.

construction inspector An individual who determines whether new construction or repairs or alterations to existing buildings meet specific codes and standards.

construction laborer An individual who supplies tools, materials, and equipment to skilled craftsmen at construction sites and performs other routine tasks.

construction machinery operator An individual who operates equipment such as bulldozers or cranes, used to move construction material. *See also* the OOH.

construction manager An individual who determines the appropriate construction methods and schedules all required construction activities. *See also* the OOH.

Construction Occupations (military) One of the twelve broad categories used by the Armed Forces to group occupations for enlisted personnel.

construction trades helper An individual who assists skilled construction workers by moving materials, supplies, and tools to and from work areas; helps with the set up and adjustment of machines; and cleans machinery.

construction unions Trade unions that organize the workers employed in the building industry. Examples: carpenters, electricians, masons, and plumbers.

consultant In the Federal civil service system, an advisor to an officer or instrumentality of the Federal Government, as distinguished from an officer or employee who carries out the agency's duties and responsibilities.

consultant, management An individual who specializes in a particular field and assists and advises businesses and organizations about a specific problem. *See also* the OOH.

consultant position In the Federal civil service

system, a position requiring the performance of purely advisory or consultant services, not including the performance of operating functions.

consultation **1)** The act of meeting with an individual or group of individuals for the purpose of obtaining an opinion or help with a problem. Usually one of more of the participants is an expert in the field or subject being discussed. **2)** The obligation of a Federal Government agency to consult a labor organization on particular personnel issues. The process of consultation lies between notification to the labor organization, which may amount simply to providing information, and negotiation, which implies agreement on the part of the labor organization.

consulting firm A company that specializes in providing consultants for businesses or governmental agencies. *See also* **consultant, management.**

consumer price index (CPI) Compiled monthly by the U.S. Bureau of Labor Statistics, an index that shows changes in the price of goods and services to a typical consumer. This index is used to calculate automatic pay increases, which are sometimes part of union contracts, and increased benefits for Social Security recipients. The index is known also as the cost-of-living index. *See also* **automatic pay increases, COLA,** and **cost-of-living adjustment/allowance.**

consumer psychologist A psychologist who studies the psychological factors that determine the behavior of an individual as a consumer of goods and services.

consumer safety inspector An individual who determines whether laws and regulations governing food, cosmetics, weights and measures, drugs, and pesticides are being obeyed.

consumer sector That part of the population which uses services and commodities.

consumerism An interest in protecting the consumer from unfair business practices.

contact lens technician An individual who teaches new users to insert, remove, and clean contact lenses.

contact person An individual designated by a business or institution to deal with prospective applicants or persons seeking information on a particular topic.

contingent employees Workers who are not regular employees but are hired on a temporary, sometimes part-time, basis and do not receive the benefits given to the regular employees.

continuance **1)** The postponement or adjournment of a hearing until some later date. **2)** In the Federal civil service system, the personnel action used to document that an employee has received a waiver from mandatory retirement or the extension of the not-to-exceed date of a previous waiver.

continuing education Additional programs for adults who want to continue learning without being in an official degree program.

continuing education (military) Courses to improve the education of enlisted personnel and help them become well-rounded individuals. Enlisted personnel may enroll in courses for a college degree, improved work skills, or personal enjoyment.

continuous mining machine operator An individual who operates a self-propelled mining machine that rips coal from the coal face and loads it onto conveyors or into shuttle cars in a continuous operation.

contract A written agreement between two parties which specifies that a particular thing will or will not be done for a stated amount of money. A properly prepared and executed contract is a legal document and enforceable in court. *See also* collective bargaining agreement.

contract specialist An individual who acts as a purchasing agent, usually for the Federal Government, when the cost of items to be purchased exceeds $25,000 and requires sealed bids and negotiated agreements.

contracting out The practice of hiring private, outside companies to perform certain services that might normally be a function of the employees of the institution or business. *Example:* a school system hiring a private company to provide food or custodial services. *See also* **vendoring out.**

contributory plan A plan, such as a pension plan or health insurance plan, that requires a contribution from the employee as well as the employer. *See also* **noncontributory plan.**

control Power, dominance, or authority over a person or situation.

controller, air traffic An individual responsible for a specified amount of air space and must direct aircraft within that area to land and take off safely and efficiently and to stay within an assigned traffic pattern. *See also* the OOH.

controller, financial An individual who is usually in charge of the budget, auditing, or accounting department of a large business or organization and oversees the preparation of financial reports, such as balance sheets, income statements, and depreciation schedules. *See also* the OOH.

convention services manager An individual who coordinates the activities of the various departments of large hotels to prepare for meetings, conventions, and other special events.

conversion In the Federal civil service system, the changing of an employee from one appointment to another appointment in the same agency without a break in service of more than three calendar days.

cook An individual who prepares food in a restaurant, hospital, private home, school, or nursing home. *See also* the OOH, **chef,** and **prep cook.**

cooking machine operator and tender An individual who operates or tends cooking equipment such as steam cooking vats, deep fry cookers, pressure cookers, kettles, and boilers to prepare food products such as meats, sugar, cheese, and grain.

co-op programs *See* **cooperative vocational education.**

co-pay *See* **coinsurance.**

cooperative vocational education (CVE) **1)** A system that combines classroom instruction with employer-paid, on-the-job training. **2)** In the Federal civil service system, a program under which a student alternates periods of education and Federal employment under terms of an agreement between the student's school and a Government agency. Co-op agreements normally provide for the student's permanent employment in the agency on satisfactory completion of the education and work assignments required by the agreement.

cop-out *Informal:* an attempt to resign from or stop an activity in order to avoid work or responsibility. *Example:* complaining of a headache as an excuse for not helping a friend move furniture on moving day.

copayment *See* **coinsurance.**

copy writer An individual who specializes in writing the copy or written part of an advertisement for radio, television, newspapers, or magazines. *See also* the OOH.

coroner An individual who officially determines the cause of death when it is not apparent that death resulted from natural causes. *See also* **forensic pathologist** and **medical examiner.**

corporate goals The stated purposes and objectives of a company that management hopes or expects to attain.

corporate image The impression held by the general public about the policies, ethical behavior, personnel, and environmental responsibility of a company.

corporate planning The act of determining a system to solve management problems or to achieve corporate goals.

correction officer An individual who maintains order in a jail or prison; supervises prisoners when eating, working, and exercising; and escorts prisoners to destinations outside the correctional facility. *See also* the OOH.

correction specialist (military) In the Army, Navy, Air Force, or Marine Corps, an individual who stands guard at gates, cellblocks, or on towers; searches inmates and cells for illegal goods; and searches vehicles entering and leaving correctional facilities. *See also* the *Military Careers* guide.

corrections careers *See* **correction officer, probation officer,** and **parole officer.**

corrective action An attempt or act intended to correct some condition or problem. *Example:* assigning extra telemarketers to a region whose sales fell drastically during the last two quarters.

corrective therapy assistant/aide *See* **physical and corrective therapy assistant/aide.**

correspondence clerk An individual who composes letters to respond to damage claims, delinquent accounts, incorrect billings, customer service complaints, and requests for merchandise or credit and other information.

correspondence course *See* **correspondence schools.**

correspondence schools Schools that offer educational instruction or skill training by mail. Instructional packets are sent to the student, who completes the work and returns it by mail for grading and evaluation.

correspondent An individual who gathers information and writes news stories printed in newspapers or magazines or broadcast on the radio or on television. *See also* the OOH.

cosmetic surgeon A doctor who specializes in the use of surgical procedures to correct or improve undesirable physical features.

cosmetologist An individual who is trained to shampoo, cut, color, bleach, and style hair, as well as give permanent waves, manicures, and facials. *See also* the OOH, **hair stylist, manicurist, pedicurist,** and **barber.**

cost-conscious *Business:* keeping a close watch on various business expenses.

cost estimator An individual who specializes in determining the cost of a construction project or an item to be manufactured. *See also* the OOH.

cost-of-living adjustment/allowance (COLA) An automatic adjustment in salaries or benefits based on changes in the cost-of-living/consumer price index and designed to compensate for increases in the cost of living.

cost-of-living index An index that shows changes in the price of goods and services to a typical consumer. This index is used to calculate automatic pay increases, which are sometimes part of union contracts. This index is known also as the consumer price index.

cost sharing A requirement that an employee share part of the cost of a benefit. *Example:* an employee who must pay a portion of the cost for group health insurance. *See also* **contributory plan** and **noncontributory plan.**

costing techniques The collection and analysis of information to obtain the cost of an item, service, or process.

counseling The practice of advising or making suggestions to individuals in order to obtain a change of behavior or to aid in the solution of some problem. *See also* **counselor.**

counseling interview An interview whose purpose is to advise the interviewee, identify an employee's personal or work-related problem, or help the employee correct a situation affecting the individual's job performance.

counseling psychologist A psychologist who uses techniques such as interviewing and testing to advise people on how to deal with problems of everyday living.

counselor 1) An individual with special training who advises and assists students, employees, disabled persons, and substance abusers. Counselors can be found in high school guidance offices, career planning and placement offices in colleges and universities, placement offices in private vocational/technical schools and institutes, vocational rehabilitation agencies, counseling services offered by community organizations, private counseling agencies or private practices, or state employment service offices affiliated with the U.S. Employment Service. *See also* the OOH, **school counselor, college career planning and placement counselor, placement counselor, rehabilitation counselor, employment counselor, and mental health counselor.** 2) A lawyer.

counselor (military) *See* **caseworker and counselor (military).**

counter attendant An individual who takes orders, serves food, and writes checks at a coffee shop, diner, cafeteria, or lunchroom.

counter clerk An individual who fills out orders, receives money, makes change, and dispenses merchandise in an establishment such as a dry cleaners. When the person works at a store that rents items such as videotapes, furniture, or machinery, or at a firm that leases automobiles,entent the individual may offer suggestions, explain rental provisions, give special instructions, calculate payments, accept returns, and note the condition of returned merchandise. *See also* the OOH.

county sheriff *See* **sheriff.**

court clerk An individual who performs clerical duties, such as preparing dockets of cases, securing information for judges, and contacting witnesses in a court of law.

court reporter An individual who uses shorthand or a stenotype machine to record legal proceedings and then produces the official record of these proceedings by transcribing the notes on a typewriter or word processor. See also the OOH.

court reporter (military) In the Navy, Air Force, Marine Corps, or Coast Guard, an individual who types text from stenotyped records, shorthand notes, or taped records of court proceedings; prepares records of hearings, investigations, courts-martial, and courts of inquiry; and maintains the legal calendar, law library, and reference file of pending cases. *See also* the *Military Careers* guide.

cover letter A letter that should accompany a resume to point out experience and relevant skills which qualify an individual for a specific job with a particular company. A cover letter also provides an opportunity to direct the resume to the proper person, show familiarity with the company's product or service, and request an appointment.

CPA An abbreviation of *certified public accountant. See* **certified public accountant.**

CPI An abbreviation of *consumer price index. See* **consumer price index.**

craft An occupation, trade, or art that requires special skill, dexterity, or artistic ability.

craft union The members of a skilled manual trade or art organization.

craftsman **1)** An individual skilled in a particular craft. **2)** An individual who has completed an apprenticeship program and advanced to the journeyman or craftsman level. *See also* **apprenticeship** and **journeyman.**

crane operator An individual who operates a crane to move heavy materials or items used in construction industries and in resource industries such as mining and logging. *See also* the OOH.

credit authorizer An individual who approves charges against customers' existing charge accounts by evaluating the customers' computerized credit records and payment history. *See also* the OOH.

credit clerk An individual who reviews applications for credit and contacts applicants, credit bureaus, and other sources for information. *See also* the OOH.

credit manager An individual who supervises the credit department in a retail establishment or bank. The credit manager establishes credit guidelines, accepts or refuses credit applications, and monitors credit purchases and delinquent accounts. *See also* the OOH.

credit union A cooperative organization composed of members from a specific occupational group or business. Credit unions provide for their members many of the same services, such as checking accounts, savings accounts, and loans, offered by private banks.

creditable military service In the Federal civil service system, the total number of years and months of military service used to determine the length of annual leave.

creditable service In the Federal civil service system, the Federal Government employment (uniformed service or civilian) that meets requirements for a particular type of appointment or benefit. For example, service may be creditable for conversion to career tenure, for completion of the waiting period for a within-grade increase, or for retirement under the civil service retirement system.

credits, Social Security *See* **Social Security work credits.**

critic An individual who prepares reviews of plays, movies, TV programs, musicals, and restaurants for newspapers or magazines or for radio or television broadcasts.

critical element A component of a Federal employee's job which is of sufficient importance that performance below the minimum standard established by management requires remedial action and denial of a within-grade increase and may be the basis for removing or reducing the grade level of that employee. *See also* **unacceptable performance.**

cronyism *Informal:* giving employment, special consideration, or favors to a friend (crony), especially in government or business. *See also* **nepotism** and **buddy system.**

cross placement The practice of increasing an employee's chance for promotion or a salary increase by moving the employee to another department or job.

crossing guard An individual who guides or controls vehicular or pedestrian traffic at street and railroad crossings.

cruiser An individual who assesses logging conditions and estimates the volume of marketable timber.

crushing, grinding, and polishing machine operator An individual who operates or tends machines that crush or grind a wide variety of materials.

curator An individual who works for a museum, zoo, or historic site. The curator may acquire items for the collection, prepare exhibits, restore materials, or conduct educational programs and tours. *See also* the OOH.

custodian An individual who cleans and maintains office buildings, stores, hospitals, schools, or apartment buildings. *See also* the OOH.

custom tailor A skilled individual who takes measurements, helps a customer with the selection of styles and fabrics, and then makes a garment tailored specifically for the customer.

customer service A company department that deals directly with the people who have purchased goods or services. This department is responsible for resolving complaints about faulty merchandise, nonperformance of services, billing, and refunds.

customer service representative An individual employed by a store or business to handle complaints about merchandise, billing problems, refunds, and questions from the people who have purchased the company's goods or services.

customer service representative, utilities An individual who interviews applicants for water, gas, electric, or telephone service or receives orders for installation, turn-on, discontinuance, or change in service.

customers' engineer An individual who services equipment such as computers, computer printers, typewriters, adding machines, cash registers, dictating machines, copying machines, and postage meters.

customs agent An individual who works for the Federal Government and enforces laws to prevent the importation of illegal items into the United States.

customs inspector An individual who checks merchandise to determine whether it can be imported or exported and, when necessary, assesses tax or duty to be paid.

cutback A reduction in personnel or wages. *See also* **downsizing** and **reduction in force**.

cutoff time A time set for an activity to stop.

cutter, apparel An individual who cuts, either by hand or machine, material that will be sewn into ready-to-wear clothing. *See also* the OOH.

cutter, welding An individual who uses heat from burning gases or an electric arc to cut and trim rather than join metals.

cutting and slicing machine operator and tender An individual who operates or tends machines that cut or slice any of a wide variety of products or materials.

cutting and slicing machine setter and setup operator An individual who sets up and operates machines that cut or slice materials to specified dimensions for further processing.

CVE An abbreviation of cooperative vocational education. *See* **cooperative vocational education.**

cyclical unemployment Unemployment that results from changes in economic conditions. Example: layoffs during a recession after a period of prosperity.

cytotechnologist An individual who prepares slides of body cells and microscopically examines these cells for abnormalities.

daily tour of duty *See* **tour of duty.**

dairy processing equipment operator and tender An individual who sets up, operates, or tends continuous-flow or vat-type equipment to process milk, cream, or other dairy products, following specified methods and formulas.

dairy scientist An individual who does research involving the selection, breeding, management, and feeding of dairy cattle.

dancer An individual who dances solo or as part of a group in a dance company or as a member of the cast of a musical or opera. *See also* the OOH.

DANTES *See* **Defense Activity for Nontraditional Education Support.**

darkroom technician An individual who develops and prints photographic film either by hand or by operating machinery that processes the film automatically.

data entry keyer An individual who types data from documents into various types of machines that convert the data into a form that can be read into a computer. *See also* the OOH.

data processing Operations performed on data, usually by computer, to produce specific results, such as numerical or alphabetical sorting in a particular order.

data processing equipment repairer An individual who maintains and repairs data processing equipment and related items, such as printers, terminals, and storage units. *See also* the OOH.

data processing manager An individual who directs, plans, and coordinates data processing activities. *See also* the OOH.

data typist *See* **data entry keyer.**

day worker An individual who goes to the employer's home during the workday to perform various types of household tasks, such as cooking, cleaning, childcare, and gardening. *See also* the OOH.

DEA An abbreviation of *Drug Enforcement Agency*. *See* **Drug Enforcement Agency.**

dead-end job *Informal:* a job that offers little chance for advancement to a better position or a higher salary.

deadheading pay A benefit to an employee in the form of free tickets to an entertainment event, free transportation tickets, or some other similar benefit for which the general public would be charged.

dealer compliance representative An individual who inspects franchised establishments to determine whether the franchisee is in compliance with the franchiser's policies and procedures. *See also* **franchise, franchiser,** and **franchisee.**

dean A broad term used in education to describe an assistant, usually to the president of a college or university, whose job may involve developing a budget, coordinating activities, working with faculty, working with students, acting as registrar, and developing programs. *See also* the OOH.

death benefit *See* **Social Security death benefit.**

decentralization Delegating decision-making power to individuals working in locations where the actual work is performed instead of having a small group of individuals make all decisions at a central location. *See also* **centralization.**

decision making The process of choosing from two or more alternatives.

deckhand An individual who performs various routine tasks aboard a ship. *See also* **boatswain, captain,** and **mate.**

deductible The amount of money that an insured individual must pay before insurance benefits are payable. *See also* **coinsurance.**

deep pockets *Informal:* an individual with a large amount of money. *Example:* a struggling company that decides to seek financial assistance from a particular investor because he is known to have deep pockets.

Defense Activity for Nontraditional Education Support (DANTES) An organization within the Department of Defense designed to support education in all of the military services. DANTES helps develop and administer educational programs including an Independent Study Program that allows enlisted personnel to take high school through graduate-level self-study courses offered by accredited colleges and universities.

deferred retirement A Federal employee with five years civilian service who separates or transfers to a position not under the Retirement Act and may receive an annuity at age 62 if the individual does not withdraw from the Retirement Fund. *See also* **retirement; disability retirement; retirement, discontinued service;** and **optional retirement.**

degree An academic title awarded by a college or university to a student after completing the required courses of study.

dehire To dismiss an employee.

Delayed Entry Program (DEP) A military program in which an applicant delays entry into active duty for up to one year for such a purpose as completing school.

delegate To give power or authority to another person to act as one's representative.

delegating The act of giving another individual the power to perform certain functions or make decisions.

demographer An individual who does research on human populations for statistics on such matters as births, diseases, and deaths.

demographics The science that deals with statistics for large populations. *See also* **demographer.**

demotion The act of moving an employee to a job with a smaller salary or less responsibility or prestige.

denial of within-grade increase In the Federal civil service system, the decision to withhold a within-grade increase to a General Schedule employee because of a determination that the employee's performance is not at an acceptable level of competence. *See also* **acceptable level of competence.**

dental assistant An individual who helps a dentist by performing a variety of tasks, such as preparing dental charts or histories, preparing instruments and materials, taking X rays, and instructing patients about follow-up or dental hygiene procedures. *See also* the OOH.

dental ceramist An individual who specializes in porcelain and acrylic restorations to make various types of dental devices, such as crowns, bridges, and dentures.

dental hygienist An individual who provides a variety of dental services under the supervision of a dentist. Depending on the state laws that regulate the services of a dental hygienist, duties may include the cleaning and scaling of teeth, the application of fluorides or sealants to prevent tooth decay, and instruction in oral health. *See also* the OOH.

dental laboratory technician A skilled individual who uses acrylics, metals, composites, or ceramics to make or repair dental devices, such as crowns, bridges, dentures, and orthodontic appliances. *See also* the OOH.

dental laboratory technician (military) In the Army, Navy, Air Force, or Coast Guard, an individual who reads instructions from dentists to make dentures, braces, and other dental devices; uses molds made from teeth impressions to make crowns or dentures; and constructs, repairs, and aligns metal braces and retainers. *See also* the *Military Careers* guide.

dental specialist (military) In the Army, Navy, Air Force, or Coast Guard, an individual who helps dentists perform oral surgery, helps dentists during examinations by preparing dental compounds and operating dental equipment, and uses scaling and polishing instruments and equipment to clean patients' teeth. *See also* the *Military Careers* guide.

dentist An individual who is licensed to perform a variety of dental services, such as filling cavities, treating gum diseases, or straightening teeth. *See also* the OOH.

dentist (military) An Army, Navy, or Air Force officer who examines patients' teeth and gums to detect signs of disease or tooth decay; examines X rays to determine the soundness of teeth and the alignment of teeth and jaws; and performs oral surgery to treat problems with teeth, gums, or jaws. *See also* the *Military Careers* guide.

DEP An abbreviation of *Delayed Entry Program* and also of *Displaced Employee Program. See* **Delayed Entry Program** and **Displaced Employee Program.**

Department of Health and Human Service A cabinet-level department of the executive branch that deals with more Americans than any other Federal agency because it administers programs which deal with Medicare, Medicaid, Social Security, drug abuse, mental health, children, families, and public health.

Department of Housing and Urban Development (HUD) The Federal agency principally responsible for housing programs, the development and preservation of communities, and the provisions of equal housing opportunities. Some of these programs include Federal Housing Administration mortgage insurance programs, rental assistance programs, fair housing programs, and the Government National Mortgage Association mortgage-backed securities program that helps ensure an adequate supply of mortgage credit.

Department of Labor A U.S. Government department responsible for the promotion and development of the welfare of wage earners and for the improvement of working conditions. *See also* **Bureau of Labor Statistics.**

Department of Veterans Affairs A cabinet-level department of the U.S. Government that replaced the Veterans Administration in 1989 and is responsible for the administration of the veterans' benefits system, health services, research, and the National Cemetery System.

deposition A form of discovery in which the testimony of a witness is given under oath, subject to cross-examination, and recorded in writing prior to a hearing.

deputy sheriff A individual who assists a sheriff in maintaining law and order, arresting offenders, and escorting defendants.

dermatologist A physician who specializes in the treatment of skin diseases.

design To prepare the preliminary plans or sketches for a project.

designer An individual who creates designs for particular objects or products, such as clothing, automobiles, floral arrangements, kitchens, appliances, or movie sets. *See also* the OOH.

detail In the Federal civil service system, a temporary assignment of an employee to a different position for a specified period. At the end of the detail, the employee returns to regular duty.

detective (military) In the Army, Navy, Air Force, Marine Corps, or Coast Guard, an individual who investigates crimes against the country and Government property; helps special agents investigate possible terrorist activities; and investigates criminal activities, such as theft, assault, and drug selling. *See also* the *Military Careers* guide.

detective, private An individual who protects property by detecting theft, conducts private investigations, and seeks missing persons.

detective, public An individual who works as part of a police department but does not usually wear a uniform and specializes in the gathering of facts and evidence in criminal cases. *See also* the OOH.

developer, film An individual who produces negatives from photographic film.

developmental psychologist A psychologist who studies the patterns and causes of behavioral change as people progress through life.

dexterity The ability to use the hands or body with great skill.

dictating-machine transcriber/typist An individual who listens to recordings and then types the information on a typewriter or word processor.

***Dictionary of Occupational Titles* (DOT)** A U.S. Department of Labor publication that focuses on occupational classifications and definitions. It contains standardized and comprehensive descriptions of job duties and related information for 20,000 occupations grouped into a systematic occupational classification system. The *Dictionary of Occupational Titles* was designed as a job placement tool to facilitate the matching of job requirements and worker skills. Each occupation is assigned an occupational code; for example, the occupation of architect is 001.061-010. *See also* ***Dictionary of Occupational Titles* codes.**

***Dictionary of Occupational Titles* codes** The occupational code numbers assigned to each job by the U.S. Department of Labor. This 9-digit code is divided into categories that identify the occupational group (digit 1); the division within the category (digit 2); the occupational group within the division (digit 3); and a rating of the tasks performed in the occupation (digit 4-data, digit 5-people, digit 6-things). Because many occupations might have the same first six digits, the last three digits are used to ensure that each occupation has a unique number.

Example:

3----Service Occupations

3**1**----Food and Beverage Preparation and Service Occupations

31**3**----Chefs and Cooks, Hotels and Restaurants

313.**1**----Task: Data----Coordinating

313.1**3** ----Task: People----Supervising

313.13**1**----Task: Things----Precision Working

313.131-**014**----Unique Identification Number: Chef (hotel and restaurant)

Thus, a restaurant chef's DOT code would be **313.131-014**. A brief description of an occupation is available by checking the appropriate code number in the *Dictionary of Occupational Titles*.

die maker A skilled individual who makes the device or die that cuts or shapes metal in a press or in a forging or stamping operation. *See also* the OOH.

diesel mechanic An individual who repairs, services, and maintains diesel engines. *See also* the OOH.

dietician A person with specialized training in nutrition who may advise individuals or groups about proper eating habits or develop and supervise food service for hospitals, nursing homes, and schools. *See also* the OOH.

dietician (military) An Army, Navy, or Air Force officer who sets policies for hospital food service operations; inspects hospital food service and preparation areas to ensure that they meet sanitation and safety standards; and plans and organizes training programs for medical food service personnel. *See also* the *Military Careers* guide.

differentials Federal Government recruiting incentives in the form of compensation adjustments justified by **1)** extraordinarily difficult living conditions, **2)** excessive physical hardships, or **3)** notably unhealthy conditions.

dining room attendant A preferred term for busboy, an individual who assists waiters and waitresses by cleaning tables, removing dirty dishes, and keeping the serving area stocked with supplies.

dinkey operator An individual who works at industrial sites or mines and operates engines that help transport coal, rock, or supplies.

diploma A written document given to high school, college, or university graduates to show that they have completed the required courses of study.

diplomate An individual who has been certified as specialist in a particular field by a national certification board.

dipper An individual who immerses racks or baskets of articles in vats of paint, liquid plastic, or other solutions.

direct To conduct, control, or manage some activity, event, or person.

direct appointment (military) A military policy that permits a fully qualified medical, legal, engineering, or religious professional to apply for an appointment as a military officer.

direct commission (military) An appointment to the military attained by a professional person who is already established in a specialty field. *See also* **direct appointment.**

direct hiring authority In the Federal civil service system, an agency recruiting plan, approved by the Office of Personnel Management, that expedites recruitment of persons for appointment to positions in shortage occupations.

directive Policy statements, regulations, or guidelines used by management to inform employees about new policies or regulations or changes in procedures.

director **1)** An individual who auditions performers for a theater, radio, movie, or television production; conducts rehearsals; and directs the cast and crew to produce a finished presentation. *See also* the OOH. **2)** An individual who serves as a member of the board of directors of a corporation or organization. *See also* **board of directors.**

director of admissions An individual responsible for having catalogs prepared, recruiting students, and overseeing the admittance procedures for a college or university.

director of student services An individual who directs and coordinates admissions, foreign student services, health services, and counseling services in an educational institution.

director, religious education and activities An individual who directs and coordinates activities of a denominational group to meet religious needs, directs religious school programs, and provides counseling and guidance services.

Directory of Accredited Home Study Schools A publication that provides information about home study programs and is available from the National Home Study Council, 1601 18th St. NW., Washington, DC 20009. Phone: (202) 234-5100.

Directory of Educational Institutions A publication that lists schools accredited by the Accrediting Commission for Independent Colleges and Schools of the Career College Association. This directory is available from Career College Association, 750 1st St. NE., Washington, DC 20002. Phone: (202) 659-2460.

disability A physical condition that may prevent an individual from performing required occupational duties. An organization that provides information on career planning, training, or public policy support for the disabled is the President's Committee on Employment of People with Disabilities, 1331 F St. NW., 3rd Floor, Washington, DC 20004. Phone: (202) 376-6200. *See also* **Americans with Disabilities Act.**

disability benefits Monies paid to individuals who can't work because of illness or injury. *See also* **Social Security disability benefit.**

disability retirement A Federal Government policy that permits payment of an immediate annuity to an employee under the retirement system who has completed five years of civilian service and has suffered a mental, emotional, or physical disability not the result of the employee's vicious habits, intemperance, or willful misconduct.

disability retirement pay (uniformed service) In the Federal civil service system, money paid by a uniformed service for disability incurred in, or as the proximate result of, the performance of active duty.

disability, Social Security *See* **Social Security disability benefit.**

disabled veteran A person who was separated under honorable conditions from active duty in the Armed Forces performed at any time and who has established the present existence of a service-connected disability or is receiving compensation, disability retirement benefits, or pension because of a public statute administered by the Department of Veterans Affairs or a military department.

discharge **1)** The action of dismissing an employee. **2)** In the Federal civil service system, an agency-initiated action to take an employee off its rolls (for work performance or for misconduct or delinquency) when the employee is serving on an appointment that does not afford the person appeal rights.

discharge during probation/trial period In the Federal civil service system, an agency-initiated action to take an employee off its rolls (for preappointment conditions or for postappointment work performance and/or misconduct or delinquency) when the employee is serving an initial appointment probation or is serving on a trial period required by civil service or agency regulations.

discharge under honorable conditions (military) An honorable or a general discharge from the Armed Forces. The term does not apply to the honorable discharge given an enlisted person to allow commissioning as an officer without a break in service. In this situation the officer's discharge must be under honorable conditions.

disciplinary action A form of punishment designed to correct rulebreaking, improve attendance, and amend undesirable actions. Punishment might include admonishment, loss of salary, demotion, or suspension.

disciplinary interview An interview whose main purpose is the reprimanding or disciplining of an employee. The interview might include a description of unacceptable job behavior or performance, a suggestion of ways to correct the poor behavior or performance, or an indication of possible consequences if the problem is not corrected.

discontinued service retirement *See* **retirement, discontinued service.**

discount An employee benefit that permits the worker to purchase merchandise, meals, housing, or travel fares at reduced rates.

discretionary income Money that can be used after taxes have been withheld and expenses for basic necessities such as food and housing have been deducted.

dishwasher An individual who scrapes the remaining food from used dishes in a food establishment and then washes them by hand or automatic dishwasher.

disk jockey An individual who plays recorded music on a radio station; reads commercials; and, depending on the size of the station, may also do the newscast or operate the broadcast equipment.

dismissal with prejudice In the Federal civil service system, the dismissal of an appeal, barring an individual from filing a later appeal on the same subject matter.

dismissal without prejudice In the Federal civil service system, the dismissal of an appeal that does not bar the individual from filing a later appeal on the same subject matter.

dismissed The status of an employee whose services were no longer needed and whose employment was terminated by the employer.

dispatcher An individual who handles calls from people requesting assistance or a service and then relays the information to the appropriate agency or individuals for necessary action. *See also* the OOH.

dispatcher (military) In the Army, Navy, Air Force, or Marine Corps, an individual who schedules the use of motor vehicles; assigns drivers for trucks, buses, and cars; and determines transportation routes. *See also* the *Military Careers* guide.

dispensing optician An individual who uses a customer's corrective eyeglass prescription to prepare eyeglasses and adjusts them so that they fit properly. In some states the dispensing optician may also fit contact lenses. *See also* the OOH.

Displaced Employee Program (DEP) A system of the Federal Government that helps find jobs for career and career- conditional employees displaced either through a reduction in force or by an inability to accept assignment to another commuting area. *See also* **career appointment, career-conditional appointment**, and **reduction in force.**

displaced homemaker An individual who has been a homemaker dependent on the income of another family member, usually a spouse, but is no longer supported by that income. Programs to provide job counseling, training, and placement for displaced homemakers are available in some areas.

displaced worker A worker who becomes unemployed for any of a number of reasons.

disposable personal income Money that can be used according to the wishes of an individual.

distributive education A type of instruction that combines classroom instruction with on-the-job training in businesses involved with distribution.

diver (military) In the Army, Navy, Marine Corps, or Coast Guard, an individual who inspects and cleans ship propellers and hulls; uses underwater welding equipment to patch damaged ship hulls; and salvages sunken equipment. *See also* the *Military Careers* guide.

dividend clerk An individual who ensures timely payments of stock or cash dividends to clients of a particular brokerage firm.

doctor, chiropractic *See* **chiropractor.**

doctor, medical *See* **physician.**

doctor, optometry *See* **optometrist.**

doctor, osteopathic *See* **osteopathic physician.**

doctor, podiatric medicine *See* **podiatrist.**

doctor, veterinary medicine *See* **veterinarian.**

document **1)** A written statement that in many cases is an official paper or record. **2)** To prove that an action took place.

dog catcher *See* **animal control officer.**

dog control officer *See* **animal control officer.**

dog warden *See* **animal control officer.**

DOL An abbreviation of Department of Labor. *See* **Department of Labor**

DOT An abbreviation of *Dictionary of Occupational Titles*. *See* ***Dictionary of Occupational Titles.***

dot etcher *See* **lithographic dot etcher.**

DOT numbers *See* ***Dictionary of Occupational Titles*** **codes.**

double-dipper *Informal:* a person who receives a pension from two different sources.

downgrading A change of a position to a lower grade with less status, less responsibility, and a lower rate of pay.

downsizing A reduction in the number of employees in a business or organization. *See also* **reduction in force.**

downtime A period of time when no work is being accomplished usually because of a mechanical or an electronic failure.

dozer operator *See* **grader, dozer, and scraper operator.**

drafter An individual who prepares detailed drawings, specifications for materials needed, and procedures to be followed for buildings, bridges, and machinery. In the past, drafting has been done by hand; however, more and more drafters are using computer-aided drafting to produce the necessary drawings. *See also* the OOH, **computer-aided design, architectural drafter, electrical drafter,** and **civil drafter.**

drafter (military) In the Army, Navy, Air Force, or Coast Guard, an individual who makes scale drawings of roads, airfields, buildings, and other military projects from engineers' instructions and sketches; draws diagrams for wiring and plumbing; and computes the cost of materials. *See also* the *Military Careers* guide.

draw To get part of a salary, wages, or commission before earning them or prior to the regular payment date.

dress code The policy of requiring a certain standard in clothing for employees. *Example:* a new employee's T-shirt and jeans that do not fit the company's dress code.

Dress for Success A 1976 book by John T. Molloy, who argued that how people dress influences significantly their career.

dressmaker An individual who makes women's apparel and repairs, hems, and restyles garments.

drier operator and tender An individual who performs operations such as removing moisture from paper, chemicals, ore, and clay products.

driver-sales worker An individual who not only delivers goods to stores and businesses but also may put the delivered items on display racks, remove outdated products, and prepare an inventory of items delivered. *See also* the OOH.

Drug Enforcement Agency (DEA) The Federal agency responsible for enforcing narcotics and controlled substances laws and regulations.

drug testing The policy of having employees take tests to detect illegal drug use. Tests may be required before employment, randomly, or at a time when such testing seems appropriate. *Example:* testing an engineer or pilot after a train or plane accident.

druggist An individual who uses specialized knowledge to fill a customer's prescription for medicines and drugs. *See also* the OOH.

drywall finisher An individual who produces a smooth surface on drywall by filling nail holes, taping and filling the joints, and then sanding the filled areas.

drywall installer An individual who attaches drywall panels to walls and cuts and prepares openings in the drywall for doors, windows, plumbing, and electric outlets. *See also* the OOH.

drywall workers and lathers *See* **drywall finisher** and **drywall installer.**

dual compensation **1)** In the Federal civil service system, the payment for more than one civilian office involving a total of more than 40 hours a week. **2)** The payment of a salary to a civilian employee who at the same time is receiving a retirement annuity from the military service.

dues Money that covers membership fees for a trade union or professional organization and is sometimes deducted monthly from wages.

dumbing down A derogatory term that means simplifying a job to accommodate unskilled workers. *Example:* installing in fast-food establishments easy cash registers that list individual items and figure change.

duplicating machine operator An individual who operates one or a variety of duplicating machines to make copies of data.

durable goods Items expected to last more than three years. *Examples:* washers, dryers, and refrigerators. *See also* **nondurable goods.**

duty (military) An assigned task to occupation.

duty assignment (military) The geographical area to which military recruits are assigned after the completion of job training.

duty station In the Federal civil service system, the city, county, and state in which the employee works. For most employees, the duty station will be more specifically the location of the employee's desk or the place where the employee normally performs duties. For those employees with no fixed work site, the duty station will be determined by the employing agency. For example, the duty station of an investigator who works in the field may be the location of the office from which assignments are normally made. For an inspector who must be on-site at many places, the duty station may be the inspector's home. Agencies will also designate the duty stations of employees who work at installations, such as military bases, whose boundaries cross county or state lines.

dyer An individual who operates a machine used by the textile industry to bleach or dye fabric. *See also* the OOH.

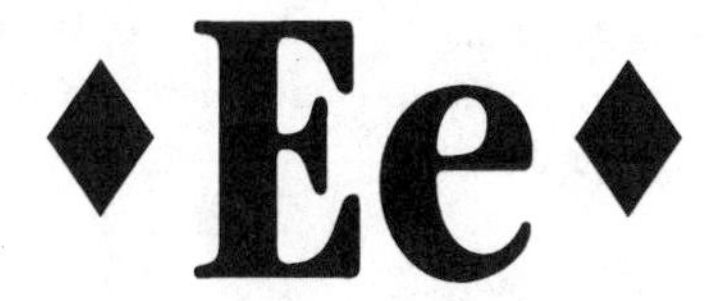

EAP An abbreviation of *Employee Assistance Program. See* **Employee Assistance Program.**

early retirement Retirement that occurs before the traditional retirement age of 65. *See also* **early retirement incentive, window,** and **Social Security retirement age.**

early retirement incentive Money or other benefits that a business or organization may offer to encourage employees to retire early. *See also* **window** and **buyout.**

earning potential Future income that is possible for a particular job.

earnings The amount of money paid to a worker as wages, salary, or commission and is usually affected by experience, level of responsibility, amount of unionization, and geographic area.

ecotourism A type of tourist activity in which travel plans emphasize ecology, such as tours of rain forests, unique animal habitats, and nature conservancies.

ecologist An individual who uses scientific training to research environmental factors, such as rainfall or pollutants, and how they relate to organisms in the environment.

economic geographer An individual who deals with the geographic distribution of an area's resources and economic activities.

economist An individual who studies how goods and services are produced, consumed, and distributed. Economists sometimes use this specialized knowledge to predict or manipulate conditions to improve economic conditions, such as inflation or recession. *See also* the OOH.

edition binding worker An individual who binds books produced in large amounts.

editor An individual who oversees the planning and production of a publication. In addition, an editor may hire writers, edit or rewrite copy, and make work assignments. *See also* the OOH.

editorial artist An individual who specializes in illustrating such items as record album, cassette, and compact-disc covers as well as magazines and theater posters. *See also* **animator, cartoonist, visual artist, fine artist,** and **graphic artist.**

editorial assistant An individual who aids an editor by performing a variety of tasks, such as checking manuscripts, doing research for writers, and preparing layouts.

editorial writer An individual who writes material of public interest for the editorial page and expresses a personal viewpoint or the opinion or editorial policy of the newspaper or magazine.

education administrator A leader in a school, college, or university who manages its daily operations. *See also* the OOH.

education and training manager An individual who supervises employee training programs that are designed to increase productivity and develop skills. *See also* the OOH.

educational assistant *See* **teacher aide.**

educational psychologist A psychologist who designs, develops, and evaluates educational programs.

educational requirements The knowledge, skills, degrees, and credentials that are necessary for a particular job.

EEG An abbreviation of *electroencephalograph* (an instrument that records brain waves) or *electroencephalogram* (the report recorded by the instrument). *See* **EEG tecnologist.**

EEG technologist An individual who operates specialized diagnostic equipment, such as an electroencephalograph (EEG) that records on an electroencephalogram (again, an EEG) a patient's brain waves. *See also* the OOH, **electroneurodiagnostic technologist,** and **neurophysiologic technologist.**

EEOC An abbreviation of *Equal Employment Opportunity Commission. See* **Equal Employment Opportunity Commission.**

effective date In the Federal civil service system, the date on which a personnel action takes place and the employee's official assignment begins.

86 *Informal:* a term used by **1)** bartenders to indicate that a customer should not be served any more alcoholic beverages, or **2)** restaurant employees to indicate that a menu item is no longer available or that something should be discarded.

EKG (or ECG) An abbreviation of *electrocardiograph* (an instrument that records heartbeats) or *electroencardiogram* (the report recorded by the instrument). *See* **EKG tecnician.**

EKG technician An individual who operates specialized diagnostic equipment, such as an electrocardiograph (EKG) that records on an electrocardiogram (again, an EKG) a patient's heartbeats. *See also* the OOH.

elder law An area of specialization that is emerging within the legal profession to serve the special needs of the increasing numbers of older Americans. Elder law deals with planning for financial security, catastrophic illness, and incapacity; handling medical problems, such as hospital care, nursing home admission, patient's rights, and home health care; and preparing such instruments as wills, trusts, health care proxies, and living wills to avoid financial problems.

elderly employees *See* **older workers and ageism.**

electric meter installer/repairer An individual who installs, tests, and repairs electric meters, and connects or disconnects service.

electric power distributor and dispatcher An individual who controls the flow of electricity through transmission lines to the users.

electric power generating plant operator An individual who oversees and regulates electric power plant equipment, such as turbines, boilers, and generators. *See also* the OOH.

electrical and electronic assembler An individual who assembles items such as electric signs, battery parts, and electric motor winders.

electrical drafter An individual who draws wiring and layout diagrams used by workers who erect, install, and repair electrical equipment and wiring in power plants, electrical distribution systems, and buildings.

electrical/electronics engineer (military) An Army, Navy, Air Force, Marine Corps, or Coast Guard officer who directs research to improve and develop computer, navigation, and other electronic systems; directs equipment installation and repair; reviews test data and report results; and recommends actions. *See also* the Military Careers guide.

electrical/electronics technician An individual who helps develop, manufacture, and service electrical and electronic products, such as radios, radar, sonar, and television. *See also* the OOH.

electrical engineer An individual who designs, develops, tests, and supervises the manufacture of electrical equipment. *See also* the OOH.

electrical inspector An individual who inspects the installation of electrical equipment to make certain that it meets building codes and specifications.

electrical powerline installer/repairer An individual who prepares for the installation of electrical cables by erecting poles----or digging trenches in an underground installation----and then attaches or inserts the cables. The electrical powerline installer/repairer also maintains and repairs the cables after their installation. *See also* the OOH.

electrical products repairer (military) In the Army, Navy, Air Force, Marine Corps, or Coast Guard, an individual who maintains, tests, and repairs electric motors in many kinds of machines, such as lathes, pumps, office machines, and kitchen appliances; inspects and repairs electrical, medical, and dental equipment; and inspects and repairs electric instruments. *See also* the *Military Careers* guide.

electrician An individual who installs, maintains, and repairs electrical systems. *See also* the OOH.

electrocardiograph technician *See* **EKG technician.**

electroencephalographic technologist *See* **EEG technologist.**

electrologist An individual who uses the process of electrolysis to remove hair from the face and body.

electromedical equipment repairer An individual who tests, adjusts, and repairs electromedical equipment.

electroneurodiagnostic technologist A new occupational title for an individual whose work resembles the duties of an EEG technologist but in addition involves some of the newer testing equipment that measures waves. *See also* **EEG technologist.**

Electronic and Electrical Equipment Repairer Occupations (military) One of the twelve broad categories used by the Armed Forces to group occupations for enlisted personnel.

electronic cottage Computer work that is done at a remote location, such as the individual's home, and is regarded as a modern version of a cottage industry. *See also* **remote work.**

electronic drafter An individual who draws wiring diagrams, schematics, and layout drawings used in the manufacture, installation, and repair of electronic equipment.

electronic home entertainment equipment repairer An individual who repairs electronic equipment, such as TVs, radios, VCRs, and CD players. *See also* the OOH.

electronic instrument repairer (military) In the Army, Navy, Air Force, Marine Corps, or Coast Guard, an individual who uses electronic and electrical test equipment to test meteorological and medical instruments, navigational controls, and simulators; reads technical diagrams and manuals in order to locate, isolate, and repair instrument parts; and replaces equipment parts, such as resistors, switches, and circuit boards. *See also* the *Military Careers* guide.

electronic semiconductor processor An individual who processes materials used in the manufacture of electronic semiconductors.

electronic weapons systems repairer (military) In the Army, Navy, Air Force, Marine Corps, or Coast Guard, an individual who installs electronic components in weapons systems; uses electronic test equipment, calibrators, and other precision instruments to test and adjust weapons firing, guidance, and launch systems; and maintains electronic weapons systems on a regular schedule. *See also* the *Military Careers* guide.

electronics engineer An individual who designs, develops, tests, and supervises the manufacture of electronic equipment, such as computers, TVs, and CD players. *See also* the OOH.

electronics engineer (military) *See* **electrical/electronics engineer (military).**

electronics repairer, commercial and industrial equipment An individual who installs and repairs electronic equipment, such as medical diagnostic equipment, transmitters, antennas, and radar systems. *See also* the OOH.

electronics technician An individual who develops, manufactures, and services electronic equipment. *See also* the OOH.

elementary school teacher An individual who teaches children in the elementary grades. *See also* the OOH.

elevator constructor *See* **elevator installer/repairer.**

elevator inspector An individual who examines elevators, escalators, and ski lifts to make certain that they meet building codes and specifications.

elevator installer/repairer An individual who assembles, installs, services, and repairs elevators and escalators. *See also* the OOH.

elevator mechanic *See* **elevator installer/repairer.**

elevator repairer *See* **elevator installer/repairer.**

eligible In the Federal civil service system, an applicant for appointment or promotion to a Federal Government job who meets the minimum qualification requirements.

eligible list In the Federal civil service system, a list of people who have been certified as qualified to hold a particular civil service position.

embalmer An individual who treats dead bodies with preservatives to prevent decay. *See also* **funeral director.**

emergency management officer (military) An Army, Navy, Air Force, Marine Corps, or Coast Guard officer who organizes emergency teams for quick responses to disaster situations, researches ways to respond to possible disaster situations, and conducts training programs for specialized disaster response teams. *See also* the *Military Careers* guide.

emergency management specialist (military) In the Army, Navy, Air Force, Marine Corps, or Coast Guard, an individual who assists in preparing and maintaining disaster operations plans; trains military and civilian personnel on what to do in an emergency; and operates and maintains nuclear, biological, and chemical detection and decontamination equipment. *See also* the Military Careers guide.

emergency medical technician (EMT) An individual who is sent to the scene of an emergency, such as an automobile accident, a heart attack, or a building collapse, to give emergency treatment and to transport the injured to an appropriate facility. *See also* the OOH.

employability All of the talents, training, or characteristics that make an individual a good prospect for a job.

Employee Assistance Program (EAP) A program that some employers provide to help employees whose personal or health problems may affect job performance. Services might include counseling or assistance with problems involving alcohol, drugs, finances, gambling, or emotional and psychological difficulties.

employee benefits Items that are granted to an employee in addition to regular wages. *Examples:* health insurance, vacation time, maternity leave, childcare, and disability insurance.

employee benefits and welfare manager An individual responsible for managing the programs for the various benefits, such as health insurance, pension plan, or profit sharing, that a company may provide for employees. *See also* the OOH.

employee development Policies or programs to develop better performance on an employee's current job, teach a new procedure, or enhance an employee's potential for advancement.

employee, exempt An employee exempt from the overtime provisions of the Fair Labor Standards Act. *See also* **Fair Labor Standards Act.**

Employee Involvement Program A program of the United States Postal Service that was designed to bring together workers and managers to address problems and improve conditions in the workplace.

employee orientation The process of familiarizing a new employee with the workplace, routines, policies, and other employees.

employee relations A personnel function that centers on the relationship between the employer and individual employees.

Employee Retirement Income Security Act (ERISA) A law that sets Federal standards for private pension plans in order to protect workers from poor business and investment practices.

employee welfare manager An individual responsible for programs covering occupational safety and health standards and practices, health promotion and physical fitness, medical examinations, and plant security.

employee with competitive status *See* **status employee.**

employment agencies Businesses that attempt to match the skills and abilities of a job seeker with a job opening.

Employment and Training Administration A Federal agency responsible for training programs to prepare unskilled and displaced workers for employment.

employment application *See* **job application.**

employment authorization expiration date The date when an alien's right to be employed in the U.S. expires.

employment benefits (military) In addition to pay and allowances, military officers' benefits that may include health care, vacation time, legal assistance, recreational programs, educational assistance, and commissary/exchange privileges. *See also* **commissary/exchange privileges.**

employment counselor An individual who advises clients who are looking for employment. An employment counselor may help the client evaluate interests and skills, administer tests, or assist in applying for a job. *See also* the OOH.

employment discrimination lawsuits Actions filed by individuals who feel that they have been dismissed or refused promotion because of their age, race, or religion. *See also* **age discrimination, Equal Employment Opportunity,** and **Equal Employment Opportunity Commission.**

employment eligibility documents Items that are accepted by the U.S. Immigration and Naturalization Service to establish the identity or employment eligibility of individuals, especially those who are not U.S. citizens. Acceptable documents include a U.S. passport, certificate of U.S. citizenship, certificate of naturalization, unexpired foreign passport, and alien registration receipt card.

employment eligibility verification requirements The regulations of the U.S. Immigration and Naturalization Service requiring employers to determine whether an employee is eligible to work. Each employee hired after Nov. 6, 1986, must fill out Form I-9 (Employment Eligibility Verification Form), and the employer is required to review and verify documents presented by the employee to prove the individual's identity and employment eligibility.

employment interviewer An individual who works with employers as well as clients seeking employment and tries to bring together a qualified individual and an available job. *See also* the OOH.

employment office *See* **state employment service.**

employment outlook An estimate of employment prospects.

employment prospects *See* **employment outlook.**

employment skills Skills that are necessary to find a job. Example: the ability to write a resume, communicate verbally, or complete a job application.

Employment Standards Administration A Federal Government agency authorized to correct a wide range of unfair employment practices, administer laws and regulations dealing with workers' compensation, and set employment standards.

empower To give power or authorization to someone. Some employers empower workers to solve problems and take more responsibility for their work. *Example:* a person who feels that his work is more important and satisfying because he has been empowered to make most of the decisions. *See also* **shared decision making.**

EMT An abbreviation of emergency medical technician. *See* **emergency medical technician (EMT).**

Encyclopedia of Associations Available in many public libraries, a multivolume publication that gives information on trade associations, professional societies, and labor unions.

endocrinologist A physician who specializes in the treatment of illnesses related to the endocrine glands and their secretions.

endodontist A dentist who specializes in root canal therapy.

endorse To approve or support some program or activity. *Example:* a union that is asked to endorse a new health insurance plan.

engine mechanic (military) In the Army, Navy, Air Force, Marine Corps, or Coast Guard, an individual who uses engine analyzers and other test equipment to troubleshoot engine problems; adjusts and repairs ignition, fuel, electrical, and steering systems; and keeps records of repairs made and parts used. *See also* the *Military Careers* guide.

engine specialist *See* **aircraft mechanic and engine specialist.**

engineer An individual with specialized training in the design, construction, and use of machinery and engines. *See also* the OOH and specific types of engineers.

engineer, ship *See* **marine engineer.**

engineer, stationary An individual who operates, services, and repairs power-generating equipment, such as diesel engines, boilers, generators, and pumps. *See also* the OOH.

engineering manager An individual who supervises engineering activities in testing, production, operations, or maintenance, and plans and coordinates the design and development of machinery, products, systems, and processes. *See also* the OOH.

engineering psychologist An individual who often works in factories and plants to develop and improve industrial products and human-machine systems.

Engineering, Science, and Technical Occupations (military) One of the broad categories used by the Armed Forces to group occupations for enlisted personnel and officers.

engineering technician An individual who uses engineering training to solve practical problems in research, sales, and manufacturing. *See also* the OOH, **civil engineering technician, electrical and electronic technician,** and **mechanical engineering technician.**

enhance To intensify, magnify, or raise something to a higher level. *Example:* to enhance the image of the company's president by a new car, a new office, and a new computer.

enlisted commissioning programs (military) Two plans that enable enlisted personnel to become officers. Enlisted personnel with outstanding performance records and a college degree may receive a direct appointment to officer training school. A second commissioning plan permits enlisted personnel to complete their college degree through a Reserve Officers' Training Corps (ROTC) program or at one of the service academies. *See also* **commissioned, direct appointment,** and **service academies.**

enlisted member (military) A member of the military below the rank of a warrant or commissioned officer and whose role is similar to that of a company employee or supervisor.

enlisted pay grades (military) New Armed Forces recruits can progress through nine pay grades beginning with E-1, E-2 usually in about 6 months, and E-3 in six to twelve months if job performance is satisfactory. E-4 to E-9 are based on job performance, leadership ability, promotion test scores, years of service, and time in present pay grade.

enlisted personnel (military) Members of the

Armed Forces who carry out and maintain the day-to-day operations of the military. Enlisted personnel are usually high school graduates and are required to meet minimum physical and aptitude requirements before enlisting.

enlistee (military) Someone who has been accepted by the military and has taken the Oath of Enlistment.

enlistment agreement/contract (military) A contract between a military service and an applicant that contains the enlistment date, term of enlistment, and other options, such as a training program guarantee or a cash bonus. If the service cannot meet its part of the agreement, the applicant is no longer bound by the contract.

Enlistment Options Program A program of the Marine Corps which guarantees before their enlistment that well-qualified applicants will be assigned to one of several military occupational specialties.

enrobing machine operator An individual who coats (enrobes) confectionery, bakery, and other food products with melted chocolate, cheese, oils, sugar, and other substances.

enrolled agent An individual with special training in Federal tax matters who is authorized to represent taxpayers before the Internal Revenue Service.

entitlement A Federal Government benefit established by law, such as Social Security, Medicare, or welfare.

entomologist An individual who uses scientific training to specialize in the study of insects and their relationship to animal and plant life.

entrance-level position A position in an occupation at the beginning level or grade.

entrepreneur An individual who organizes and manages a business that may involve a new concept or service and requires initiative and risk.

entry-level job *See* **entrance-level position.**

entry on duty In the Federal civil service system, the process by which a person completes the necessary paperwork and is sworn in as an employee.

entry on duty date In the Federal civil service system, the date on which a person completes the necessary paperwork and is sworn in as an employee.

environmental differential Additional pay authorized for a Federal employee for duty involving unusually severe hazards or working conditions.

environmental health inspector An individual who enforces government regulations and standards that apply to the cleanliness and safety of food, water, and air.

environmental health officer (military) An Army, Navy, Air Force, or Coast Guard officer who determines methods to collect environmental data for research projects and surveys, analyzes data to identify pollution problem areas, and conducts health education programs. *See also* the *Military Careers* guide.

environmental health specialist (military) In the Army, Navy, Air Force, Marine Corps, or Coast Guard, an individual who inspects food service, storage, and dining facilities; inspects foods for quality and freshness; and plans the disposal of radioactive and toxic wastes. *See also* the *Military Careers* guide.

EOE An abbreviation of *Equal Opportunity Employer*. *See* **Equal Opportunity Employer.**

Equal Employment Opportunity Law A Federal law to provide equal employment opportunity for all; to prohibit discrimination on the grounds of age, race, color, religion, sex, national origin, or physical or mental handicap; and to promote the full realization of employee potential through a continuing affirmative action program.

Equal Employment Opportunity Commission (EEOC) A Federal commission that is the primary enforcement agency to ensure that individuals are not discriminated against in employment because of race, color, sex, religion, age, handicap, or national origin. The main office of the Equal Employment Opportunity Commission is located at 1801 L St. NW., Washington, DC 20507. Phone: (202) 663-4264.

Equal Employment Opportunity counselor/representative An individual who works with both employers and minority employees to see that unfair employment practices are eliminated.

Equal Opportunity Employer (EOE) A business or government that complies with the Equal Employment Opportunity law. *See also* **Equal Employment Opportunity Law.**

equal pay for equal work A policy that provides the same pay for work at the same level of difficulty and responsibility regardless of sex.

equipment cleaner An individual who cleans machinery, vehicles, and storage tanks.

equipment rental clerk An individual who deals with customers renting various types of equipment. The equipment rental clerk writes out orders, gets or directs the customer to the rental item, and accepts returns and payment.

ergonomics The study of people's use of modern technology in order to adapt the workplace to the worker's needs to be efficient, comfortable, and safe.

ergonomist An individual who designs equipment so that it is comfortable and compatible for the user.

ERISA An acronym for *E*mployee *R*etirement *I*ncome *S*ecurity *A*ct. *See* **Employee Retirement Income Security Act.**

escalation clause A union contract provision that is tied to some economic indicator, such as the consumer price index, and which gives workers an automatic increase if the indicator rises.

esthetic Related to or appreciative of beauty and taste, especially in art. *Variant of* **aesthetic.**

esthetician An individual who gives facials and specializes in skin care and the correction of minor skin problems. *Variant of* **aesthetician.**

estimate The act of forming an opinion or evaluation of the cost, quantity, or extent of something.

estimator *See* **cost estimator.**

ethical conduct *See* **ethics** and **standards of conduct.**

ethics The system of values, principles of right and wrong, and moral conduct of a culture. *See* **standards of conduct.**

ethnobotanist A scientist who studies plants and their relationship to people.

euphemism A pleasant term substituted for an unpleasant term to soften or modify the harsh reality underlying the unpleasant idea. *Example:* speaking of downsizing or of a reduction in force instead of saying that employees are being fired.

euthanasia technician An individual who destroys unwanted or sick animals at animal shelters and kennels.

evaluate To determine the amount or worth of something.

examination A means of measuring, in a practical and suitable manner, qualifications of applicants for employment in specific positions. *See also* **examination, assembled; examination, fitness-for-duty;** and **examination, unassembled.**

examination, assembled In the Federal civil service system, an examination for a Federal job that includes, as one of its parts, a written or performance test for which applicants are required to assemble at appointed times and places.

examination, fitness for duty In the Federal civil service system, an examination given by a Federal medical officer or an employee-designated, agency-approved physician to determine the employee's physical, mental, or emotional ability to perform assigned duties safely and efficiently.

examination, unassembled In the Federal civil service system, a Federal examination in which applicants are rated on their education, experience, and other qualifications, as shown in the formal application and any supportive evidence that may be required without assembling for a written or performance test.

excavating and loading machine operator An individual who operates and tends heavy machinery equipped with scoops, shovels, or buckets to move construction materials or manufactured goods.

excepted position In the Federal civil service system, a position in the Excepted Service. *See also* **Excepted Service.**

Excepted Service In the Federal civil service system, an unclassified service, unclassified civil service, or positions outside the competitive service and the Senior Executive Service. Excepted Service positions have been excepted from the requirements of the competitive service by law, Executive order, or Office of Personnel Management regulation. *See also* **Office of Personnel Management; Senior Executive Service;** and **Executive order.**

Excepted Service agencies In the Federal civil service system, the Federal agencies that do not havetofollowcompetitiveserviceproceduresand can establish their own evaluation criteria and hiringsystems.

exclusive bargaining agent *See* **exclusive recognition.**

exclusive bargaining representative *See* **exclusive recognition.**

exclusive recognition The status conferred on a labor organization that receives a majority of votes cast in a representation election and entitles it to act for and negotiate agreements covering all employees included in an appropriate bargaining unit.

exclusive representative *See* **exclusive recognition.**

execute To perform or carry out some action.

executive An individual who has supervisory authority over the employees in a business or organization.

Executive, Administrative, and Managerial Occupations (military) One of the nine broad categories used by the Armed Forces to group occupations for officers.

executive chef A chef who does little hands-on work in a restaurant, hotel, or resort but instead is responsible for the management and administration of the food program.

executive housekeeper An individual who ensures that guest rooms, meeting and banquet rooms, and public areas in hotels, resorts, and conference centers are clean, orderly, and well maintained.

executive inventory An Office of Personnel Management computerized file that contains background information on all members of the Senior Executive Service and persons in Federal positions at GS (General Schedule) grades 16 through 18 or equivalent, as well as individuals at lower grades who have been certified as meeting the managerial criteria for the Senior Executive Service (SES). The inventory is used as an aid to Federal agencies in executive recruiting and as a planning and management tool.

Executive order A directive issued by the President of the United States.

executive recruiter An individual who finds people to fill top-level management positions. *See also* **headhunter** and **executive search firm.**

Executive Resources Board A panel of top Federal agency executives responsible under the law for conducting the merit staffing process for career appointment to Senior Executive Service positions in the agency.

executive schedule The salary schedule that covers top officials in the executive branch of the Federal Government.

executive search firm An employment agency that specializes in the recruitment of management level individuals. *See also* **headhunter** and **executive recruiter.**

expedite To speed up or move a process along.

expediter An individual responsible for the efficient routing and timely dispatch of some product or service.

expediting clerk An individual responsible for the flow of work and material according to production schedules.

expense account Funds expended by an employee for various business expenses that, after an accounting, will be reimbursed by the employer.

experimental psychologist A psychologist who studies behavior processes and works with human beings and animals.

expert **1)** An individual who has special training or experience in a particular area and is considered an authority in that field. **2)** In the Federal civil service system, a person with excellent qualifications and a high degree of attainment in a professional, scientific, technical, or some other field. The person's attainment is such that the individual usually is regarded as an authority or as a practitioner of unusual competence and skill by other persons in the profession, occupation, or activity.

expert position In the Federal civil service system, a position that can be satisfactorily performed only by someone who is an expert in that field.

extractive metallurgist A metallurgist who removes metals from ores and refines and alloys them to obtain useful metal.

extruding and forming machine operator and tender An individual who operates or tends machines to shape and form any of a wide variety of manufactured products by means of extruding, compressing, or compacting.

extruding and forming machine setter and setup operator An individual who sets up, or sets up and operates, machines to manufacture a wide variety of products by means of extruding, compressing, or compacting.

eyeball *Informal:* to look at something and make a judgment about its size, quality, or relationship to another item, without doing any actual measuring.

FAA An abbreviation of *Federal Aviation Administration. See* **air safety inspector** and **aviation safety inspector.**

facialist An individual in a beauty salon or spa who specializes in giving facials.

facilitator An individual who assists in solving problems or aids in the process of running an operation smoothly and without difficulty.

Fair Labor Standards Act A Federal law that established standards for minimum wages, maximum hours, child labor, equal pay, and overtime pay for employees of companies engaged in interstate commerce.

faller An individual who cuts down trees as part of a timber-cutting or logging operation.

family daycare provider An individual who cares for young children during normal working hours. The family daycare provider may furnish these services at a daycare facility or at home.

family issues *See* **work-family issues.**

family service worker An individual who assists and counsels families who are experiencing social adjustment problems.

farm and home management advisor An individual who advises, instructs, and assists individuals and families engaged in agriculture and related processes or home economics activities.

farm equipment mechanic An individual who services and repairs various types of farm machinery, such as tractors, combines, and hay balers. *See also* the OOH.

farm labor contractor An individual who secures farm laborers for farmers and fruit growers.

farm manager An individual who oversees the operation of a farm for the owner. *See also* the OOH.

farm operator An individual who owns or rents farmland and is responsible for the farming operation from the planning stage to the marketing of final products. *See also* the OOH.

farm worker An individual who performs a variety of duties, such as planting, cultivating, harvesting, and storing crops or tending livestock and poultry.

fashion artist/illustrator An individual who specializes in drawing sketches of the newest styles in clothing.

fashion designer An individual who specializes in the design of clothing and accessories.

fashion model *See* **model.**

fast-food cook An individual who prepares some of the items served in food establishments that specialize in a rapid turnover of customers and a high percentage of take-out orders.

fast-food worker An individual who works at the counter of a fast-food establishment and takes orders, accepts money, gives change, and gathers ordered items.

fast tracker *Informal:* an individual who probably will advance in a career faster than others doing similar jobs.

fax number A number that permits copies of information to be transmitted from one place to another by telephone lines and a facsimile machine (fax) or fax/modem board in a computer.

FBI An abbreviation of *Federal Bureau of Investigation See* **Federal Bureau of Investigation.**

FBI special agent An individual employed by the Federal Bureau of Investigation to investigate violations of Federal law, such as kidnapping, bank robbery, espionage, and organized crime.

Federal Bureau of Investigation (FBI) The agency responsible for gathering and reporting facts, locating witnesses, and compiling evidence in cases involving Federal jurisdiction.

Federal Cooperative Education Program An educational program for high school or college students that combines academic studies with on-the-job experience. *See also* **cooperative vocational education.**

Federal Employees' Retirement System A retirement system that provides three benefit plans----Basic Benefit, Social Security, and Thrift Savings Plan----for Federal Government employees. *See also* **Federal Retirement Thrift Investment Board.**

Federal Government service In the Federal civil service system, the total of all periods of military and civilian Federal service considered for retirement, reduction in force, and leave purposes.

Federal Insurance Contribution Act (FICA) The law that established who was eligible to contribute to Social Security.

Federal Job Information Centers Offices set up in major cities of the United States to provide information on employment with the Federal Government. The main office is located at 1900 E St. NW., Room 1416, Washington, DC 20415. Phone: (202) 606-2700.

Federal Labor Relations Authority The agency that oversees the Federal service labor-management relations program and administers the law that protects the rights of employees of the Federal Government to organize, bargain collectively, and participate through their labor organizations in decisions affecting them.

Federal Mediation and Conciliation Service A service that helps to prevent interstate commerce disruptions caused by labor-management disputes. Mediators assist in resolving disputes at the request of either labor or management when the problem may cause a substantial interruption of interstate commerce.

Federal Merit System A complete system of personnel selection and management based on an integrated set of personnel policies, procedures, and practices designed to accomplish three basic objectives: **1)** to recruit a competent work force, **2)** to ensure a stable work force, and **3)** to provide equal opportunity for employment.

***Federal Personnel Manual* (FPM)** In the Federal civil service system, the official publication of the Office of Personnel Management that contains Federal personnel instructions, operational guidance, policy statements, and related information to other agencies.

Federal Personnel Manual Bulletin In the Federal civil service system, notices that contain temporary instructions and an expiration date.

Federal Personnel Manual Letter In the Federal civil service system, letters containing continuing instructions that, because of urgency, cannot be put in the *Federal Personnel Manual* or its supplements at the time of issue.

Federal Personnel Manual Supplements Publications that expand, amplify, or explain in greater detail various subjects covered in the basic *Federal Personnel Manual.*

Federal Retirement Thrift Investment Board An independent agency of the Federal Government that administers the Thrift Savings Plan, which provides Federal employees the opportunity to save for additional retirement security. The Thrift Savings Plan is a tax-deferred contribution plan open to employees covered under the Federal Employees' Retirement System.

Federal Service Impasses Panel (FSIP) An administrative body created to resolve bargaining impasses in the Federal Service. This panel may recommend procedures, including arbitration, for settling impasses, or may itself settle the impasses.

The panel is considered the legal alternative to strikes in the Federal sector.

Federal wage employees *See* **wage employees.**

Federal Wage System In the Federal civil service system, the job grading and pay system that applies to most trade, craft, and labor positions (blue-collar). Under this system, pay is adjusted according to the rates paid by private industry for similar jobs in the same area. Included are Federal employees in recognized unskilled, semiskilled, or skilled manual labor occupations, and other persons, including foremen or supervisors, in positions in which trade, craft, or labor experience or knowledge is the main requirement.

fellowship An award made to an individual from a governmental agency, foundation, or institution to be used for further education or research.

FICA An acronym for the *F*ederal *I*nsurance *C*ontribution *A*ct. FICA is used on payroll and tax-withholding forms as the designation for the amount deducted from an employee's wages for Social Security tax. *See also* **Federal Insurance Contribution Act.**

field engineer 1) In the broadcast industry, an individual who sets up and operates the broadcasting equipment when the program originates outside the studio. **2)** In the computer service industry, an individual who goes to a business establishment to service computers, printers, and disk drives. **3)** In the office machine maintenance sector, an individual who services and repairs office machines, such as typewriters, dictating machines, and duplicating equipment.

field technician *See* **field engineer.**

field trip Visit or excursion to a location outside a school or workplace to see something or gain information. *Example:* students going to a historical site, aquarium, or museum.

50 *See* **Standard Form 50.**

52 *See* **Standard Form 52.**

file clerk An individual who files and retrieves records according to some classification system. *See also* the OOH.

film developer An individual who operates equipment that develops photographic film automatically.

film mounter, automatic *See* **automatic mounter.**

financial aid officer An individual who works with college or university students who are interested in applying for loan programs, scholarships, grants, or fellowships.

financial manager An individual who supervises the various types of financial departments in businesses and institutions. *See also* the OOH.

financial manager (military) An Army, Navy, Air Force, Marine Corps, or Coast Guard officer who sets policies for the use of military funds, directs the preparation of budgets and financial forecasts, and directs the budget and accounting staff. *See also* the *Military Careers* guide.

financial planner An individual who attempts to advise clients and to select appropriate investments for them after analyzing their financial objectives and assets.

financial records processor An individual who computes, records, and reviews financial data in order to maintain systematic billing, payroll, and other accounting records. *See also* the OOH.

financial services sales representative An individual who calls on various businesses to solicit applications for loans and new deposit accounts for a bank or savings and loan association, locates and presents to prospective customers the bank's financial services, and ascertains custormers' banking needs. *See also* the OOH.

fine artist An individual who creates art as a means of self-expression instead of producing art to fulfill the requirements of a client. *See also* the OOH.

fire inspector An individual who ensures that structures meet fire-code requirements.

firearms inspector *See* **alcohol, tobacco, and firearms inspector.**

fired Dismissed from a job.

firefighter An individual who operates equipment to put out fires in homes and buildings. *See also* the OOH.

firefighter (military) In the Army, Navy, Air Force, Marine Corps, or Coast Guard, an individual who operates pumps, hoses, and extinguishers; forces entry into aircraft, vehicles, and buildings to fight fires and rescue personnel; and inspects aircraft, buildings, and equipment for fire hazards. *See also* the *Military Careers* guide.

fireman The preferred unisex term is *firefighter*. *See* **firefighter.**

firing Terminating the employment of an individual.

first-line supervisor *See* **blue-collar worker supervisor.**

fiscal year (FY) A twelve-month period used by governmental units and businesses as their accounting year. The fiscal year may not coincide with the calendar year. *Example:* a fiscal year that begins on July 1 and ends on June 30.

fish cleaner An individual who cuts, scales, and dresses fish in fish processing plants and wholesale and retail fish markets.

fish cutter *See* **butcher and meat, poultry, and fish cutter.**

fisher *See* **fisherman.**

fisherman A collective term for individuals who may do any of the various tasks associated with fishing occupations, such as captain, boatswain, and deckhand. *See also* **captain, boatswain,** and **deckhand.**

fishing guide An individual who assists people who want to fish, leads them to areas where good fishing is available, advises them on fishing techniques, and may set up a camp.

fitness-for-duty examination *See* **examination, fitness-for-duty.**

fitness trainer An individual who devises and supervises physical fitness exercises for classes or private clients.

five-point veterans preference *See* **preference, tentative.**

flexi-employee In the United States Postal Service, a part-time flexible-schedule employee who is a career employee but whose work schedule varies and who is not guaranteed a 40-hour workweek.

flexible benefits plan A plan that permits employees to choose from a number of available benefits to fit their particular needs. *See also* **cafeteria plan.**

flexible spending account An employee benefit program in which an employee puts pretaxed money into the account and then designates the specific benefit(s) to be paid from the account. These benefits might include childcare expenses, an optical plan, or dental insurance.

flexible workplace employment A policy that sometimes permits a Federal employee to work at home.

flexitime *See* **flextime.**

flextime A system that permits an employee to select the hours or days to be worked rather than a traditional 8-hour-day, 5-day workweek.

flight attendant An individual who provides airline patrons with services, such as describing emergency procedures, serving food and beverages, and answering questions. *See also* the OOH.

flight engineer A pilot who assists the other pilots by operating and monitoring many of the sophisticated electronic systems found on large, modern aircraft.

flight engineer (military) In the Navy, Air Force, Marine Corps, or Coast Guard, an individual who inspects aircraft before and after flights, following pre- and post-flight checklists; plans and monitors the loading of passengers, cargo, and fuel; and informs the pilot of aircraft performance problems and recommends corrective action. *See also* the *Military Careers* guide.

flight instructor An individual who teaches people to fly planes and helicopters.

flight operations specialist (military) In the Army, Navy, Air Force, Marine Corps, or Coast Guard, an individual who helps plan flight schedules and air crew assignments, keeps air crew flying records and flight operations records, and plans aircraft equipment needs for air evacuation and dangerous cargo flights. *See also* the *Military Careers* guide.

floor covering installer An individual who lays carpets and rugs in homes, schools, and offices. *See also* the OOH.

floral designer An individual who designs and makes a flower arrangement according to a particular specification. *Example:* a red-and-white contemporary arrangement.

florist An individual who provides and arranges flowers for bouquets, floral pieces, and corsages.

food and beverage manager An individual who directs the food and beverage services of hotels by overseeing the operation of the restaurants, cocktail lounges, and banquet facilities.

food and beverage service occupations *See* **bartender, host/hostess, waiter/waitress, counter attendant, fast-food cook, fast-food worker, chef, cook,** and **pastry chef/baker.**

food inspector An individual who inspects meat and poultry to ensure that they are wholesome and safe for public consumption.

food service manager An individual responsible for the efficient operation of a food establishment. The food service manager usually hires employees, orders food and supplies, and supervises daily operations. *See also* the OOH.

food service manager (military) An Army, Navy, Air Force, Marine Corps, or Coast Guard officer who manages the cooking and serving of food at mess halls; directs the operation of officers' dining halls; and determines staff and equipment needed for dining halls, kitchens, and meat cutting plants. *See also* the Military Careers guide.

food service specialist (military) In the Army, Navy, Air Force, Marine Corps, or Coast Guard, an individual who orders, receives, and inspects meat, fish, fruit, and vegetables; uses cleavers, knives, and band saws to prepare standard cuts of meat; and bakes breads, cakes, pies, and pastries. *See also* the *Military Careers* guide.

food technologist An individual who uses scientific training to study the nature of food to learn how to process, preserve, package, distribute, and store it safely. *See also* the OOH.

forecasting The act of calculating or predicting something in advance, such as employment trends or the weather.

foreign imports Goods from a foreign country that are brought into the United States to be sold. *See also* **trade adjustment assistance.**

foreman/forewoman An individual who is in charge of a group of workmen, usually in a factory. The preferred unisex term for this occupation is supervisor. *See also* **blue-collar worker supervisor.**

forensic pathologist A physician who specializes in medical situations that may be the subject of legal action. Many times the forensic pathologist conducts autopsies and performs tests to establish the cause of death and provide information for law enforcement officers. *See also* **coroner** and **medical examiner.**

forensic psychiatrist A psychiatrist who specializes in problems that are the subject of legal action. Example: the determination of legal insanity.

forest and conservation worker An individual who develops, maintains, and protects forests and woodlands through such activities as raising and transporting tree seedlings; combating insects, pests, and diseases harmful to trees; and controlling erosion and leaching of forest soil.

forester An individual who plans and supervises the growing, protection, and harvesting of trees. *See also* the OOH.

forklift operator An individual who operates a forklift or industrial truck that moves materials around a factory or warehouse.

Form I-9 The Employment Eligibility Verification form required by the U.S. Department of Immigration and Naturalization. *See also* **employment eligibility verification requirements.**

forming machine operator/tender An individual who maintains the machinery that produces manufactured fiber.

Fortune 500 company One of the top five hundred companies as determined annually by Fortune magazine.

Forty Plus A nationwide organization of individuals who are over 40 years of age and without a job.

foundation An institution funded by corporations or wealthy individuals for such purposes as dispensing funds for projects or research and providing educational opportunities.

401(k) plan A retirement plan that allows an employee to put before-tax money into an account whose growth is not taxed until the employee retires. At retirement, withdrawals from the plan are taxed at rates favorable to retired persons. Many employers contribute a percentage of the employee's salary to the employee's account or match the amount of the employee's contribution.

403(b) plan A retirement plan that allows some public employees to put before-tax money into an account that is not taxed until funds are withdrawn at retirement.

FPM See ***Federal Personnel Manual.***

frame wirer An individual who connects or disconnects the telephone wires or cables that run to the central office. The frame wirer is also responsible for the inspection and repair of these telephone wires and cables.

franchise A right granted, for a fee, by a corporation to sell a product or offer a service. *Example:* a franchise to open a McDonald's Restaurant.

franchisee An individual who has been granted a franchise to sell a product or offer a service.

franchiser An individual or corporation that offers franchises.

franchising The system of offering a franchise in order to expand the selling of a product or service.

free enterprise system The American economic system that encourages competition, private ownership, and a minimum of government control.

free-lance To work independently and often intermittently for different employers. *See also* **free lancer.**

free-lancer An individual who performs a service but does not work regularly for one employer. *Examples:* writers and photographers who work independently. *See also* **contingent employees.**

friendly takeover A company's agreeable acquiring of another company that gives to acquired company some new advantage, such as more working capital or access to new markets. *See also* **hostile takeover.**

fringe benefits Items granted to employees in addition to wages. *Examples:* vacation, sick leave, life insurance, disability insurance, childcare leave, and profit sharing.

front-end mechanic An individual who aligns and balances wheels and repairs steering mechanisms and suspension systems.

front office manager An individual who coordinates hotel or motel reservations and room assignments and trains and directs the front desk personnel who deal with the public.

frozen service In the Federal civil service system, the total years and months of civilian and military service, creditable for calculation of the service computation date (leave), at the time an employee first becomes covered by FICA and other retirement plans.

FSIP *See* **Federal Service Impasses Panel.**

fuel and chemical laboratory technician (military) In the Army, Navy, Air Force, or Coast Guard, an individual who tests fuels and oils for water, sediment, and other contaminants; analyzes chemicals for strength, purity, and toxic qualities; and performs chemical and physical tests on clothing, food, paints, and plastics. *See also* the *Military Careers* guide.

full field investigation A personal investigation of an applicant's background to determine whether the individual meets fitness standards for a critical-sensitive Federal position.

full retirement, Social Security *See* **Social Security retirement age.**

full-time regular employee In the United States Postal Service, an employee with a career appointment and a regular schedule of five 8-hour days in a service week.

full-time work schedule In the Federal civil service system, a full-time work schedule which requires that most employees work 40 hours during the work week.

function A specific action or natural activity required of someone in an occupation.

funeral attendant An individual who assists a funeral director by greeting mourners, aiding family members, and driving funeral cars.

funeral director An individual who supervises and coordinates preparations for funeral services and the burial of dead persons. *See also* **embalmer** and **funeral attendant.**

furlough **1)** To lay off an employee temporarily. **2)** To grant leave to a member of the Armed Forces. **3)** In the Federal civil service system, to place an employee in a temporary nonpay status and nonduty status (or to designate the employee as absent from duty) because of a lack of work or funds or for other nondisciplinary reasons.

furlough without pay One of the disciplinary or nondisciplinary personnel actions against an employee that is sometimes taken by a Federal agency.

furnace installer An individual who installs various types of heating equipment, such as gas or oil furnaces, air ducts and vents, fuel lines, and pumps. *See also* the OOH.

furnace operator/tender An individual who performs such operations as annealing glass, roasting sulfur, converting chemicals, or processing petroleum.

furniture and wood finisher An individual who is skilled in the precision work needed to complete furniture or wood items.

furniture upholsterer An individual who attaches webbing, springs, padding, and fabric to the framework of new furniture or performs similar operations to old furniture in need of reconditioning. *See also* the OOH.

FY An abbreviation of *fiscal year*. See **fiscal year.**

G-man *Informal:* a term used in previous years to identify an FBI agent (*G*overnment *man*).

gainsharing plan A program designed to increase productivity by encouraging employee involvement and the sharing of the resulting profits.

GAO An abbreviation of *General Accounting Office*. *See* **General Accounting Office.**

garde manger chef *See* **chef de garde manger.**

gardener An individual who plants and cares for trees, plants, and lawns. *See also* the OOH.

garment sewing machine operator An individual who sews clothing for men, women, and children.

garment worker *See* **apparel worker.**

gas plant operator An individual who distributes or processes gas for utility companies and others.

gate agent An individual who assists boarding airline passengers by directing them to the correct boarding area; checking flight tickets; making boarding announcements; and assisting elderly, disabled, or young passengers when they board or depart from the airplane.

gatekeepers *Informal:* personnel executives or other individuals who act as barriers or obstacles between a business or organization and the general public.

gauger An individual who gauges and tests oil in storage tanks and regulates the flow of oil into pipelines at wells, refineries, and rail terminals.

gemologist An individual who specializes in the appraisal of the quality and market value of gemstones.

gender-blind companies Businesses that consider the individual and the person's abilities instead of hiring and promoting on the basis of sex or sexual stereotypes. *Examples:* companies that hire women as executives as well as secretaries, or hospitals that employ men as nurses as well as electricians.

genealogist An individual who conducts research into the ancestry of specific persons or families. This research is usually used as a basis for a written narrative or a chart showing lines of descent.

General Accounting Office (GAO) An investigative agency of Congress that conducts audits and evaluations of Government programs and activities to examine all matters dealing with public funds.

general discharge (military) A discharge granted under honorable conditions.

general houseworker An individual who dusts, sweeps, mops, waxes, washes, and performs other routine household tasks. *See also* **housekeeper** and **executive housekeeper.**

general maintenance mechanic An individual who performs a variety of services relating to the upkeep of a facility. Tasks might include repairing machinery, building or altering partitions, painting, or making minor plumbing repairs. *See also* the OOH.

general manager/top executive An individual who formulates policies and directs the operation of a company, institution, or organization. *See also* the OOH and **chief executive officer.**

general office clerk An individual who performs a variety of duties in an office instead of one specialized task. A general office clerk may file, type, answer telephones, deliver messages, or operate copiers or other office equipment. *See also* the OOH.

general position A position with the Federal Senior Executive Service that may be filled by a career, noncareer, or limited appointment.

General Schedule (GS) In the Federal civil service system, the listing of rankings and salaries for the various classifications in the civil service. Rankings begin at GS-1 and progress to GS-18. *See also* **Senior Executive Service.**

geochemical oceanographer An individual who studies the chemical composition, dissolved elements, and nutrients of oceans.

geodetic surveyor An individual who uses new technologies, such as satellite observations, to measure large areas of the earth's surface.

geographer An individual who studies the distribution of physical and cultural phenomena over an area. *See also* **economic geographer, political geographer, physical geographer, urban geographer, regional geographer,** and **medical geographer.**

geological oceanographer An individual who studies the ocean floor.

geologist An individual who studies the composition, structure, and history of the earth's crust. *See also* the OOH.

geophysical prospecting surveyor An individual who marks sites for subsurface exploration, usually for petroleum-related purposes.

geophysicist An individual who uses the principles of physics and mathematics to study the earth's internal composition, surface, and atmosphere and its magnetic, electrical, and gravitational forces. *See also* the OOH.

geriatric aide A nursing aide who works with elderly patients in a nursing home. *See also* **nursing aide.**

gerontologist An individual who studies aging and the special problems of the aged.

gerontology aide An individual who works in a group home or institution and provides a variety of routine services for elderly patients.

ghostwriter An individual who writes an article or book for another person who receives credit as the author.

GI Bill benefits Money provided under the Montgomery GI Bill Program to military personnel who entered active duty after June 30, 1985. Military personnel who choose to participate have their basic pay reduced by $100 per month for their first 12 months of service; on completion of three years of continuous active duty, these individuals are eligible for $300 per month for 36 months in basic benefits for full-time schooling. Individuals who complete a two-year obligation receive $250 per month for 36 months.

Girl Friday *Informal:* an assistant or especially helpful employee who may perform a variety of general services for an executive. Girl Friday is considered a sexist term, and *administrative assistant* is preferred. *See also* **administrative assistant.**

glass ceiling *Informal:* an invisible barrier that prevents a woman from advancing to a top position in a company or profession because of her sex.

glazier An individual who selects, cuts, installs, and removes all types of glass or materials such as plastic that are used in place of glass. *See also* the OOH.

GNP An abbreviation of *gross national product. See* **gross national product.**

go-between *Informal:* an individual who "goes between" two groups or persons in order to settle some dispute or arrange a business deal. *See also* **intermediary.**

goal setting Formulating aims or results in order to reach a particular objective.

goals The objectives or results that an individual hopes to achieve.

golden parachute *Informal:* generous benefits granted to an executive before retirement or termination.

goods-producing industries Industries that produce a product rather than render a service. Examples: construction, manufacturing, mining, and agriculture. *See also* **service-producing industries.**

governess An individual who works for and sometimes lives with a wealthy family and is responsible for the care of older children. *See also* **nanny** and **au pair.**

government chief executive and legislator An elected or appointed official who tries to meet the needs of constituents through effective and efficient government. Government chief executives have the responsibility for the performance of a governmental unit. Legislators make laws or amend existing ones in order to remedy problems or to promote certain activities. *See also* the OOH.

Government Printing Office (GPO) The agency that prints, binds, and distributes the publications of the Federal Government. Purchases can be made directly by mail order or through Government bookstores.

GPO *See* **Government Printing Office.**

grade In the Federal civil service system, all classes of Federal positions that, although different with respect to kind or subject matter of work, are sufficiently equivalent in **1)** level of difficulty and responsibility and **2)** level of qualification requirements of the work to warrant the inclusion of such classes of positions within one range of rates of basic compensation.

grade restoration action In the Federal civil service system, an action taken to restore to an employee the grade the individual held prior to the reduction in grade that was effective during the retroactive period of title VIII of the Civil Service Reform Act. The grade restoration action records the employee's retained grade in the Office of Personnel Management's data system.

grade retention action In the Federal civil service system, an action taken to retain the grade held by an employee prior to a grade reduction that was effective during the retroactive period of title VIII of the Civil Service Reform Act. The grade retention action documents, for official personnel action purposes, the employee's step in the retained grade and the rate of basic pay to which the individual is entitled.

grade retention entitlement In the Federal civil service system, the right of an employee to retain for two years, for pay and benefits purposes, the grade of the position from which the individual was reduced.

grader An individual who compares products such as eggs, poultry, and cheese against standards or specifications to see whether the products are acceptable.

grader, dozer, and scraper operator An individual who operates heavy machines, such as graders, bulldozers, and scrapers, that are equipped with blades to remove, distribute, level, and grade earth. *See also* the OOH.

grandfather clause A policy statement or regulation that exempts individuals who have previously enjoyed a benefit, privilege, or advantage from losing it. *Example:* an employee who doesn't have to move into the city to keep a job, because a grandfather clause in the new regulation gives the employee the right to remain living outside the city limits.

grant A monetary award to an individual to be used for education or research.

graphic artist An individual who uses a variety of film and print media to create art that meets a client's commercial needs. *See also* the OOH.

graphic designer An individual who designs items such as packaging, promotional displays, logos, and annual reports. *See also* **graphic artist.**

graphic designer and illustrator (military) In the Army, Navy, Air Force, or Marine Corps, an individual who draws graphs and charts to represent budgets or numbers of troops, develops ideas and designs posters and signs, and produces computer-generated graphics. *See also* the *Military Careers* guide.

green card *Informal:* the identification card issued by the U.S. Immigration and Naturalization Service to some immigrants to the United States. The card includes an alien registration number, expiration date, identification photo, and signature and gives the alien's residence status, which affects the individual's employability. *See also* **employment eligibility documents, employment eligibility verification requirements,** and **employment authorization expiration date.**

greenskeeper An individual who maintains a golf course and equipment such as ball washers, benches, and tee markers.

grievance Under a negotiated contract, any complaint or expressed dissatisfaction by an employee against an action by management in connection with the employee's job, pay, or other aspects of employment.

grievance interview A meeting whose purpose is the discussion or resolution of a grievance usually because of a violation of a provision of the collective bargaining agreement between labor and management.

grievance procedure A procedure, either administrative or negotiated, by which employees may seek redress of any matter subject to administrative control or negotiated contract.

grinder and polisher, hand An individual who grinds and polishes by hand a wide variety of metal, stone, clay, plastic, and glass objects or parts.

grocery clerk An individual who performs a variety of tasks in a grocery store or supermarket, such as operating the cash register, bagging purchases, and stocking shelves.

gross domestic product A measurement of the total output of goods and services within the United States.

gross national product (GNP) A measurement of the total output of goods and services inside the United States and overseas.

gross pay Wages before any deductions have been made for taxes, FICA, and dues.

groundskeeper An individual who cares for athletic fields, golf courses, cemeteries, and parks. *See also* the OOH.

GS *See* **General Schedule.**

GS grades *See* **General Schedule.**

guaranteed pay **1)** In certain wage systems, guaranteed employment and pay for a day or week. **2)** The payment of wages for the day even if the task rate was not reached.

guard An individual who patrols and inspects property to protect it against theft, vandalism, and illegal entry. *See also* the OOH.

guard, crossing *See* **crossing guard.**

guidance counselor *See* **school counselor.**

guide *See* **fishing guide** and **hunting guide.**

gunsmith An individual who makes or repairs guns.

gynecologist A physician who specializes in the diseases and conditions of women.

♦Hh♦

hair colorist An individual who specializes in the bleaching and dyeing of hair.

hair stylist An individual who is trained to cut hair in a variety of styles to suit patrons' requirements. *See also* **cosmetologist** and **barber.**

hand cutter An apparel worker who does cutting by hand on delicate or valuable items.

hand packer/packager An individual who manually packages or wraps materials.

hand presser An apparel worker who hand presses finished products.

hand sewer A highly skilled apparel worker who specializes in sewing buttonholes and adding lace or trimmings.

hand trimmer An apparel worker who removes loose threads and basting stitches from finished products.

Handbook of Accredited Private Trade and Technical Schools A publication that lists schools accredited by the Accrediting Commission for Trade and Technical Schools. Copies are available from the Career College Association, 750 1st St. NE., Washington, DC 20002. Phone: (202) 659-2460.

Handbook of Occupational Groups and Series A U.S. Office of Personnel Management publication that is the official guide for positions in the General Schedule and determines the occupational categories within which a position falls. It lists the occupational groups and series of classes, defines them, and assigns a number to each. This publication is available from the U.S. Office of Personnel Management, 1900 E St. NW., Washington, DC 20415-0001.

Handbook X-118 In the Federal civil service system, the manual that lists the official qualification standards for General Schedule (white-collar) positions. Qualification standards describe the knowledge, abilities, and skills needed to perform the duties of a position and are intended to ensure the recruitment of a competent, stable work force on the basis of merit and fitness for the work to be done. These standards are arranged by series code number in numerical order. This publication is available from the U.S. Office of Personnel Management, 1900 E St. NW., Washington, DC 20415-0001.

Handbook X-118C In the Federal civil service system, the manual that lists the official qualification standards for wage system (blue-collar) positions. This publication is available from the U.S. Office of Personnel Management, 1900 E St. NW., Washington, DC 20415-0001.

handicapped person An individual who has a physical or mental impairment that substantially limits one or more of the person's major life activities, such as taking care of oneself, performing manual tasks, walking, seeing, hearing, speaking, breathing, learning, and working.

handler **1)** An unskilled worker who moves materials to and from storage areas and unloads trucks. **2)** An individual who shapes the public image of a political candidate by advising the candidate about what to say, how to act, and what to wear.

hard hat *Informal:* a construction worker who traditionally wears hard headgear to protect the individual from falling objects.

harnessmaker An individual who is a skilled leather worker and specializes in making the straps and bands used as a harness for animals such as horses.

hazard pay Extra wages paid to workers because of the dangerous nature of their work. *Examples:* extra wages given to oil well firefighters and demolition experts.

hazard pay (military) Extra wages paid to Armed Forces members because of the dangerous nature of their work. *Examples:* extra wages given to parachute jumpers and those on submarine duty or flight deck duty.

headhunter *Informal:* an individual who recruits management-level people for employment.

health benefit The health service and insurance programs established by businesses and organizations for their employees. *See also* specific benefits.

Health Care Occupations (military) One of the broad categories used by the Armed Forces to group occupations for enlisted personnel and officers.

Health Diagnosing and Treating Practitioner Occupations (military) One of the nine broad categories used by the Armed Forces to group occupations for officers.

health inspector An individual who checks food, drugs, and cosmetics to see whether they meet public health and safety regulations.

health insurance A benefit provided by many employers for employees and their families. Health insurance may take the form of hospitalization coverage, health maintenance organization membership, preferred providers, or dental insurance. *See also* **health maintenance organization, coinsurance,** and **deductible.**

health maintenance organization (HMO) A prepaid health plan that provides medical care to employees at a central health care facility.

health psychologist A psychologist who counsels the public in health maintenance to help people avoid serious emotional or physical illness and does research on the psychological aspects of medical problems.

health services administrator (military) An Army, Navy, Air Force, or Coast Guard officer who develops and manages budgets for health care facilities or programs; directs personnel activities, such as hiring, employee evaluation, staff development, and recordkeeping; and meets with hospital department heads to plan services and keep the health care facility running smoothly. *See also* the *Military Careers* guide.

health services manager An individual responsible for the staff, budget, programs, and services of a health care facility, such as a hospital, clinic, nursing home, or rehabilitation center. *See also* the OOH.

hearing In the Federal civil service system, an opportunity for contending parties under a grievance, complaint, or other remedial process to introduce testimony and evidence and to confront and examine or cross-examine witnesses.

hearing examiner *See* **administrative law judge.**

hearing officer *See* **administrative law judge.**

heater An individual employed in a metalworking plant who tends the machines that reheat steel before it is rolled into sheets.

heating, air-conditioning, and refrigeration mechanic An individual who installs, maintains, and repairs heating, air-conditioning, and refrigeration systems. *See also* the OOH.

heating and cooling mechanic (military) In the Army, Navy, Air Force, Marine Corps, or Coast Guard, an individual who installs and repairs furnaces, boilers, and air conditioners; recharges cooling systems with refrigerant gases; and installs copper tubing systems that circulate water or cooling gases. *See also* the *Military Careers* guide.

heating equipment technician *See* **furnace installer.**

heavy equipment mechanic (military) In the Army, Navy, Air Force, Marine Corps, or Coast Guard, an individual who locates engine problems, places engines and transmissions in bulldozers and other heavy equipment, and replaces or repairs hydraulic arms or shovels and grader blades. *See also* the *Military Careers* guide.

heavy equipment operator *See* **material moving equipment operator.**

heavy mobile equipment mechanic An individual who services and repairs equipment such as graders, trenchers, backhoes, and shovels. *See also* the OOH.

helicopter pilot *See* **aircraft pilot.**

helicopter pilot (military) An Army, Navy, Air Force, Marine Corps, or Coast Guard officer who prepares flight plans showing air routes and schedules; flies helicopters by controlling engines, flight controls, and other systems; and performs combat maneuvers, spots and observes enemy positions, transports troops and equipment, and evacuates wounded troops. *See also* the *Military Careers* guide.

help wanted ad A classified advertisement, appearing usually in a newspaper, that gives information about an available job and invites response from qualified persons who are interested in filling the position. *See also* **blind ad, situations wanted ad,** and **classified ad.**

helper, construction trades An individual who performs a variety of tasks and supplies much of the routine physical labor at a construction site.

herpetologist An individual who studies the behavior, diseases, and life processes of snakes.

highway maintenance worker An individual who maintains highways, roads, and airport runways by patching broken or eroded pavement or erecting and repairing guard rails, highway markers, and snow fences.

highway patrol officer An individual who enforces the laws and regulations of the state and whose duties may include issuing tickets, investigating accidents, enforcing criminal laws, and aiding stranded motorists.

Hispanic worker An individual who is an immigrant or the descendent of a recent immigrant from a Spanish-speaking country. An organization to aid low-income, older Hispanics is the Asociacion Nacional Por Personas Mayores (National Association for Hispanic Elderly), 2727 W. 6th St., Suite 270, Los Angeles, CA 90057. Phone: (213) 487-1922.

histology technician An individual who cuts and stains tissue specimens for microscopic examination by pathologists.

historian An individual who does research about the past and may specialize in a particular time period or country.

historic site director An individual responsible for the operation of a property that has historic significance and is open to the public.

HMO An abbreviation of *health maintenance organization. See* **health maintenance organization (HMO).**

hoist and winch operator An individual who tends and operates machines that use power-operated cable equipment to lift and pull loads.

holiday premium pay Extra pay for working on holidays, such as Thanksgiving, Christmas, or Easter.

Holland system A system developed by John L. Holland, Ph.D., that attempts to match an individual to the appropriate occupational group. Occupations are divided into categories involving **1)** realistic occupations, such as skilled trades, technical occupations, and some service occupations; **2)** investigative occupations, such as scientific occupations and some technical occupations; **3)** artistic occupations, such as artistic, musical, and literary occupations; **4)** social occupations, such as educational and social welfare occupations; **5)** enterprising occupations, such as managerial and sales occupations; and **6)** conventional occupations, such as office and clerical occupations.

home appliance and power tool repairer An individual who installs, services, and repairs appliances, such as washers, dryers, toasters, and vacuum cleaners, and power tools, such as hedge trimmers, saws, and drills. *See also* the OOH.

home entertainment electronic equipment repairer An individual who repairs entertainment equipment, such as radios, televisions, CD players, VCRs, and stereo systems. *See also* the OOH.

home health aide *See* **homemaker-home health aide.**

home study courses Educational courses offered by private businesses to prepare students for an occupation. Instructional packets are mailed to students at their home. When completed, the packets are returned for grading and evaluation. Home study courses are also called correspondence courses.

homemaker-home health aide An individual who works in private homes, usually part-time, and provides a variety of services determined by the needs of the client. Tasks of the homemaker-home health aide may include cleaning, shopping, doing laundry, preparing meals, bathing the patient, or administering medicine. *See also* the OOH.

horizontal move A career change that is considered neither a promotion nor a demotion but a move to a job with roughly the same status and responsibility.

horticulturist An individual who uses scientific training to improve the quality, yield, and disease resistance of fruits, vegetables, and ornamental plants.

hospital administrator An individual responsible for the overall direction of a hospital. *See also* the OOH.

hospital attendant *See* **nursing aide.**

hospital nurse A nurse on the staff of a hospital who provides bedside nursing care; carries out the medical orders of physicians; and supervises licensed practical nurses, aides, and orderlies.

host/hostess An individual who acts as a personal representative of a food establishment and welcomes guests as they enter, directs or escorts them to their table, and provides menus.

hostile takeover A company's acquiring of another company against the wishes of the officers, board of directors, or stockholders of the acquired company. Hostile takeovers often result in a loss of positions in the acquired company.

hot line A direct communication link to an individual or organization for quick and easy exchange of information or assistance.

hotel manager/assistant An individual responsible for the efficient and profitable operation of a hotel. *See also* the OOH.

hotel/motel clerk An individual who performs a variety of services for hotel or motel guests, such as assigning rooms, answering questions about services, and keeping records. *See also* the OOH.

hourly wage Payment to a worker that is based on the number of hours worked instead of a salary. *See also* **salary, piece work,** and **commission.**

house detective An individual who patrols a business, hotel, resort, or conference center to ensure acceptable behavior of guests and visitors and to protect the premises against theft and vandalism.

housekeeper **1)** An individual who works in a private home and is responsible for the smooth operation of the household. **2)** An individual employed by a hotel or institution to supervise the department responsible for the cleaning, maintenance, and supplying of rooms and other housekeeping services. *See also* **executive housekeeper.**

housing allowance (military) An extra amount of money allotted to military personnel who live off of a military base.

HUD An acronym for *Department of Housing and Urban Development. See* **Department of Housing and Urban Development.**

Human Services Occupations (military) One of the broad categories used by the Armed Forces to group occupations for enlisted personnel and officers.

human services worker An individual who may work in a group home, mental health center, or drug abuse clinic and, under the direction of a professional, may perform a variety of tasks, such as organizing activities, leading discussions, interviewing clients, and keeping records. *See also* the OOH.

hunter An individual who tracks, stalks, and kills predatory animals, animal pests, and large game animals whose numbers are out of control.

hunting guide An individual who assists hunters by leading them to areas where the desired animals are present, advising them on tracking and stalking techniques, and setting up a camp.

hydrologist An individual with scientific training who specializes in the study of the distribution, circulation, and physical properties of underground and surface waters.

hygienist, dental *See* **dental hygienist.**

hypnotherapist *See* **hypnotist.**

hypnotist An individual who hypnotizes people for entertainment or to control such conditions as smoking or overeating.

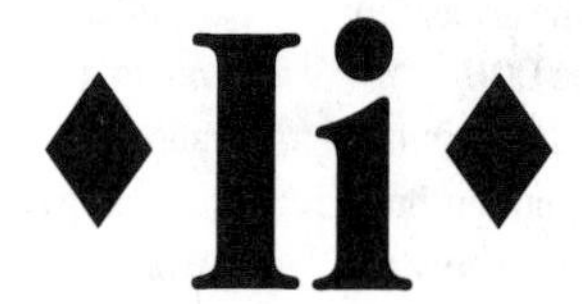

ichthyologist An individual who studies the origin, behavior, diseases, and life processes of fish.

ILIA *See* **retirement-in lieu of involuntary action.**

illusionist A magician. Some magicians prefer illusionist as the name of their occupation. *See also* **magician.**

illustrator An individual who paints or draws pictures for books, magazines, or film.

image consultant An individual who is paid to help people change their appearance and attitudes in order to communicate a different style, personality, or image.

immigration inspector An individual who enforces the laws and regulations relating to immigration. The immigration inspector may interview and examine people entering the United States, inspect passports to verify citizenship, and process applications. *See also* **alien** and **green card.**

immunology technologist An individual who examines elements and responses of the human immune system to foreign bodies.

impartial Free from bias, prejudice, or unfairness.

impasse procedures Procedures for resolving collective bargaining deadlocks between employers and unions.

implement To devise and carry out a plan to achieve some objective.

in-house Within a business or organization instead of outside it. *Example:* using company personnel to publish a company newsletter, perform specialized computer operations, repair equipment, or create media productions instead of hiring free-lance writers, editors, computer programmers, computer technicians, or graphics designers to do these projects or operations.

in-the-can *Informal:* finished, particularly with regard to the creation of a movie or TV production. The term originated in the motion picture industry in which reels of film for a movie were stored in metal canisters after it was completed.

in the field Outside an office or work site. Some jobs, such those of inspectors, surveyors, and engineers, require field work.

inactive Reserve duty Affiliation with the military in a nontraining or nonpaying status after competing a minimum obligation of active duty service.

incentive and special pay (military) In addition to basic pay, money paid for certain types of duty, such as submarine and flight duty, parachute jumping, flight deck duty, and explosive demolition. Special pay is provided also for officers in certain occupations, such as doctors, dentists, and veterinarians.

incentive awards **1)** A reward granted to a Federal employee for a suggestion adopted by management; **2)** a special achievement award for performance exceeding job requirements; or **3)** an honorary award in the form of a certificate, emblem, or pin.

incentive pay Extra wages to an employee who suggests ways to save money, increase productivity, or improve services. *See also* **incentive awards.**

indefinite appointment/tenure The tenure of a nonpermanent Federal employee hired for an unlimited time.

induction (military) *See* **entry on duty.**

industrial buyer An individual who purchases goods, supplies, and services for a company or organization. *See also* **purchasing agent** and **manager.**

industrial designer An individual who specializes in the development and design of manufactured products, such as cars, appliances, computers, and sports equipment. *See also* the OOH.

industrial electronic equipment repairer *See* **commercial and industrial electronic equipment repairer.**

industrial electronics technician *See* **commercial and industrial electronic equipment repairer.**

industrial engineer An individual who determines the best ways for a company or organization to utilize its machines, materials, information, and employees. *See also* the OOH.

industrial engineer (military) An Army, Navy, Air Force, Marine Corps, or Coast Guard officer who studies how workers and tasks are organized; studies and improves the way work is done and equipment is used; and plans and directs quality control and production control programs. *See also* the *Military Careers* guide.

industrial engineering The application of engineering principles and techniques to the design, installation, or improvement of some system or facility to increase its efficiency and productivity.

industrial engineering technician An individual who studies the efficient use of personnel, materials, and machines in factories, stores, repair shops, and offices.

industrial machinery repairer An individual who maintains and repairs the many types of machines used in factories and industrial plants. *See also* the OOH.

industrial nurse An individual who specializes in providing first aid and minor nursing care to the employees of a factory or industrial plant. *See also* **registered nurse.**

industrial production manager An individual responsible for the production schedules, staff, equipment, quality control, inventory control, and coordination of activities with other departments in a factory. *See also* the OOH.

industrial psychologist A psychologist who applies psychological techniques to personnel administration, management, and marketing problems.

industrial relations The association or connection between management and labor in areas such as labor policy, collective bargaining agreements, and grievance procedures.

industrial safety and health inspector An individual who enforces the laws and regulations that protect employees in their workplace. The industrial safety and health inspector checks the safety of equipment and tries to detect unhealthy conditions. *See also* **Occupational Safety and Health Act** and **occupational safety and health inspector.**

industrial sales worker An individual who works for a manufacturer and sells company products to other producers, wholesalers, or retailers. The industrial sales worker, unlike other manufacturers' sales representatives, usually sells some type of technical product. *See also* the OOH.

industrial truck and tractor operator An individual who drives and controls industrial equipment used to lift and move goods or equipment inside a factory or between factories, warehouses, or outdoor storage areas. *See also* the OOH.

infant nurse An individual who dresses, feeds, bathes, and performs other routine tasks associated with caring for an infant. *See also* **nanny** and **au pair.**

infantry officer An Army or Marine Corps officer who gathers and evaluates intelligence on enemy strength and positions, develops offensive and defensive battle plans, and develops and supervises infantry unit training. *See also* the *Military Careers* guide.

infantryman In the Army or Marine Corps, an individual who operates, cleans, and stores automatic weapons; parachutes from troop transport airplanes while carrying weapons and supplies; and digs foxholes, trenches, and bunkers for protection against attacks. *See also* the *Military Careers* guide.

inform To communicate information either orally or in writing.

information clerk An individual involved with gathering information from and providing information to the public. This occupational term includes hotel/motel clerks, interviewing clerks, and receptionists. *See also* the OOH, **hotel/motel**

clerk, interviewing clerk, and **receptionist.**

information officer An individual employed by the U.S. Government to provide the public with information about the activities of a particular Government agency. *See also* **public relations specialist.**

information scientist An individual who designs information storage and retrieval systems and develops procedures for collecting, organizing, interpreting, and classifying information.

informational interview A meeting designed to communicate facts about new policies, benefits, promotions, demotions, and problems or to solicit information from the interviewee.

inhalation therapist *See* **respiratory therapist.**

inhibition The checking or restraining of an action. Example: a person who disagrees with his boss and wants to express his point of view but has inhibitions that keep him from opening his mouth.

initiate To start, begin, or introduce. *Example:* to initiate a new system for checking the production of widgets.

injury compensation In the Federal civil service system, the compensation and medical care provided to civilian Federal employees for disability due to personal injuries sustained while in performance of duty or to diseases relating to this employment.

injury, traumatic Under the Federal Employees' Compensation Act, for continuation of pay purposes, a wound or other condition of the body caused by external force, including stress or strain. The injury must be identifiable by time and place of occurrence and member or function of the body affected and be caused by a specific event or incident or series of events or incidents within a single day or work shift.

injury, work-related Under the Federal Employees' Compensation Act, an injury sustained by an employee while performing the individual's duties. *See also* **injury, traumatic.**

inside collector An individual who works for a bank, department store, or hospital and is responsible for the collection of customers' overdue accounts.

inspect To examine something to detect imperfections, problems, or violation of laws.

inspector and compliance officer, except construction An individual who enforces the laws and regulations that protect the public on matters such as health, safety, food, immigration, licensing, and interstate commerce. *See also* specific types of inspectors.

inspector, construction and building An individual who examines the construction, alteration, or repair of various structures, such as buildings, bridges, streets, and highways. *See also* specific types of inspectors.

inspector, tester, and grader An individual who checks products to make certain that they meet the standards and specifications established by the manufacturer of the item or the producer of a service. *See also* the OOH.

institutional cook An individual who cooks in institutions such as schools, hospitals, nursing homes, and correctional facilities.

instruct To teach, train, give knowledge to, or give an order or direction.

instructor An individual who teaches. *See also* **adult education teacher, college/university faculty, kindergarten teacher, elementary school teacher,** and **secondary school teacher.**

instructor (military) *See* **teacher/instructor (military).**

instrument repairer An individual who uses hand tools and power tools to repair, test, and modify communications equipment, such as telephones, teletypewriters, and switchboards.

instrumental musician An individual who plays a musical instrument in an orchestra, band, rock group, or jazz "combo."

insulation worker An individual who installs insulation in buildings, boilers, and tanks. *See also* the OOH.

insurance adjuster *See* **claim adjuster.**

insurance agent *See* **insurance sales worker.**

insurance examiner *See* **claim examiner.**

insurance man The preferred nonsexist term is *insurance agent* or *insurance sales worker. See* **insurance sales worker.**

insurance processing clerk An individual who processes new policies, modifies existing policies, and reviews insurance applications to ensure that all questions have been answered. *See also* the OOH.

insurance sales worker An individual who helps clients select the right insurance policy for their needs. Policies may be for life, health, or disability insurance or for coverage against fire and theft. *See also* the OOH.

intangible Something that cannot be touched or seen, such as an idea, value, or goal. *Example:* time, which cannot be touched, seen, or heard, compared to a clock that can be touched, seen, and heard.

intelligence officer (military) An Army, Navy, Air Force, Marine Corps, or Coast Guard officer who directs sea, ground, and aerial surveillance; prepares plans to intercept foreign communications transmissions; and oversees the writing of intelligence reports. *See also* the *Military Careers* guide.

intelligence specialist (military) In the Army, Navy, Air Force, Marine Corps, or Coast Guard, an individual who studies aerial photographs of foreign ships, bases, and missile sites; studies foreign troop movements; and uses computers to store and retrieve intelligence data. *See also* the *Military Careers* guide.

interest inventory tests To assist individuals in making career decisions, tests which identify concepts that arouse a person's curiosity, attention, or concern.

intergovernmental personnel assignment An assignment of personnel to and from the Executive branch of the Federal Government, state and local government agencies, and institutions of higher education up to two years, although a two-year extension may be permitted. The purpose of such an assignment is to provide technical assistance or expertise where needed for short periods of time.

interim geographic adjustment In the Federal civil service system, an additional payment made to a General Schedule, Foreign Service, or Veterans Health Administration employee, or to an officer of the U.S. Park Police whose official duty station is in an area where the President has determined that significant pay disparities and recruitment or retention problems exist.

interior designer An individual who plans and furnishes the interiors of private homes, public buildings, or offices. *See also* the OOH.

intermediary An individual who acts as an agent between two people or groups in order to settle a dispute, arrange a business deal, or negotiate a settlement. *See also* **go-between.**

intermittent Recurrent at irregular intervals or occasionally. *Example:* a light bulb that blinks off and on irregularly.

intermittent employment/service Less than full-time employment requiring irregular work hours that cannot be prescheduled.

intermittent work schedule In the Federal civil service system, a work schedule that requires employees to work irregularly and for which there is no prearranged, scheduled tour of duty.

intern An individual who acts as an aide or assistant in order to add practical experience to formal education. *Example:* a political science student who acts as an intern in the office of a U.S. Senator.

internal revenue agent An individual responsible for the various operations involved in the collection of Federal income taxes.

interpersonal skills An individual's skills or abilities that are useful in relationships with other persons.

interpret **1)** To give, explain, or judge the meaning of something. **2)** To translate a statement into a different language.

interpreter/translator (military) In the Army, Navy, Air Force, or Marine Corps, an individual who translates written and spoken foreign language material to and from English; interrogates prisoners of war, enemy deserters, and civilian informers in their native languages; and records foreign radio transmissions. *See also* the *Military Careers* guide.

intervenor An individual who is not a party to a proceeding but who participates in the proceeding because its outcome may affect the person's rights or duties. *See also* **intervenors as a matter of right** and **permissive intervenors.**

intervenors as a matter of right Those parties who have a statutory or legal right to intervene. *Example:* the Director of the Office of Personnel Management.

interview A meeting in which questions are asked and answered about a particular topic. Interviews can be of several types. In an **appraisal interview**, a prospective employer makes preliminary assessments of an applicant's abilities and potential value to the business or organization. An employer might use a **counseling interview** to identify an employee's personal or work-related problem that is affecting job performance and to help the employee correct the situation. In a **disciplinary interview**, an employer might point out unacceptable job behavior or performance and suggest remedies or potential consequences should the problem persist. An employer might use an **informational interview** to communicate facts about new policies, benefits, promotions, or demotions. In a **grievance interview**, an employer might focus on reasons for the grievance, contract provisions relating to it, and possible solutions.

interviewee An individual who is being interviewed.

interviewer An individual who asks questions of a job applicant during an interview. *See also* **interview.**

interviewing clerk An individual who helps people complete different types of forms, verifies information, and processes the forms. *See also* the OOH.

inventory specialist (military) *See* **stock and inventory specialist (military).**

investigator *See* **detective, private**; and **detective, public.**

investigator, insurance *See* **claim representative, claim adjuster,** and **claim examiner.**

involuntary separation In the Federal civil service system, a separation against the will of, and without the consent of, the employee, and other than separation for cause on charges of misconduct or delinquency. *Examples:* separation due to a reduction in force, an abolishment of position, an expiration of a term of office, a lack of funds, or inefficiency (apart from any employee misconduct).

ironworker An individual who erects steel frameworks for buildings, bridges, and other structures, and positions steel bars and wire mesh to reinforce concrete structures. *See also* **structural and reinforcing ironworker.**

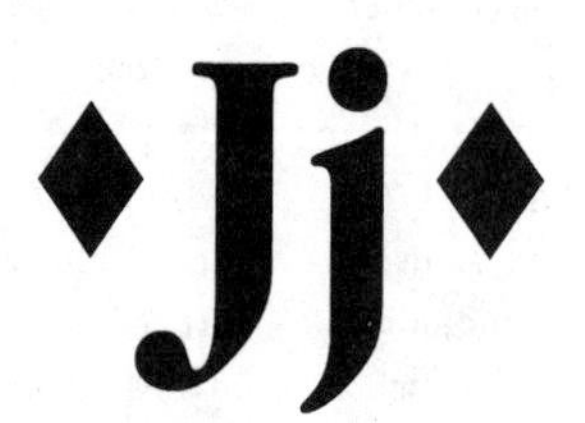

jack-of-all-trades *Informal:* an individual who can do a variety of routine maintenance, alteration, or building tasks. The term is part of an old saying, "Jack of all trades and master of none."

jailer An individual responsible for people confined in a jail or prison. *See also* **correction officer.**

janitor An individual who cleans office buildings, hospitals, schools, and apartment buildings. *See also* the OOH.

jargon Informal or special technical vocabulary used in certain trades or professions. *Example:* librarians who "read" shelves and "accession," "shelve," and "slip" books.

jeweler An individual who makes, repairs, and sells jewelry. *See also* the OOH.

job A group of tasks performed for payment.

job action A type of protest in which employees refuse to perform some part of their duties in an effort to force their employer to agree to some demand. This type of action is used many times by groups who are not legally permitted to strike. *See also* **work to rule** and **blue flu.**

job ad *See* **classified ad, help wanted ad, situations wanted ad,** and **blind ad.**

job analysis A technical review and evaluation of a position's duties, responsibilities, and level of work and of the skills, abilities, and knowledge needed to do the work.

job analyst An individual who collects and examines detailed information about job duties and uses this data to prepare job descriptions. *See also* **job description.**

job application A written form for gathering information about an individual applying for a job. Typical information requested might include name, address, telephone number, Social Security number, education, employment experience, special skills or qualifications, and references.

job bank **1)** A computerized listing of public and private-sector job openings that is updated daily and available at most state employment service offices. **2)** A program in which individuals can register and make themselves available for employment in a particular job or industry. Some corporations have started job banks that hire retired employees when a special need arises. *Example:* retired claims adjusters returning to work during natural disasters such as earthquakes and hurricanes.

***Job Bank* series** A group of books containing information such as the name, address, and telephone number of a company; contact person; description of the firm's primary business; listing of common positions; educational background needed; fringe benefits offered; and industries cross-indexed to pinpoint employers in a particular field for the major metropolitan areas or states. *Examples:* Job Bank----Chicago; Job Bank----Los Angeles.

job binding worker An individual who binds books produced in small quantities.

job burnout Physical and emotional distress caused by an individual's job.

job classification A grouping of jobs into logical categories according to similarity of tasks, subject matter of the work, and level of difficulty.

job club A group formed to work together with a leader or facilitator to learn job-search techniques, interpersonal skills, and self-analysis. The goal of most job clubs is to find a job or improve job prospects.

Job Corps A U.S. Department of Labor program that provides basic education and vocational skills training in residential centers to young adults.

job description A listing of the duties and responsibilities for a particular job.

job enrichment A work assignment or training that is carefully planned to use and upgrade employee skills, abilities, and interests; to provide opportunity for growth; and to encourage self-improvement.

job evaluation A determination of whether the various duties, tasks, and responsibilities of a job are being done satisfactorily. *See also* **performance appraisal.**

job fair An event sponsored by a business or industry to provide information to attendees and to answer their questions about particular companies, available jobs, and benefits.

job freeze A temporary suspension of the hiring of personnel.

Job Grading System for Trades and Labor Occupations A publication that provides detailed standards for grading trades and labor jobs in various occupations under the prevailing rate system (blue-collar jobs). It is the official guide for use in determining job families and occupational series for trades and labor jobs. These standards are arranged in numerical order by series code. This publication is available from the U.S. Office of Personnel Management, 1900 E St. NW., Washington, DC 20415-0001.

job-growth areas Areas in which the increase in the number of jobs is expected to be higher than average.

job hopper An individual who changes jobs frequently.

job hunt A search for employment.

Job Information Centers *See* **Federal Job Information Centers.**

job interview One of the steps in the employment process that may involve questions about the applicant's past experience, salary history, expectations, availability, and references. *See also* **interview.**

job lead Information that may prove valuable for finding a job.

job market The overall condition of employment. A poor job market results when the number of job seekers is greater than the number of jobs available.

job opening An available job. Sources to check for job openings include state employment service offices, civil service announcements, classified ads, labor unions, professional associations, libraries, community centers, women's counseling and employment programs, youth programs, school or college placement services, employment agencies, career consultants, employers, parents, friends, and neighbors.

job order Written instructions indicating to a worker tasks that are to be done.

job outlook The future prospects for employment with regard to a particular job or occupation.

job performance An employee's work evaluated according to the job's objectives. *See also* **performance appraisal.**

job ready The status of an individual who does not need counseling or testing before a job search is started.

job resume *See* **resume.**

job retention An employer's act or policy of keeping or retaining an employee in a job.

job rotation The practice of having employees change jobs periodically to learn other tasks and to have the experience and ability to fill in for another employee if necessary.

job satisfaction The feeling of contentment, happiness, pleasure, or fulfillment that an employee might have in a particular job.

job scams Illegal business schemes that **1)** charge large fees and promise lists of good foreign jobs but which do not exist, or **2)** offer work-at-home jobs that promise large fees for stuffing envelopes or making items. Individuals seeking jobs should be suspicious if a large fee or a credit card number is requested in advance, if claims about success seem exaggerated, or if a call must be made to a 900 phone number that may have heavy charges.

job search The process of going through the necessary steps to find a job.

job security Confidence that an individual's job will not be eliminated or jeopardized.

job service *See* **state employment service.**

job sharing A new work strategy that permits two individuals to work part-time and share one position.

job sheet *See* **position description.**

job specialty (military) A specific job or occupation in one of the five services.

job ticket A card or piece of paper that is sent along with a job to give instructions or to record the amount of time spent accomplishing the job.

job title The formal name of a position as determined by official classification standards. *Examples:* secretary, police officer, and librarian.

job training Skill or technical training taken as preparation for a particular job.

Job Training Partnership Act (JTPA) A law to promote the job training and placement of individuals, especially those from disadvantaged or minority groups.

job vacancy announcement A notice which indicates that a position is available and gives pertinent information, such as duties, qualifications needed, date of availability, contact person, salary, or grade.

jobber An individual who buys large quantities of items from a manufacturer or importer and then resells the merchandise to a retailer or wholesaler.

jobless rate A statistic that shows the percentage of people who are seeking employment.

Jobs Offered The heading for a classified ad section used by some newspapers instead of the traditional Help Wanted heading. *See also* **help wanted ad.**

Jobs Wanted The heading for a classified ad section used by some newspapers instead of the traditional Situations Wanted heading. *See also* **situations wanted ad.**

journalist An individual who works as a writer, editor, columnist, reporter, correspondent, or radio or television broadcaster. *See also* the OOH and specific types of journalists.

journeyman An individual who has completed an apprenticeship program and advanced from the apprentice level. *See also* **apprenticeship** and **apprentice.**

journeyman (military) A status level that can be achieved after satisfactory completion of training in one of the military occupational specialties, such air traffic control, electricity, or surveying.

journeyman level The lowest level of a career ladder position at which an employee has learned the full range of duties in a specific occupation.

JTPA *See* **Job Training Partnership Act.**

judge An individual who oversees the legal process in courts of law. *See also* the OOH.

judgment The ability to make reasonable decisions after considering the facts or conditions involved.

junior college A two-year college similar to a community college. *See also* **community college.**

jury duty pay Wages or salary paid to an employee while serving on a court jury panel.

keeper An individual who works in a steel mill and operates equipment that taps liquid iron and removes impurities from the furnace.

Keogh plan A retirement plan for self-employed individuals that allows them to contribute pretax dollars into an account whose growth is not taxed until accumulated funds are withdrawn at retirement.

kettle operator and tender An individual who performs such operations as boiling soap or melting antimony or asphalt materials.

keypunch operator *See* **data entry keyer.**

kickback The illegal practice of returning part of an employee's wages to an employer or supervisor in order to get or keep a job or obtain special privileges.

kiln operator and tender An individual who performs such operations as heating minerals, drying lumber, firing greenware, annealing glassware, or baking clay products.

kindergarten teacher An individual who introduces children in kindergarten classes to such subjects as language, numbers, science, and social studies. *See also* the OOH.

kitchen worker An individual who assists the cook or chef by weighing and measuring ingredients; stirring and straining soups and sauces; cleaning, peeling, and slicing vegetables and fruits; and cleaning work areas, equipment, and dishes. *See also* the OOH.

kosher cook An individual who prepares food for a restaurant according to Jewish dietary laws.

♦Ll♦

labor force trends The direction the need for workers is likely to take. Various factors such as population, age, sex, and ethnic composition of the work force are considered. Future projections indicate a slowdown in people added to the labor force because of the nation's declining rate of population growth. Other expected changes involve greater diversity as the percentage of minority workers increases, the number of women joining the labor force grows, the number of young people between the ages of 16 and 24 becomes a smaller percentage of the labor force, and the percentage of workers from 25 to 55 and above increases.

labor-management relations Dealings and relationships between employee unions and management.

labor organization An organization composed in whole, or in part, of members who participate and pay dues and whose purpose is dealing with employers concerning wages, working conditions, and grievances. *See also* **grievance, collective bargaining,** and **collective bargaining agreement.**

labor pool The number of workers available for employment.

labor relations A general term used for the relationship between management and labor.

labor relations manager An individual who is knowledgeable in the areas of labor law, current wage information, and economic conditions, and uses this expertise to provide background data to support the position of management when a contract is being negotiated with employees. *See also* the OOH.

laboratory animal technician An individual who works in a laboratory and provides daily care of animals by giving prescribed dosages and medications, taking specimens, performing laboratory tests, and assisting with minor surgery. *See also* **laboratory animal technologist** and **assistant laboratory animal technician.**

laboratory animal technologist An individual who works in a laboratory and supervises the daily care and maintenance of animals by a laboratory animal technician and assistant laboratory animal technician and may also assist in surgical care or laboratory procedures. *See also* **laboratory animal technician** and **assistant laboratory animal technician.**

laboratory technician, dental *See* **dental laboratory technician.**

laboratory technician, film An individual who develops photographic film, makes slides or prints, and does enlarging and retouching.

laboratory worker, medical An individual who uses specialized equipment to perform medical tests, interprets the results, and relays this information to the patient's physician. *See also* specific types of laboratory workers.

laborer An individual who performs many of the routine physical tasks at a construction site. These tasks might include supplying tools or materials to the skilled workers, digging trenches, and cleaning up work sites.

Lamaze instructor An individual who acts as a teacher for pregnant women who want to use the Lamaze Method, a form of natural childbirth, when having their babies.

land surveyor An individual who measures distances, directions, and angles between points and elevations of points, lines, and contours on the earth's surface in order to establish land and water boundaries, and writes descriptions of land for deeds, leases, and other legal documents. *See also* the OOH.

landscape architect An individual who designs parks, college campuses, golf courses, and shopping centers to make them attractive as well as functional. *See also* the OOH.

landscape curator An individual who usually works at a historic site and attempts to restore the grounds to their original design, using the same type of plants, shrubs, and trees. If available, site drawings, old photographs, account books, and journals are used to research the project.

landscape gardener An individual who follows the plans of a landscape architect and plants trees, hedges, and flowering plants.

landscape maintenance worker An individual who maintains the lawns and plantings for office buildings, shopping malls, apartment buildings, and hotels.

lather An individual who forms a base for plaster coatings by installing metal or gypsum lath to walls or ceilings. *See also* the OOH.

laundromat attendant An individual who performs a variety of services in a laundromat, such as providing change, assisting customers, and in some cases doing the laundry for customers.

laundry and dry cleaning machine operator and tender An individual who operates and tends washing or dry cleaning machines to clean or dry-clean commercial, industrial, or household articles.

law The group of rules and regulations made by a government to control the conduct of the members of that society.

law enforcement A collective term for the many occupations whose members are responsible for the enforcement of local, state, and Federal laws. *Examples:* police officer, highway patrol officer, sheriff, and military police.

law enforcement director (military) An Army, Navy, Air Force, Marine Corps, or Coast Guard officer who develops policies and programs to prevent crime and reduce traffic accidents, directs programs to patrol coastal waters and harbors, and assigns military police and detectives to patrols and investigations. *See also* the *Military Careers* guide.

lawn and garden equipment mechanic An individual who maintains and repairs equipment such as lawn mowers, garden tractors, and chain saws.

lawn service worker An individual who specializes in maintaining lawns and shrubs for a fee.

lawyer An individual who uses legal training in a variety of situations, such as representing clients in court, giving advice about the law in personal or business situations, and preparing legal documents. *See also* the OOH.

lawyer (military) An Army, Navy, Air Force, Marine Corps, or Coast Guard officer who gives legal advice about Government real estate, commercial contracts, patents, and trademarks; acts as prosecuting attorney, defense attorney, or judge in court cases; and presides over court cases and makes judgments based on the Uniform Code of Military Justice. *See also* the *Military Careers* guide.

lay off To instruct a worker not to return to work for an indefinite period of time. *See also* **furlough.**

layoff **1)** The act of instructing a worker not to return to work indefinitely. **2)** An indefinite period of inactivity.

layout worker, apparel An individual who spreads out the layers of material to be cut for a garment, determines the most efficient arrangement of the pattern, and draws the outline of the pattern.

lead agency Under the Federal Wage System, the Federal agency with the largest number of Federal wage workers in a geographical area. This lead agency has the primary role for determining wage rates for all Federal employees who work in that area and are covered by the system.

leadership skills The abilities necessary to convince people to follow an individual's guidance, advice, direction, or plan of action. Leadership skills might include a sense of confidence, an ability to communicate effectively, and personal charm.

leadership training (military) Leadership and management classes designed primarily for noncommissioned officers to help them deal more effectively with the day-to-day operations of their units.

leather repairer An individual who maintains and repairs leather products, such as shoes, saddles, handbags, and belts. *See also* the OOH.

leather worker An individual who uses leather to make products such as shoes, jackets, boots, handbags, and luggage. *See also* the OOH.

leave *See* **leave, annual; leave, court; leave, military; leave, sick; leave with pay; leave without pay;** and **leave policy.**

leave, annual In the Federal civil service system, a paid leave of absence allowed for personal, emergency, and other purposes. With certain exceptions, employees earn or accrue leave at the rate of 13 to 26 working days a year, depending on length of service.

leave, court In the Federal civil service system, the time allowed to Federal employees for jury duty and certain types of witness service.

leave, military In the Federal civil service system, a leave of absence with pay allowed for employees who are members of the Reserve or National Guard to perform active military duty.

leave policy The course of action taken by a business, governmental agency, or organization relating to the number of days and the reasons an employee may be absent without loss of pay. *See also* other types of leave.

leave, sick In the Federal civil service system, the leave of absence with pay allowed for employees when the employee is physically incapacitated for the performance of duties; receives medical, dental, or optical examination or treatment; or is required to give care and attendance to an immediate family member afflicted with a contagious disease. With certain exceptions, all civilian employees of the Federal Government earn sick leave at the rate of 13 working days a year.

leave with pay In the Federal civil service system, an absence from duty with pay granted at the employee's request following the approval of a disability retirement application or after application for optional retirement due to disability.

leave without pay In the Federal civil service system, a temporary nonpay status and absence from duty granted by a Federal agency at the employee's request.

legal assistant *See* **paralegal.**

legal authority suffix In the Federal civil service system, a word or phrase added to the legal authority to identify more precisely the circumstances under which the authority is being used or the action is being taken. *Examples:* RIF = reduction-in-force, Mil = military, and Reas = reassignment.

legal secretary An individual who uses skills such as typing, shorthand, and filing to assist a lawyer in the preparation of legal documents.

legal technician (military) In the Army, Navy, Air Force, or Marine Corps, an individual who researches court decisions and military regulations; processes legal claims, appeals, and summonses to appear in court; and maintains law libraries and trial case files. *See also* the *Military Careers* guide.

legislator An individual elected to make laws or amend existing ones in order to remedy problems or to promote certain activities for the welfare of the people the individual represents. *See also* the OOH.

letter carrier *See* **mail carrier.**

letter of commendation A letter citing some project, problem, or situation that was handled in a superior manner and extending thanks or congratulations to the individual receiving the letter. Usually a copy of a letter of commendation is placed in an employee's personnel file.

letter of recommendation A letter from an individual who has knowledge of a job applicant's background, skills, and experience and seeks to impress a prospective employer with the applicant's positive qualities. *See also* **references.**

level of difficulty A Federal Government category for ranking classified duties and responsibilities.

level playing field *Informal:* an equal chance for all of the participants (players) in a particular project or event to succeed (win). *Example:* a potential contractor who, after getting all of the available information on a proposed new building, feels that there is a level playing field for developing a competitive bid.

liaison An individual who acts as a bridge between two groups in order to maintain or further communications, advance some project, or coordinate an activity.

liberal arts education A college or university education that promotes broad exposure to the sciences, social sciences, philosophy, literature, foreign languages, and fine arts, rather than a curriculum that is mainly technical.

librarian An individual who makes information available to patrons by selecting, acquiring, organizing, and lending books, magazines, audio and video tapes, and computer programs. *See also* the OOH, **public librarian, school librarian, academic librarian, cataloger, bibliographer, adult services librarian, media specialist, children's librarian, classifier,** and **special librarian.**

library assistant An individual who sorts returned books, publications, and other items and returns them to shelves, files, or other designated storage areas.

library binding worker A bindery employee who repairs books and provides other specialized binding services to libraries.

library media specialist In some states, a term for school librarian. *See* **school librarian.**

library technician An individual who performs many routine library tasks, such as organizing and maintaining periodicals, filing cards, operating and maintaining audiovisual equipment, doing computer searches, and helping patrons find information. *See also* the OOH.

licensed occupations Occupations for which a license must be obtained after the worker meets certain requirements. *Examples:* architects, barbers, cosmetologists, and insurance agents.

licensed practical nurse (L.P.N.) An individual who works under the direction of physicians and registered nurses to provide care for the sick. *See also* the OOH.

licensed vocational nurse (L.V.N.) In some states, a term for licensed practical nurse. *See* **licensed practical nurse.**

licensing requirements The specific items that must be met or fulfilled to be licensed. *Examples:* technical training, experience, and physical examination.

lie detector test *See* **polygraph test.**

life insurance agent *See* **insurance sales worker.**

life scientist (military) An Army, Navy, or Air Force officer who studies bacteria and parasites to determine how they invade and affect humans or animals, studies ways of protecting humans through immunization from disease, and conducts experiments and writes technical reports. *See also* the *Military Careers* guide.

life skills Abilities an individual needs in order to function successfully from day to day. *Examples:* living alone; holding a job; and managing money, a checking account, or credit.

life underwriter *See* **insurance sales worker.**

lifeguard An individual responsible for the safety of people at beaches or in the water and for the enforcement of rules at that particular site.

limited appointment *See* **appointment, temporary limited.**

limited duty officer (military) A Navy program that permits career enlisted personnel to advance to commissioned officer status without a college education.

limnologist A scientist who specializes in the study of fresh water organisms.

line installer and cable splicer An individual who places poles and then attaches equipment that carries electric, telephone, or fiber optic cables. *See also* the OOH.

line installer and repairer (military) In the Army, Navy, Air Force, Marine Corps, or Coast Guard, an individual who erects utility poles, strings overhead communications and electric cables between utility poles; and installs street lights and airfield lighting systems. *See also* the *Military Careers* guide.

linguist An individual who speaks several languages. *See also* **interpret; interpreter/translator.**

literary agent An individual who represents a professional writer and whose responsibilities may include finding a publisher for the writer's work; arranging meetings; assisting with editing; discussing prospective literary proposals; creating an awareness of the current literary market; and promoting the literary work through book fairs, exhibitions, and conferences.

lithographic and photoengraving worker An individual who photographs or scans material to be printed and makes a printing plate from the film. The printing plate is then inked and pressed against a rubber blanket that transfers the ink to paper. This process is also called offset printing. *See also* the OOH; **camera operator, offset printing; scanner operator, offset printing; lithographic etcher; stripper;** and **platemaker.**

lithographic dot etcher An individual involved in offset printing who retouches negatives by sharpening or reshaping images on the negatives.

load dispatcher *See* **electric power distributor and dispatcher.**

loan officer and counselor An individual who evaluates, authorizes, or recommends commercial, real estate, or credit loans or advises borrowers on financial status and methods of payment.

loan processing clerk An individual who prepares loan applications for underwriters by reviewing loan applications; writing credit bureaus; and contacting employers, banks, and references to verify personal and financial information.

lobby attendant An individual who assists patrons at entertainment events, such as plays or motion pictures, by collecting admission tickets, giving out information, checking ticket stubs, and helping people find their seats.

lobbyist An individual who works for a trade or professional association or other special interest group and tries to influence laws and regulations that would have an effect on the group represented.

locality adjustment In the Federal civil service system, the annual total dollar amount representing the difference between an employee's "rate of basic pay" and "adjusted basic pay." This amount may include an interim geographic adjustment, a locality comparability payment, and a special pay adjustment for law enforcement officers.

lockout The practice of an employer who refuses to permit employees to enter a factory or business to begin work. Lockouts usually occur because labor and management have been unable to come to an agreement on a contract or because of a contract provision dispute.

locksmith An individual who installs and repairs various kinds of locks, opens doors in houses or automobiles when keys have been misplaced or lost, and makes keys.

locomotive engineer An individual who operates locomotives in yards, stations, and on the road between stations and transports cargo and passengers between stations.

lodging The industry that deals with the housing of travelers in hotels, motels, lodges, resorts, conference centers, and spas.

lodging specialist (military) In the Army, Navy, Air Force, or Coast Guard, an individual who registers personnel and assigns them rooms, receives payments and keeps financial records, arranges hotel accommodations when lodging on base is not available. *See also* the *Military Careers* guide.

log grader/scaler An individual who inspects logs for defects, measures logs to determine their volume, and estimates the marketable content or value of logs or pulpwood.

log handling equipment operator An individual who operates tracked or wheeled equipment to load or unload logs and pulpwood onto or off trucks or gondola railroad cars.

log marker An individual who determines the bucking (cutting) points at which logs will be sawed into sections.

logging equipment mechanic An individual who services and repairs the mobile heavy equipment used in the logging industry.

logging occupations Jobs that involve the selection, marking, cutting, and hauling of logs and pulpwood. *See* individual occupations, such as **faller, bucker, choke setter, logging tractor operator, log handling equipment operator, log grader/scaler, cruiser, brush clearing laborer, tree trimmer, pulp piler, river, rigging slinger,** and **chaser.**

logging operations inspector An individual who reviews contract logging operations, prepares reports, and issues remedial instructions for violations of contractual agreements and of fire and safety regulations.

logging tractor operator An individual who drives the wheeled tractors or harvesting machines used to move logs.

longevity pay Extra money paid to an employee because of many years of service. *Example:* a teacher paid an additional amount after completing 20 years of teaching.

loss prevention manager An individual who trains, supervises, and develops a loss prevention staff (security force) for a store, factory, or business.

L.P.N. An abbreviation of *licensed practical nurse. See* **licensed practical nurse.**

luggage maker An individual who makes luggage by fastening leather to a frame, attaching a handle and other hardware, cutting and securing a lining inside the frame, and sewing or stamping decorations onto the luggage.

lupinologist An expert in the study of wolves.

L.V.N. An abbreviation for *licensed vocational nurse. See* **licensed vocational nurse** and **licensed practical nurse.**

♦Mm♦

machine assembler An individual who assembles items such as air-conditioning coils, ball bearing rings, and fuel injection systems, which do not require the highest degree of precision work.

machine feeder and offbearer An individual who works under the supervision of skilled workers and feeds materials into various machines.

Machine Operator and Precision Work Occupations (military) One of the twelve broad categories used by the Armed Forces to group occupations for enlisted personnel.

machine readable An item with a code that can be read electronically. *See also* **bar code.**

machine-tool operator, numerical control An individual who sets up and uses machine tools that are controlled electronically. *See also* the OOH.

machine-tool operator/tender An individual who monitors, adjusts, loads, or unloads machines that make metal or plastic parts.

machine-tool setter/setup operator An individual who prepares machines that make metal or plastic parts.

Machine Trades Occupations One of the nine primary categories for grouping occupations in the *Dictionary of Occupational Titles. Examples:* layout worker, tool dresser, and turbine-blade assembler.

machinery mechanic, industrial An individual who performs preventive maintenance on industrial machinery and makes any necessary repairs or adjustments. Preventive maintenance may include regular inspections, performance checks, adjustments, and testing.

machinist A skilled individual who sets up and operates machine tools to make machined products that meet precise specifications. *See also* the OOH.

machinist (military) In the Army, Navy, Air Force, or Marine Corps, an individual who sets up and operates lathes to make parts such as shafts and gears, studies blueprints or written plans of the parts to be made, and uses power tools to cut metal stock. *See also* the *Military Careers* guide.

magician An individual who entertains by performing sleight-of-hand tricks. A newer term for this occupation is illusionist.

maid **1)** An individual who works under the supervision of a housekeeper in a hotel or motel and whose tasks may include changing beds, vacuuming rooms, cleaning bathrooms, and disposing of discarded items. **2)** An individual who performs a number of personal services for a family in a private home.

mail carrier A United States Postal Service employee who delivers mail either on foot or by motor vehicle in a prescribed area. *See also* the OOH, **postal clerk,** and **mailhandler.**

mail clerk An individual who sorts and delivers incoming mail and packages within large corporations or organizations and may also prepare items for mailing. *See also* the OOH.

mail order business A type of selling that solicits customers by sending catalogs to their homes or through advertisements in newspapers and magazines. Ordered merchandise is shipped from the company warehouse or factory to the customer by mail or a delivery service. *See also* **nonstore retailing.**

mailhandler A United States Postal Service employee who loads, unloads, and moves mail; cancels stamps; and performs other duties related to the moving and processing of mail in a postal facility.

mailman The preferred nonsexist term is *mail carrier*. *See* **mail carrier.**

maintenance administrator An individual who works for a telephone company, tests circuits by entering instructions into a computer terminal, and updates and maintains computerized files of trouble status reports.

maintenance data analyst (military) In the Army, Navy, Air Force, Marine Corps, or Coast Guard, an individual who reviews maintenance schedules and notifies mechanics about the types of service needed, prepares charts and reports on maintenance activities, and operates computers and calculators to enter or retrieve maintenance data. *See also* the *Military Careers* guide.

maintenance manager (military) *See* **transportation/maintenance manager.**

maintenance mechanic, general An individual who performs a variety of services in small establishments. These services may include small mechanical repairs, building or repairing simple wooden items, and minor electrical and plumbing repairs. *See also* the OOH.

maintenance review A formal, periodic review of all positions in an organization to ensure that classifications are correct and position descriptions are current.

maintenance technician An individual who sets up, adjusts, services, and repairs electronic broadcasting equipment.

major duty Any duty or responsibility, or group of closely related tasks, of a position that **1)** determines qualification requirements for the position, **2)** occupies a significant amount of the employee's time, and **3)** is a regular or recurring duty.

makeup artist An individual who specializes in the application of makeup, usually for models or entertainers.

mall manager An individual in charge of a shopping mall and whose tasks include the leasing of space to mall tenants, providing an environment that encourages shoppers to come to the mall, dealing with tenant problems, attending to public relations, and planning special events.

mammalogist A scientist who specializes in the study of the origins, behavior, diseases, and life processes of mammals.

manage The act of controlling, handling, directing, or arranging some operation or condition.

management **1)** The group of individuals responsible for handling or controlling the operations of a company or organization. **2)** The process of directing, managing, or controlling a business or organization.

management analyst (military) An Army, Navy, Air Force, Marine Corps, or Coast Guard officer who measures work load and calculates how many persons are needed to perform the work; studies the information needs of managers and designs manual or computerized systems to satisfy them; and designs organizations for new or existing offices. *See also* the *Military Careers* guide.

management analyst/consultant An individual who collects, reviews, and analyzes information and then makes recommendations to solve a particular problem for a business or industry. *See also* the OOH.

management consultant *See* **management analyst/consultant.**

management dietician A dietician who specializes in the planning and preparation for large-scale meals in hospitals, nursing homes, prisons, schools, or colleges.

management effectiveness A measure of how well the individuals responsible for directing or controlling a business or organization achieve their objectives.

management official A Federal agency employee whose duties and responsibilities require or authorize the individual to formulate, determine, or influence the policies of the agency.

management rights The rights of management to make day-to-day personnel decisions and to direct the work force without mandatory negotiation with the exclusive bargaining representative.

management trainee An individual who is learning the various techniques of management through on-the-job experience, and on successful completion of this training is usually offered a management position.

manager An individual in charge of an operation or activity.

managerial Concerning or pertaining to managers or management.

manicurist An individual who usually works in a beauty shop and cleans, shapes, and applies polish to a customer's fingernails. *See also* **nail technician.**

manifold binding worker A printing industry worker who binds business forms, such as ledgers and books of sales receipts.

manipulator operator A steel mill worker who tends the machinery that controls the position of the steel ingot on the roller.

manpower The people available to do a particular job.

manpower development specialist *See* **employment interviewer.**

manpower shortage **1)** Fewer qualified workers than positions available. **2)** In the Federal civil service system, a category of positions for which the Office of Personnel Management authorizes agencies to pay interview expenses or travel and transportation expenses to the first post of duty.

manual dexterity Skill in using one's hands, which is an important skill for certain occupations.

manufacturers' agent An individual in the sales industry who is self-employed and contracts services to all types of companies.

manufacturers' representative *See* **manufacturers' sales representative.**

manufacturers' sales representative An individual who works for a company and visits manufacturers, wholsalers, retailers, government agencies, and other institutions to show samples, pictures, and catalogs that describe the company's products. *See also* the OOH.

manufacturing The act of making, producing, processing, or fabricating a product either by hand or machinery and usually in large quantities.

manufacturing optician *See* **ophthalmic laboratory technician.**

map editor An individual who uses aerial photographs and other reference materials to develop and verify maps. *See also* **surveyor, cartographer, photogrammetrist, geodetic surveyor, geophysical prospecting surveyor, marine surveyor, mapping scientist,** and **land surveyor.**

mapping The act of making a drawing of some part of the earth.

mapping manager *See* **surveying and mapping manager (military).**

mapping scientist An individual who collects information for maps and then uses this data to prepare maps and charts.

marble setter A stonemason who specializes in setting marble. *See also* the OOH, **bricklayer,** and **stonemason.**

margin clerk An experienced worker in the securities industry who posts accounts, monitors activity in customers' accounts, and ensures that customers make their payments and stay within legal boundaries concerning stock purchases.

marine biologist A scientist who specializes in the study of salt water organisms.

Marine Corps A member of the U.S. Armed Forces with close ties to the U.S. Navy. Marine Corps responsibilities include serving on U.S. Navy ships, protecting naval bases, guarding U.S. embassies abroad, and serving as a strike force to protect the interests of the U.S. and its allies.

marine engine mechanic (military) In the Army, Navy, Air Force, or Coast Guard, an individual who repairs and maintains shipboard gasoline and diesel engines, locates and repairs machinery parts, and repairs ship propulsion machinery. *See also* the *Military Careers* guide.

marine engineer An individual who operates, maintains, and repairs propulsion engines, boilers, generators, pumps, and other machinery on ships and boats. *See also* the OOH.

marine engineer (military) A Navy or Coast Guard officer who studies new ways of designing and building ship hulls, develops and tests shipboard combat and salvage equipment, and manages research programs to solve naval engineering problems. *See also* the *Military Careers* guide.

marine geologist *See* **geological oceanographer, physical oceanographer,** and **geochemical oceanographer.**

marine oiler An individual who lubricates gears, shafts, bearings, and other moving parts of engines used in ships and boats.

marine surveyor An individual who surveys harbors, rivers, and other bodies of water to determine shorelines, topography of the bottom, and water depth.

marker, apparel An individual who determines the best arrangement of pattern pieces to minimize the amount of material needed.

market **1)** A place where various items are sold. **2)** The business of buying and selling various types of goods.

market research The study of the various factors that affect the buying and selling of a product. *Example:* as part of market research, a company survey of the preferences of housewives.

market research analyst An individual concerned with the design, promotion, price, and distribution of a product or service. *See also* the OOH.

marketable skills Those skills that would help an individual obtain a job.

marketing All of the factors involved in buying or selling a product or service.

marketing manager An individual who develops the marketing strategy of a company after studying the demand for the product or service and identifying potential customers. *See also* the OOH.

masculine career stereotypes The perception or idea that certain occupations should be filled by men only. *Examples:* plumber, minister, farmer, carpenter, and miner.

mass layoff A high percentage of workers who have been told not to report to work, usually for an indefinite period of time.

mass market The large market that exists for a product or service.

mass transfer In the Federal civil service system, the movement of an employee and the employee's position to a different agency with no change in the employee's position, grade, or pay when a transfer of function or an organizational change takes place.

massage therapist A skilled individual who uses body massage techniques to relieve muscular problems and improve circulation.

masseur A man who gives massages. *See also* **massage therapist.**

masseuse A woman who gives massages. *See also* **massage therapist.**

master An individual who, with the captain, supervises the operation of a marine vessel and its crew.

Master of Business Administration (MBA) A graduate degree which emphasizes courses that are useful in business, such as accounting, economics, and administration.

mate An individual who works as a deck officer on a ship and assists with overseeing the operation of the vessel. Large ships may have a first mate, second mate, and third mate.

material mover, hand An individual who loads, unloads, or moves items in a variety of working places, such as grocery stores, factories, and ships.

material moving equipment operator An individual who uses bulldozers, cranes, and loaders to move manufactured and construction materials. *See also* the OOH.

material recording, scheduling, dispatching, and distributing occupations The various jobs done for a variety of communications and record keeping operations in business and government and that involve the coordinating, expediting, and record keeping of orders for personnel, equipment, and materials. *See also* **dispatcher, traffic clerk, shipping and receiving clerk, stock clerk, procurement clerk,** and **expediting clerk.**

materials engineer An individual who determines which metal, plastic, ceramic, or other material is best for a particular use. *See also* the OOH.

maternity leave The leave time that may be taken from a job before the birth of a baby, including time to care for the new infant. *See also* **parental leave.**

mathematician An individual who translates economic, scientific, and managerial problems into mathematical terms. Mathematicians are sometimes divided into two areas of specialization: theoretical mathematicians and applied mathematicians. *See also* the OOH.

maxillofacial surgeon A dentist who specializes in jaw surgery.

MBA An abbreviation of *Master of Business Administration*. *See* **Master of Business Administration.**

mean/average The method of figuring the average salary for an occupation. The total of the salaries for a particular job is divided by the number of people doing that job. *See also* **median.**

measurer An individual who measures materials, supplies, and equipment for the purpose of keeping relevant records.

meatcutter *See* **butcher and meat, poultry, and fish cutter.**

mechanic *See* the specific type of mechanic.

mechanical aptitude The ability to understand and operate machines and tools.

mechanical drafter An individual who draws detailed working diagrams of machinery and mechanical devices, including dimensions, fastening methods, and other engineering information.

mechanical engineer An individual who designs and develops power-producing machines for the production, transmission, and use of mechanical power and heat. *See also* the OOH.

mechanical engineering technician An individual who helps engineers design and develop machinery and other equipment.

mechanical inspector An individual who inspects the installation of mechanical equipment.

mechanical metallurgist An individual who develops and improves metalworking processes, such as casting, forging, rolling, and drawing.

mechanization The use of machinery, trucks, and automatic equipment to accomplish a task.

Media and Public Affairs Occupations (military) One of the broad categories used by the Armed Forces to group occupations for officers and enlisted personnel.

media specialist An individual who teaches students how to use the library/media center; works with teachers to develop curricula; and acquires books, magazines, and computer/audiovisual software. *See also* **school librarian.**

median In a sequence of numbers, the midpoint at which half of the numbers are below the midpoint, and the other half are above the midpoint. *Example:* the point at which half of the salaries of people in a particular occupation are below the median, and the other half are above the median. *See also* **mean/average.**

mediation The intervention of a third party who attempts to bring two disputing groups together to settle a conflict, such as a labor-management controversy. *See also* **conciliation** and **arbitration.**

mediator An individual who attempts to prevent or resolve labor and management disputes by making suggestions and recommendations. *See also* **arbitrator** and **conciliator.**

Medicaid A hospital and medical insurance program for individuals in certain, usually lower, income brackets. Medicaid is financed by the

Federal, state, and local governments.

medical assistant An individual who works under the direction of a physician and helps with the examination and treatment of patients and with routine office duties. *See also* the OOH.

medical examiner An individual employed by a governmental unit to examine the circumstances of a suspicious death. The medical examiner may order an inquest or an autopsy. *See also* **forensic pathologist** and **coroner.**

medical geographer An individual who studies health care delivery systems, epidemiology (the study of disease in populations), and the effect of the environment on health.

medical illustrator An artist who draws illustrations of the human body, animals, and plants.

medical laboratory technician An individual who works under the supervision of a medical technologist or laboratory supervisor and performs a wide range of routine tests and laboratory procedures.

medical laboratory technician (military) In the Army, Navy, Air Force, or Coast Guard, an individual who uses laboratory equipment to analyze specimens of tissue, blood, and body fluids; tests specimens for bacteria or viruses; and draws blood from patients. *See also* the *Military Careers* guide.

medical leave An approved absence from a job because of a physical condition, disease, or illness.

medical microbiologist An individual who studies the relationship between organisms and disease or the effects of antibiotics on microorganisms.

medical records administrator An individual who develops systems for documenting, storing, and retrieving medical information in a hospital or other medical facility.

medical records clerk An individual who usually works under the supervision of a medical records technician in a large health care facility or nursing home and is responsible for maintaining the medical records system.

medical records personnel *See* individual occupations, such as **medical record administrator, medical records technician, medical records clerk,** and **medical records transcriptionist.**

medical records technician An individual who organizes, evaluates, and codes the medical records of a patient in a hospital or other medical facility. *See also* the OOH.

medical records technician (military) In the Army, Navy, Air Force, or Coast Guard, an individual who fills out admission and discharge records for patients entering and leaving military hospitals; assigns patients to hospital rooms; and organizes, files, and maintains medical records. *See also* the *Military Careers* guide.

medical records transcriptionist An individual who types physicians' records and notes from dictating or recording equipment or, occasionally, from written notes.

medical secretary An individual who combines secretarial skills and an understanding of medical terminology and laboratory and hospital procedures to aid physicians in the preparation of correspondence, reports, and records.

medical service technician (military) In the Army, Navy, Air Force, or Coast Guard, an individual who examines and treats emergency or battlefield patients, interviews patients and records their medical histories, and gives shots and medicines to patients. *See also* the *Military Careers* guide.

medical social worker An individual who uses social worker training to counsel and assist patients in hospitals and other health care facilities.

medical technologist An individual who performs complicated chemical, biological, hematological, immunologic, microscopic, and bacteriological tests. *See also* **clinical chemistry technologist, blood bank technologist, phlebotomist, immunology technologist,** and **cytotechnologist.**

Medicare The country's basic health insurance program for people 65 or older and some disabled individuals. Medicare is divided into Part A----hospital insurance and Part B----medical insurance.

melter An individual who works in a steel mill and supervises the workers who control the furnace (furnace operators) and their assistants, directs the loading of the furnace with raw materials, and supervises the taking of samples.

membership secretary An individual whose

work involves the membership of an organization and may be responsible for maintaining records, collecting dues, and sending out newsletters.

mental health assistant *See* **psychiatric aide.**

mental health careers *See* **social worker, psychiatric aide, mental health counselor,** and **mental health technician.**

mental health counselor An individual who uses training as a counselor to assist individuals and groups suffering from various types of mental and emotional problems.

mental health technician An individual who works with individuals in mental health facilities in a variety of ways, such as through music, art, or dance therapy; individual and group counseling; and teaching communication or everyday living skills.

MEPS *See* **Military Entrance Processing Stations.**

merchandise discounts A benefit that permits employees to buy goods at a reduced price.

merchant marine A nation's ships that are used for commerce instead of defense.

merged records personnel folder In the Federal civil service system, a folder of records that requires special handling because the records document employment under the civil service system and under another Federal civilian employment system.

merger The combining of two businesses or organizations. *See also* **hostile takeover** and **friendly takeover.**

Merit Pay System In the Federal civil service system, the pay system established for General Schedule employees in grades 13 through 15 who were in supervisory, managerial, or management official positions. The Merit Pay System was replaced by the Performance Management and Recognition System. *See* **Performance Management and Recognition System.**

merit promotion program *See* **merit staffing program.**

merit raise A salary increase because of a positive evaluation or an outstanding achievement instead of an automatic cost-of-living increase or one required by a contract.

merit staffing program In the Federal civil service system, the program under which agencies consider the personal merit of an employee to fill a vacant position. Vacant positions are usually filled through competition, in which applicants are evaluated and ranked by their experience, education, skills, and performance record.

merit system A system that hires and promotes people on the basis of their ability rather than political influence.

Merit Systems Protection Board (MSPB) An agency that protects the rights of Federal employees working under the merit system. The Merit Systems Protection Board conducts special studies of the merit system, hears and decides charges of wrongdoing and employee appeals, and can order corrective and disciplinary actions against an agency or employee when appropriate.

messenger An individual who picks up and delivers letters and packages within a limited geographic area. *See also* the OOH.

metallographic technician An individual skilled in working with the structure of metals and their compounds.

metallurgical engineer An individual who may work in one of the three branches of metallurgical engineering. **1)** *Extractive* metallurgists deal with the removal, refining, and alloying of metals. **2)** *Physical* metallurgists are concerned with the nature, structure, and physical properties of metals and alloys. **3)** *Mechanical* metallurgists develop and improve casting, forging, rolling, and drawing processes. *See also* the OOH.

metalworking and plastics-working machine operator An individual who runs machines that produce small parts used in the manufacture of various items. *See also* the OOH.

metalworking machine operator An individual who operates machines that form metal parts for manufactured products. *See also* the OOH.

meteorologist An individual who uses scientific training to study the atmosphere and in many cases to forecast the weather. *See also* the OOH.

meteorologist (military) An Army, Navy, Air Force, or Marine Corps officer who directs personnel who collect weather data, interprets weather data received from satellites and weather balloons, and trains staff in data collection and interpretation. *See also* the *Military Careers* guide.

meter reader, utilities An individual who checks electric, gas, or water meters to determine the consumption of the resource for the period between the preceding reading and the new reading.

metropolitan area A large city and its immediate surroundings.

microbiologist An individual who uses scientific training to study the growth and characteristics of bacteria, viruses, and fungi.

microbiology technologist An individual who uses scientific training to examine and identify bacteria and other types of microorganisms.

middle manager An individual who is part of the management team in a large corporation or organization. On an organizational chart, a middle manager is below the chief executive officer, president, and vice presidents but above management trainees and other lower-level management personnel. *See also* **management trainee** and **chief executive officer.**

middleman An individual who acts **1)** as an intermediary between a buyer and seller, or **2)** as a liaison in a business arrangement between two groups. *See also* **go-between, intermediary,** and **liaison.**

midwife A woman who assists pregnant women when they have their babies. *See also* **nurse midwife.**

migrant worker An individual, sometimes from another nation, who moves about the country harvesting crops as they ripen. *See also* **seasonal employee.**

mileage reimbursement Payment to employees for the use of their personal automobiles by giving them a specified amount for each mile used for business purposes.

Military Career Paths Entries in the Military Careers guide that describe typical duties and assignments for individuals advancing along any one of 38 sample career paths (25 for enlisted personnel, 13 for officers). Information in this section of the *Military Careers* guide includes profiles of individuals working in a particular military occupation; related military occupations; military services offering employment in a particular occupation; an introduction summarizing job duties; a duty assignment description; skill, qualities, and abilities needed for advancement; possible areas of specialization; training provided; a description of a typical career path, and a timeline illustrating the average time it takes to move through the various career levels.

Military Careers A U.S. Department of Defense publication that lists the various occupations open to both enlisted personnel and officers in the Armed Forces and Coast Guard, as well as information about enlistment procedures, testing, and promotion possibilities. Cited in this dictionary's cross-references as the *Military Careers* guide.

Military Entrance Processing Stations (MEPS) Located around the country, stations at which the enlistment process occurs.

military police In the Army, Navy, Air Force, or Marine Corps, individuals who patrol areas on foot, by car, or by boat; arrest and charge criminal suspects; and interview witnesses, victims, and suspects in the course of investigating crimes. *See also* the *Military Careers* guide.

millwright An individual who unloads, installs, or dismantles machinery used in various industries. *See also* the OOH.

mine cutting and channeling machine operator An individual who cuts or channels along the face or seams of coal, quarry stone, or other mining surfaces to facilitate the blasting, separating, or removing of minerals or materials from mines or from the earth's surface.

mine inspector An individual who visits mines to make certain that health and safety regulations are enforced.

mineralogist An individual who uses scientific training to analyze and classify minerals and gems according to their composition and structure.

minimalizing *See* **downsizing.**

minimum qualifications The least number of qualifications an individual must have in order to be considered for a position.

minimum wage The lowest hourly wage that can be paid to employees who work for companies engaged in interstate commerce. *See also* **Fair Labor Standards Act.**

mining engineer An individual who finds, extracts, and prepares various minerals for use in industry. *See also* the OOH.

mining equipment repairer An individual who specializes in the repair of the heavy equipment used in the mining industry.

mining machine operator An individual who operates mining machines, such as self-propelled or truck-mounted drilling machines, continuous mining machines, channeling machines, and cutting machines, to extract coal, metal or nonmetal ores, rock, stone, or sand from underground or surface excavation.

mining, quarrying, and tunneling occupations *See* **rock splitter, quarry; mining machine operator; continuous mining machine operator;** and **mine-cutting and channeling machine operator.**

minister, Protestant An individual who provides religious leadership to the congregation of a Protestant church by administering various rites of the church, delivering sermons, counseling, and visiting members of the congregation. *See also* the OOH, **clergy, Roman Catholic priest,** and **rabbi.**

minor An individual under legal age. Minors are not permitted to hold certain jobs. *Example:* a 16-year-old teenager who was not hired for a job at a neighborhood tavern because alcoholic beverages were served and he was a minor. *See also* **prohibited occupations.**

minorities Particular groups who are sometimes the victims of discrimination. *Examples:* blacks, Hispanics, Asians, Native Americans, women, handicapped, and older workers. The following organizations work with minority groups on career planning:

Blind: Job Opportunities for the Blind Program, National Federation for the Blind, 1800 Johnson St., Baltimore, MD 21230. Phone: toll-free, (800) 638-7518.

Disabled: President's Committee on Employment of People with Disabilities, 1331 F St. NW., 3rd Floor, Washington, DC 20004. Phone: (202) 376-6200.

Minorities: National Association for the Advancement of Colored People (NAACP), 4805 Mount Hope Dr., Baltimore, MD 21215-3297. Phone: (212) 358-8900. National Urban League, Employment Dept., 500 E. 62nd St., New York, NY 10021. Phone: (301) 310-9000. National Urban League, Washington Operations, 1111 14th St. NW., 6th Floor, Washington, DC 20005. Phone: (202) 898-1604.

Older workers: National Association of Older Workers Employment Services, c/o National Council on the Aging, 409 3rd St., SW., Suite 2000, Washington, DC 20024. Phone: (202) 479-1200. American Association of Retired Persons (AARP), Worker Equity, 601 E St. NW., Floor A5, Washington, DC 20049. Phone: (202) 434-2040. Asociacion Nacional Por Personas Mayores (National Association for Hispanic Elderly), 2727 W. 6th St., Suite 270, Los Angeles, CA 90057. Phone: (213) 487-1922. National Caucus/Center on Black Aged, Inc. 1424 K St. NW., Suite 500, Washington., DC 20005. Phone: (202) 637-8400. Veterans: Regional office of the Department of Veterans Affairs.

Women: U.S. Department of Labor, Women's Bureau, 200 Constitution Ave., NW., Washington, DC 20210. Phone: (202) 523-6652. Catalyst, 250 Park Ave., South, 5th floor, New York, NY 10003. Phone: (212) 777-8900. Wider Opportunities for Women, 1325 G. St. NW., Lower Level, Washington, DC 20005. Phone: (202) 638-3143.

Miscellaneous Occupations One of the nine primary categories for grouping occupations in the *Dictionary of Occupational Titles. Examples:* dump-truck driver, jackhammer operator, and mud-plant operator.

missile system officer An Army, Navy, or Air Force officer who stands watch as a member of a missile launch crew, directs testing and inspection of missile systems, and directs early-warning launch training exercises. *See also* the *Military Careers* guide.

mixing and blending machine operator and tender An individual who operates or tends machines to mix or blend any of a wide variety of materials, such as spices, dough batter, tobacco, fruit juices, chemicals, livestock feed, and food products.

mixologist A job title preferred by some bartenders. *See* **bartender.**

mobile heavy equipment mechanic An individual who repairs and maintains heavy equipment, such as graders, backhoes, shovels, and trenchers. *See also* the OOH.

mobilization In the Federal civil service system, the readiness provisions for operating the Federal Personnel System in time of national emergency.

model (1 An individual who poses for photographs to be used in magazines, newspapers, catalogs, and flyers. (2 An individual who shows clothes and accessories for a designer at a fashion show. (3 An individual who poses for an artist. (4 A smaller version of an object that is usually built to scale and is used to show how the completed full-size object will look.

molding and casting machine operator An individual who tends steel mill machines that release molten steel from a ladle into water-cooled molds at a controlled rate.

monitor To observe, supervise, or oversee an action.

moonlighting *Informal:* having a second job, usually part time, in addition to a regular occupation.

morale The general feelings of employees about their jobs and their willingness to perform their work. Workers with good morale usually do their work cheerfully and in good spirits, but workers with poor morale usually are dissatisfied and unhappy about their tasks and work environment.

mortgage broker An individual who represents many banks and other lenders, determines the best lender for a prospective borrower, and brings the lender and the borrower together.

mortgage loan officer An individual who originates the loan application, provides information required by law, and determines the next step in the loan process.

mortgage processor An individual who collects the documents for a loan and verifies the information submitted.

mortgage underwriter An individual who controls the funds for a mortgage loan and makes the final decision about whether a mortgage loan will be given.

mortician *See* **funeral director**

motel clerk *See* **hotel/motel clerk.**

motion picture camera operator An individual who uses a 35- or 16-millimeter camera to photograph movies, television programs, or commercials. *See also* **cinematographer.**

motion picture camera operator (military) In the Army, Navy, Air Force, Marine Corps, or Coast Guard, an individual who sets up and operates motion picture equipment, including cameras, sound recorders, and lights; operates television cameras in TV studios and remote sites; and follows script and instructions of film or TV directors to move cameras, zoom, pan, or adjust focus. *See also* the *Military Careers* guide.

motion picture projectionist An individual who sets up and operates projection equipment in a movie theater.

motion study The analysis of the physical movements of employees to try to find more efficient ways to accomplish the same task.

motivated Stimulated to take action. *Example:* a company president who has received an important contract and is motivated to do the best possible job. *See also* **unmotivated.**

motivating Encouraging or persuading someone to act in a particular manner. *Example:* a foreman who is an expert at motivating workers to increase production.

motor vehicle body repairer An individual who removes dents, straightens parts, and replaces body parts on damaged motor vehicles.

motor vehicle inspector An individual who checks motor vehicles to see whether they comply with emission and safety regulations.

motor vehicle repairer An individual who repairs and services automobiles.

motorboat mechanic An individual who repairs and adjusts the engines and electrical and mechanical equipment of inboard and outboard marine engines.

motorcycle mechanic An individual who repairs and adjusts the engines and electrical and mechanical equipment on motorcycles.

movie projectionist *See* **motion picture projectionist.**

MSPB An abbreviation of *Merit Systems Protection Board. See* **Merit Systems Protection Board.**

multilevel selling/marketing A plan in which individuals work as independent contractors and sell the products of a company and also recruit others who help sell and then pay the independent contractor a part of their commission. Multilevel selling is a popular plan used by cosmetic companies and other organizations that sell products mainly through personal contacts and parties. *See also* **nonstore retailing.**

multinational companies Large companies that do business in more than one country.

municipal clerk An individual who records minutes of meetings, answers correspondence, keeps fiscal records, and prepares reports for town or city governments.

museum curator An individual responsible for the care and management of a museum and its collections.

musical instrument repairer and tuner An individual who repairs and adjusts various musical instruments, such as pianos and pipe organs. *See also* the OOH and **piano tuner.**

musician An individual who may play a musical instrument, sing, write music, or conduct musical performances. *See also* the OOH.

musician (military) In the Army, Navy, Air Force, Marine Corps, or Coast Guard, an individual who plays in or leads bands, orchestras, combos, and jazz groups; sings in choral groups or as soloists; and performs for ceremonies, parades, concerts, festivals, and dances. *See also* the *Military Careers* guide.

musicologist An individual involved with the systematic study of music rather than the art of composition or performance.

♦Nn♦

NAACP An abbreviation of National Association for the Advancement of Colored People. See **minorities.**

nail technician An individual who applies artificial fingernails; various types of wraps, filler materials, and extensions; and affixes sculptured nails and decorations.

nanny An individual who is hired to care for an infant in a private home. *See also* **infant nurse, governess,** and **au pair.**

national agency check and inquiries In the Federal civil service system, the investigation of applicants for, and new appointees to, nonsensitive or low-risk Federal positions by means of a name check through national investigative files and voucher inquiries. *See also* **background check/investigation.**

National Apprenticeship Program and Apprenticeship Information A pamphlet that provides information about apprenticeship programs and is available from the Bureau of Apprenticeship and Training, U.S. Department of Labor, 200 Constitution Ave., NW., Washington, DC 20210. Phone: (202) 535-0545. *See also* **apprenticeship, apprentice,** and **journeyman.**

National Business Employment Weekly A

publication that combines a week's worth of help wanted ads from all of the regional editions of the *Wall Street Journal.*

National Credit Union Administration In the executive branch of the Federal Government, an independent agency responsible for chartering, insuring, supervising, and examining Federal credit unions. Credit unions are financial cooperatives formed by groups of employees, and credit union members are provided with many services usually associated with banks, such as savings accounts, certificates of deposit, and loans.

National Home Study Council An organization that provides information about home study programs in the Directory of Accredited Home Study Schools, available from the National Home Study Council, 1601 18th St. NW., Washington, DC 20009. Phone: (202) 234-5100.

National Labor Relations Board (NLRB) An independent Federal Government agency that administers the National Labor Relations Act. The National Labor Relations Board has the power to safeguard employees' rights to organize, to determine through elections whether workers want unions as their bargaining representatives, and to prevent and remedy unfair labor practices by private sector employers and unions.

National Mediation Board A board that mediates disputes over wages, hours, and working conditions which arise between rail and air carriers and organizations representing their employees.

National Security Agency An agency responsible for the centralized coordination, direction, and performance of highly specialized technical functions in support of U.S. Government activities to protect communications and produce foreign intelligence information.

Naval Reserve Officers' Training Corps (NROTC) A U.S. Navy program that offers at many colleges and universities tuition and other financial benefits to students who can use their NROTC training to obtain a commission as a Navy officer.

NC *See* **numerical-control tool operator.**

NCO *See* **noncommissioned officer.**

negotiability A determination as to whether a matter is within the obligation to bargain or negotiate.

negotiated agreement *See* **collective bargaining agreement.**

negotiated contract *See* **collective bargaining agreement.**

negotiated grievance procedure A procedure for considering grievances applicable to members of a bargaining unit (union). The coverage and scope of grievances are negotiated by the parties to the agreement (labor and management). *See also* **grievance** and **grievance interview.**

negotiations The bargaining process used to reach a settlement between labor and management over conditions of employment and wages.

neighborhood work center An office equipped with computers and other telecommunication tools that can be used by remote workers employed by one of the businesses which share the cost of the work center. *See also* **remote work, telecommuting, satellite office,** and **electronic cottage.**

neonatologist A physician who specializes in the care of ill or premature babies.

nepotism The practice of favoring relatives in business or politics, which may result in the hiring or promoting of relatives on the basis of relationship instead of merit or ability.

net/net pay The wages or salary left after taxes and FICA contributions have been withheld. *See also* **gross pay.**

network A chain or connection linking a number of objects or persons. Examples: a broadcasting system, an electricity distribution system, and interrelated people. *See also* **networking.**

networking An informal system used by individuals who want to improve their chances for advancement or for a better job by establishing or maintaining contact with people who might be helpful.

neurophysiologic technologist A newer term for an individual who operates machinery for measuring the electrical activity of the brain. *See also* **EEG technologist.**

new accounts clerk An individual who works for

a bank or other financial institution and interviews and assists prospective customers who want to open an account. *See also* the OOH and **interviewing clerk.**

new broom *Informal, Great Britain:* an individual who starts to make a number of changes as soon as the person begins a new job. The term comes from the saying, "a new broom sweeps clean."

news anchor An individual who works for a radio or television studio, presents news stories, and introduces in-depth videotaped news or live air transmissions from on-the-scene reporters.

newscaster An individual who works for a radio or television studio and presents the news. *See also* **sportscaster, weathercaster, broadcast news analyst, commentator, announcer,** and **news anchor.**

newsletter A small publication sent to a select group, such as employees, members of an organization, and subscribers to a service, for the purpose of informing, improving morale, and announcing changes.

newsman Preferred nonsexist terms are *reporter and correspondent. See also* **reporter/correspondent** and **news anchor.**

newspaper reporter An individual who gathers information and prepares stories for a newspaper.

newswriter An individual who gathers and organizes information on a topic and then writes the information in a form that meets the needs of the prospective readers. *See also* the OOH, **editor, copy writer, columnist,** and **reporter/correspondent.**

night differential In the United States Postal Service, a 10 percent compensation added to an employee's base hourly rate for work time between 6 p.m. and 6 a.m.

night-owl shift *See* **night shift.**

night school Evening classes offered by a high school, college, or university to accommodate individuals who must work during the day.

night shift Employees who work during evening or early morning hours instead of during the day. A night shift is scheduled for factories operating 24 hours per day, as well as for workers such as police officers and firefighters. *See also* **shift differential** and **night differential.**

NLRB An abbreviation of *National Labor Relations Board. See* **National Labor Relations Board.**

no layoff policy A policy of shifting workers to other positions in a company instead of laying off or dismissing the workers.

noise pollution technician An individual who operates equipment for determining the noise level, checks the sound level of equipment, and redesigns equipment for quieter operation.

nominating officer A subordinate officer of a Federal agency to whom the agency head has delegated the authority to nominate employees for appointment, but not actually to appoint them.

nonappropriated fund employees In the Federal civil service system, persons paid from nonappropriated funds of agencies of the United States. Generally, these employees are responsible for the comfort, pleasure, and contentment of personnel of the Armed Forces.

noncareer appointment In the Federal civil service system, the political appointment of an individual rather than a person who has a civil service rating.

noncommissioned officer (NCO) An enlisted member in pay grades E-4 or higher.

noncompetitive actions In the Federal civil service system, a personnel action based on prior service and made without regard to civil service registers of eligibles or to the priorities required for making temporary appointments outside the register.

noncontributory plan An employee benefit plan, such as insurance, that does not require a contribution from the employee.

nondestructive tester (military) In the Navy and Air Force, an individual who inspects metal parts and joints for wear and damage; takes X rays of aircraft and ship parts and examines X-ray film to detect cracks and flaws in metal parts and welds; and operates ultrasonic, atomic absorption, and other kinds of test equipment. *See also* the *Military Careers* guide.

nondurable goods Items meant to be used up, such as food or fuel. *See also* **durable goods.**

nongarment sewing machine operator An individual who operates machinery that sews items such as towels, sheets, and curtains.

nonmonetary perks Job benefits, such as job satisfaction and easy commuting, that do not concern money. *See also* **job satisfaction.**

nonprofit sector Organizations, such as foundations, museums, and historic sites, that operate without seeking to make a profit.

nonstore retailing Selling other than sales in an establishment where the public shops in person. *Example:* a TV channel that displays merchandise and accepts purchases by phone from buyers at home. *See also* **mail order business** and **multilevel selling/marketing.**

nonunion contractors Contractors who hire workers who are not members of a trade union.

nonverbal communication/cues Communication without the use of words. Communication may be accomplished by gestures, facial expressions, or position of the body. *Examples:* a thumbs-up or thumbs-down gesture, wave, frown, smile, or slouch.

notarized Certified by a notary public that an individual has signed a document in the presence of the notary public.

notary public An official who has been authorized to certify documents. *See also* **notarized.**

NROTC An abbreviation of *Naval Reserve Officers' Training Corps. See* **Naval Reserve Officers' Training Corps.**

nuclear engineer An individual who designs, develops, monitors, and operates nuclear power plants. *See also* the OOH.

nuclear engineer (military) An Army, Navy, Air Force, or Marine Corps officer who directs projects to improve nuclear power plants in ships and submarines, directs research on the uses and effects of nuclear weapons, and assists high-level officials in creating policies for developing and using nuclear technology. *See also* the *Military Careers* guide.

nuclear medicine technologist An individual who is trained to use radiopharmaceuticals and, working under the supervision of a physician, may conduct laboratory studies and do research. *See also* the OOH.

nuclear pharmacist *See* **radiopharmacist.**

Nuclear Regulatory Commission An independent Federal Government agency that regulates uses of nuclear energy to protect the health and safety of the public and environment. Some employees of nuclear power facilities must be licensed by the Nuclear Regulatory Commission.

nuclear technician An individual who operates nuclear test and research equipment, monitors radiation, and assists nuclear engineers and physicists in research.

numerical-control machine-tool operator An individual who operates a machine tool that can be programmed to make parts of different dimensions automatically. *See also* the OOH.

numerical-control tool programmer An individual who writes computer programs that direct numerically controlled (NC) equipment to produce precision-machined parts.

nurse *See* **registered nurse.**

nurse anesthetist A nurse with special training who administers anesthesia under the direction of a physician.

nurse clinician A nurse with special training or expertise in a clinical area, such as pediatrics or gerontology/geriatrics.

nurse midwife A nurse with graduate training in assessing and diagnosing prenatal conditions and assisting with the birth of a baby.

nurse practitioner A nurse with graduate school training in how to diagnose and assess patients, which enables them to perform certain duties normally performed by a physician.

nursery worker An individual who works in a nursery and may plant, cultivate, harvest, or transplant shrubs, trees, or plants.

nurse's aide *See* **nursing aide.**

nursing The profession involved with the care of sick people, rehabilitation of recovering patients, and emotional and physical well being of patients.

nursing aide An individual who works under the supervision of a registered nurse or licensed practical nurse and whose duties may include answering the call bell of patients, making beds, bathing patients, and serving meals. *See also* the OOH.

nursing home administrator An individual who manages the personnel, finances, and general operations of a nursing home. *See also* the OOH.

nursing home nurse A nurse who manages nursing care for residents of a nursing home.

nursing technician (military) In the Army, Navy, or Air Force, an individual who provides bedside care in hospitals, serves food and feeds patients requiring help, and drives ambulances and assists doctors and nurses in providing emergency treatment. *See also* the *Military Careers* guide.

nutrition adviser *See* **nutrition counselor.**

nutrition counselor An individual who advises groups or individuals on healthy eating habits or may assist in devising special diets.

nutritionist An individual who uses knowledge of the principles of nutrition to help people develop good eating habits. The term nutritionist is used interchangeably with dietician. *See also* the OOH, **clinical dietician, dietician, community dietician, management dietician, research dietician,** and **registered dietician.**

objective An aim or goal that an individual, business, or organization wants to achieve.

obligation The period of time an individual agrees to serve on active military duty, in the Reserve, or a combination of both.

OBRA An acronym for the *O*mnibus *B*udget *R*econciliation *A*ct of 1989. *See* **Omnibus Budget Reconciliation Act of 1989.**

obsolete Out-of-date, discarded, or no longer in use. *See also* **occupationally obsolete.**

obstetrician A physician who specializes in the birth of children and in the care of the mother before and after childbirth. *See also* the OOH.

occupation The main work of an individual in order to earn a living. *See also* **profession, trade,** and **job.**

occupational analyst An individual who conducts research pertaining to occupational classification systems and the effects of industry and occupational trends on worker relationships.

occupational disease A disease or condition caused by some element of the job or workplace, such as exposure to radiation, chemicals, or dust. *Example:* miners who get black-lung disease.

occupational education Education that emphasizes practical courses geared to technical skills and paraprofessional jobs.

occupational group Positions of differing kinds but within the same field of work.

occupational hazard A risk associated with a particular job, such as exposure to harmful chemicals, radiation, or dust.

occupational health nurse An individual who uses nursing training to provide care to employees in industry and government. Persons in this nursing specialty are referred to also as industrial nurses. *See also* **registered nurse, hospital nurse, nursing home nurse, public health nurse, private duty nurse, office nurse, school nurse, and industrial nurse.**

occupational neurosis A negative reaction to a job that may result in mental stress or physical symptoms which hinder an individual's ability to perform the duties of the job.

***Occupational Outlook Handbook* (OOH)** A U.S. Department of Labor publication that is issued every two years and lists important information about the occupations most commonly held by Americans. The OOH includes information about the nature of the work; working conditions; employment; training, other qualifications, and advancement; job outlook; earnings; related occupations; and sources of additional information. The OOH is available in most libraries.

occupational preparation The various types of preparation for a career, such as the best type of education---academic, vocational, or apprenticeship.

Occupational Safety and Health Act (OSHA) A law that covers almost every employer in the country and was enacted to reduce the incidence of personal injuries, illness, and deaths among American workers resulting from their employment.

Occupational Safety and Health Administration (OSHA) The agency that has responsibility for occupational safety and health activities in the workplace, as outlined in the Occupational Safety and Health Act. *See also* **Occupational Safety and Health Act (OSHA)** and **Occupational Safety and Health Review Commission.**

occupational safety and health inspector An individual who visits places of employment to detect unsafe equipment or unhealthy working conditions.

Occupational Safety and Health Review Commission An independent quasi-judicial agency established to rule on cases forwarded to it by the Department of Labor when disagreements arise over the results of safety and health inspections performed by the Occupational Safety and Health Administration (OSHA). These cases involving alleged health and job-safety violations found during OSHA inspections can be brought by employers or employees.

occupational therapist An individual who helps persons who are mentally, physically, or developmentally disabled to develop, recover, or maintain daily living and work skills. *See also* the OOH.

occupational therapist (military) An Army, Navy, or Air Force officer who plans and manages occupational therapy programs, tests and interviews patients to diagnose the extent of their disabilities, and supervises occupational therapy specialists in treating patients. *See also* the *Military Careers* guide.

occupational therapy An activity to aid in the physical or mental recovery of a patient. *See also* **occupational therapist.**

occupational therapy aide/assistant An individual who assists an occupational therapist in administering medically oriented occupational programs to help rehabilitate disabled patients.

occupational therapy specialist (military) In the Army, Navy, Air Force, or Coast Guard, an individual who tests patients to determine physical and mental abilities, fits and adjusts artificial limbs, and teaches patients new mobility skills. *See also* the *Military Careers* guide.

occupational trends The factors likely to influence occupations in the future. Example: a higher proportion of older people in the U.S. in the future, making health care occupations more important because older people require more medical care.

occupationally obsolete Occupations that are no longer needed and are considered out-of-date. *Examples:* buggy whip makers and corset or bustle makers.

oceanographer An individual who uses scientific training to study the oceans. *See also* **geological oceanographer, physical oceanographer,** and **geochemical oceanographer.**

oceanographer (military) A Navy or Coast Guard officer who directs personnel who collect oceanographic data, conducts research on the effects of water and atmosphere on military warning and weapon systems, and oversees the preparation of oceanographic and weather forecasts. *See also* the *Military Careers* guide.

OCS An abbreviation of *Officer Candidate School. See* **Officer Candidate School.**

odd jobs Small, miscellaneous jobs or pieces of work.

off-the-books *Informal:* the illegal practice of paying a worker without entering the payment in the business records or withholding income or Social Security taxes. *See also* **underground economy** and **black economy.**

off-the-clock Not officially at work and therefore

is without pay. The expression originated from the practice of using a time clock to "punch in" the time of arrival and departure. *Example:* A person who is at a job site but is off-the-clock and not expected to work.

office clerk, general An individual who may perform a variety of office duties, such as filing, typing, and using equipment such as copiers, calculators, and computers.

office electrician An individual who works for a telephone company and makes operating adjustments in submarine cable repeater and terminal circuits and related equipment.

office machine and cash register servicer *See* **computer and office machine repairer.**

office machine repairer *See* **computer and office machine repairer.**

office manager An individual responsible for the efficient operation of an office and whose duties may include hiring new employees, instructing workers in their duties, and planning the work of subordinates. *See also* the OOH.

office nurse An individual who uses nursing training to assist physicians in private practice, clinics, or health maintenance organizations.

Office of Personnel Management (OPM) An agency that administers for Federal employees a merit system which includes recruiting, examining, training, and promoting people. The Office of Personnel Management administers also health benefits, life insurance, and retirement benefits for Federal merit system employees. This agency superseded the U.S. Civil Service Commission. *See also* **area offices of the Office of Personnel Management.**

office politics Employee practices such as choosing sides in a dispute, trying to manipulate some situation, or plotting for or against some person or group in an office or workplace.

office temp An employee hired for temporary work from an agency that provides workers to offices for short periods of time when regular workers are unavailable or unable to handle the current work load.

Officer Candidate School (OCS) A program for college graduates with no prior military training who want to become military officers. Qualified enlisted members also may attend OCS. After successful completion, candidates are commissioned as military officers.

officer-in-charge In the United States Postal Service, a postal employee appointed temporarily to fill a postmaster vacancy, usually for no longer than 180 days.

officer pay grades (military) Military officers can progress through ten pay grades. Most newly commissioned officers begin at pay grade O-1 and after two years usually move to O-2.

Officer Training School (OTS) One of the pathways to a commission as a military officer in the Air Force and open to college graduates. Applicants for OTS enter the service as enlisted personnel. After they complete their training successfully, they are commissioned as military officers.

officers (military) Members of the Armed Forces who are the professional leaders of the military and develop plans, set objectives, and direct the efforts of other military personnel. Officers are usually college graduates, are required to meet physical and academic standards developed by the various branches of the Armed Forces, and hold the rank of second lieutenant or ensign or above.

Official Personnel Folder (OPF) The official place for the employment records and documents of personnel actions occurring during an employee's Federal civilian service or service with the United States Postal Service.

older workers Workers age 55 and above. *See* **Minorities** for agencies that assist older workers.

Older Workers Benefit Protection Act Federal law effective in 1992 that revises certain provisions of the Age Discrimination in Employment Act of 1967.

Omnibus Budget Reconciliation Act of 1989 (COBRA) An amendment to the Comprehensive Omnibus Budget Reconciliation Act of 1985 (COBRA). A major amendment clarified when an employer could terminate an employee's COBRA coverage. *See also* **Comprehensive Omnibus Budget Reconciliation Act of 1985.**

on-break Released from work for a brief period of time.

on-call employee An individual who works when needed during heavy work loads.

on his/her/their watch *Informal:* on duty, usually for a specified period of alertness or responsibility. *Example:* a break-in that occurs while the night security guard is on his watch.

on-site Located where some activity is taking place. *Example:* an architect, engineer, and contractor who spend a lot of time on-site because of a project's importance.

on-the-carpet *Informal:* reprimanded or disciplined. Said of an employee reprimanded by the employer.

on-the-clock At work and working for pay. The term originated from the practice of having workers use time cards with a time clock that recorded arrival and departure times.

on-the-job *Informal:* not only at work but also alert to personal responsibilities.

on-the-job training Practical job training that takes place in an actual work situation. *See also* **Job Training Partnership Act.**

oncologist A physician who specializes in the treatment of tumors, especially malignant tumors (cancer).

One Hundred Best Companies to Work for in America By Robert Levering and others, a book that uses interviews and comments by employees and executives about their particular companies' benefits and policies which qualify their companies to be considered among the one hundred best companies in America.

171 *See* **Standard Form 171.**

open-ended question A question that encourages an unrehearsed, informative answer and is used especially during employment interviews. *Example:* What do you think you can contribute to our organization?

operating engineer An individual qualified to operate various types of construction equipment. *See also* specific types of equipment.

operating room technician *See* **surgical technologist.**

operating room technician (military) In the Army, Navy, Air Force, or Coast Guard, an individual who prepares patients for surgery, sterilizes instruments, and passes sterile instruments and supplies to surgeons. *See also* the *Military Careers* guide.

operational meteorologist An individual who studies information on air pressure, temperature, humidity, and wind velocity and applies physical and mathematical relationships to make short- and long-range weather forecasts.

operations research analyst An individual who helps organizations plan and operate in the most efficient and effective manner. *See also* the OOH.

operations research analyst and mathematician (military) An Army, Navy, Air Force, Marine Corps, or Coast Guard officer who develops research designs for analyzing and evaluating military operations and processes; designs new or improved operational and management procedures based on results of studies; and develops and analyzes war games to find ways to improve the nation's defenses. *See also* the *Military Careers* guide.

OPF An abbreviation of *Official Personnel Folder. See* **Official Personnel Folder.**

ophthalmic dispenser *See* **dispensing optician.**

ophthalmic laboratory technician An individual who makes eyeglass lenses according to prescriptions from an ophthalmologist or optometrist. *See also* the OOH.

ophthalmologist A physician who specializes in medical diagnosis and treatment of eye and vision disorders, especially diseases and injuries to the eye. *See also* the OOH.

OPM An abbreviation of *Office of Personnel Management. See* **Office of Personnel Management.**

optical goods worker *See* **ophthalmic laboratory technician.**

optical mechanic *See* **ophthalmic laboratory technician.**

optician (military) In the Army or Navy, an individual who calculates the correct lens size and thickness from written prescriptions, uses power grinders and polishers to grind and polish lenses, and uses optical tools to assemble eyeglass frames and lenses. *See also* the *Military Careers* guide.

optician, dispensing *See* **dispensing optician**

optional retirement The minimum combinations of age and Federal service for this kind of immediate annuity are age 62 with 5 years of service, age 60 with 20 years of service, and age 55 with 30 years of service. *See also* **deferred retirement; disability retirement;** and **retirement, discontinued service.**

optometric technician (military) In the Army, Navy, or Air Force, an individual who performs screening tests of patients' vision, orders eyeglasses and contact lenses from prescriptions, and fits eyeglasses to patients. *See also* the *Military Careers* guide.

optometrist An individual who examines people's eyes to diagnose and treat vision problems. *See also* the OOH.

optometrist (military) An Army, Navy, or Air Force officer who checks patients' vision, examines eyes for glaucoma and other diseases, and prescribes corrective lenses. *See also* the *Military Careers* guide.

oral pathologist A dentist who specializes in diseases of the mouth.

oral surgeon A dentist who specializes in surgery of the mouth.

orchestra conductor An individual who leads an orchestra or band.

order clerk An individual who receives and processes incoming orders for materials, merchandise, or services. *See also* the OOH.

orderly An individual who works in a hospital or nursing home and performs various duties of a nonmedical nature, usually for male patients.

ordnance mechanic In the Army, Navy, Air Force, Marine Corps, or Coast Guard, an individual who loads nuclear and conventional explosives and ammunition on aircraft, ships, and submarines; repairs and maintains tank weapons and fire control systems; and assembles and loads explosives. *See also* the *Military Careers* guide.

organic chemist A chemist who studies the chemistry of the vast number of carbon compounds.

organization A group of people whose jobs have been arranged to achieve some particular work or purpose.

organizational chart A diagram that shows an organization's various job titles and their relationship to each other. *Example:* a chart displaying the president at the top; the vice presidents, managers, and supervisors below the president; and then on still lower levels the other members of the organization according to their status, rank, and responsibilities.

organizational psychologist An individual who applies psychological techniques to personnel administration, management, and marketing problems.

orientation *See* **employee orientation.**

ornithologist A scientist who specializes in the study of the origin, behavior, diseases, and life processes of birds.

orthodontic technician An individual who makes appliances for straightening teeth and treating speech impediments.

orthodontist A dentist who specializes in straightening teeth.

orthopedic technician (military) In the Army, Navy, or Air Force, an individual who makes and applies plaster casts for broken bones, constructs splints for setting broken bones, and prepares patients for orthopedic surgery. *See also* the *Military Careers* guide.

orthotic specialist (military) In the Army or Air Force, an individual who designs orthotic devices as requested by physicians, makes plaster casts for injured arms or legs, and adjusts devices to fit patients. *See also* the *Military Careers* guide.

orthotist An individual who works under the direction of a physician and fits and prepares orthopedic braces for injured or disabled people.

OSHA An acronym for *O*ccupational *S*afety and *H*ealth *A*ct/*A*dministration. *See* **Occupational Safety and Health Act** and **Occupational Safety and Health Administration.**

osteopathic physician A physician who places special emphasis on the importance and treatment of the body's musculoskeletal system.

OTS An abbreviation of *Officer Training School.* *See* **Officer Training School.**

out-of-pocket expense A collective term for the various items for which employees must pay from their own funds. *Examples:* health insurance deductibles, coinsurance payments, and noncovered services. *See also* **coinsurance** and **deductible.**

out-of-the-loop *Informal:* without important information, instructions, and privileges that are available to others.

outdoor occupations Jobs in farming, recreation, soil conservation, forestry, water conservation, and fish and wildlife management.

outlook A forecast that something will happen. *Example:* an outlook that more jobs will be available because of a shortage of skilled workers.

outplaced employee An employee who has been dismissed from a position usually because of a downsizing or plant closing rather than poor job performance. *See also* **outplacement.**

outplacement An organized program financed by a business or organization to assist employees whose jobs are being eliminated. Assistance may take the form of resume writing help, counseling, relocation information, skill training, or job referral service.

outplacement consultant An individual who helps workers find new jobs when their old jobs are being eliminated. *See also* **outplacement.**

outsourcing The practice of contracting for a service with an outside firm instead of handling the service within the business or organization. *Examples:* hiring outside companies to provide food services, print newsletters, and do payroll checks. *See also* **vendoring out.**

oven operator/tender An individual who operates or tends heating equipment other than basic metal or plastic processing equipment and performs such operations as baking fiberglass or painted products, fusing glass or enamel to metal products, carbonizing coal, or curing rubber.

overseas jobs Jobs in countries outside the United States. *Examples:* jobs in the foreign service, diplomatic corps, construction, oil companies, and multinational companies.

overstaffing Hiring too many people for a particular project, business, or organization.

overtime Work in excess of eight hours a day or 40 hours per week.

overtime pay Wages, usually at a higher rate, paid for hours of work that exceed the normal work day/week.

♦Pp♦

PA An abbreviation of *physician assistant. See* **physician assistant.**

PACE An acronym for the Federal program Professional and Administrative Career Examination, which was a competitive examination used from 1974 to Sept. 1, 1982, to rate, rank, and hire entry-level applicants for a wide range of professional and administrative careers with the Federal Government. PACE has been replaced by the Professional and Administrative Career Program (PAC).

package designer An individual who specializes in the design of packaging items that are attractive but easy to handle and store.

packaging and filling machine operator An individual who operates or tends machines that package or fill a wide variety of products.

painter An individual who applies paint, stain, varnish, and other finishes to the interior or exterior of buildings. *See also* the OOH.

painter, visual artist An individual who works in a variety of media and methods to communicate ideas, thoughts, or feelings. *See also* the OOH, **graphic artist, graphic designer, cartoonist, animator,** and **fine artist.**

painting and coating machine operator An individual who operates and tends various types of machines that apply paints and coatings to manufactured items. *See also* the OOH, **dipper, tumbling barrel painter, spray-machine operator, paper coating machine operator, silvering applicator,** and **automotive painter.**

painting, coating, and decorating worker, hand An individual who applies paint or coating, or decorates manufactured items, such as furniture, glass, lamps, jewelry, books, and leather products.

paleontologist An individual who uses scientific techniques to study fossils in geological formations to trace the evolution of plant and animal life and the geologic history of the earth.

pamphlet binding worker An individual who works in a bindery and produces leaflets and folders.

panhandler An individual who approaches people on the street or other public areas to beg for money.

paper carrier An individual who sells newspapers on the street or delivers them to homes.

paper coating machine operator An individual who sprays "size," a coating mixture, on the surface of paper to give it its gloss or finish.

paper goods machine setting and setup operator An individual who sets up and operates paper goods machines to manufacture a variety of items, such as toilet tissue, napkins, and bags.

paperboy The preferred nonsexist term is *paper carrier*. *See* **paper carrier.**

paperhanger An individual who applies paper, vinyl, or fabric to walls and ceilings. *See also* the OOH.

paralegal An individual who works under the direction of a lawyer and assists with the preparation of legal documents, conducts research, and prepares reports. *See also* the OOH. Paralegals are sometimes called legal assistants.

paramedic An individual who uses special medical training to assist injured or wounded people at the scene of an emergency. When victims require transportation for treatment, the paramedic transports the patient to a hospital or other appropriate facility. Paramedics are also called emergency medical technicians. *See also* **emergency medical technician.**

paraprofessional An occupation that requires some training or formal education and is near or close to another occupation requiring more formal education. *Examples:* a paraprofessional library technical assistant, who works with a professional librarian; and a paraprofessional legal assistant (paralegal), who works with an attorney.

parental leave Time off from work that some companies grant to male or female employees who need to care for infants or young children. *See also* **maternity leave.**

parking lot attendant An individual who assists customers in parking their cars in parking lots or garages, collects the fees, and issues identification tickets.

parole officer An individual who works with people who have been released from a jail or penitentiary on parole. The parole officer counsels and assists parolees to help them adjust to life outside the penal institution. *See also* **social worker.**

part-time employment Work that is less than full-time. Part-time work usually means working fewer hours than 40 hours per week and without employee benefits normally given to full-time employees.

part-time flexible employees United States Postal Service workers who are career employees and who do not have a regular work schedule or weekly guarantee of hours. These workers replace absent workers and help with extra work as the need arises.

part-time regular employees United States Postal Service workers assigned to a regular schedule of fewer than 40 hours in a service week.

part-time service In the Federal civil service system, the service of an employee who works on a part-time work schedule. *See* **part-time work schedule.**

part-time work schedule In the Federal civil

service system, a schedule that requires an employee to work less than full-time but for a specific number of hours (usually 16 to 32 hours per administrative workweek) on a prearranged scheduled tour of duty. *See also* **administrative workweek** and **tour of duty.**

partner An individual associated with a person----or persons----in a business arrangement. *See also* **partnership.**

partnership A contract between two individuals in which they agree to engage in a business, contribute a specified amount of capital, and fix the percentage of profit for each party.

parts manager An individual who orders, inventories, and sells replacement parts, maintenance items, and accessories for motor vehicles.

pass over The elimination from appointment consideration of a veteran preference eligible on a certificate (candidate list) to appoint a lower-ranking nonveteran when an agency submits reasons that the Office of Personnel Management finds sufficient.

passenger-booking clerk *See* **ticket agent.**

passenger rate clerk An individual who works for a bus company and arranges trips by planning travel routes, computing rates, and selling tickets.

pastry chef/baker An individual who produces baked goods for restaurants, institutions, and retail bakery shops.

pathologist, speech-language An individual who identifies, assesses, and treats persons with speech and language disorders. *See also* the OOH.

patience The quality of calmness, tolerance, and understanding.

patternmaker, apparel An individual who creates the master pattern that can be reduced or enlarged to make different size patterns from which garments are cut.

paving equipment operator (military) In the Army, Navy, Air Force, or Marine Corps, an individual who operates rock crushers and other quarry equipment to make gravel, operates mixing plants to make batches of concrete and asphalt, and spreads asphalt and concrete with paving machines. *See also* the *Military Careers* guide.

paving, surfacing, and tamping equipment operator An individual who operates equipment for applying concrete, asphalt, or other materials to roadbeds, parking lots, or runways.

pay adjustment In the Federal civil service system, any increase or decrease in an employee's rate of basic pay when there is no change in the duties or responsibilities of the employee's position. A pay adjustment may include a change in the step at which an employee is paid. A change in the pay system under which the employee is paid is also a pay adjustment.

pay cap In the Federal civil service system, the ceiling or limitation placed on the retired or retainer pay of an employee who retired from a uniformed service on or after 01-11-79.

pay equity The policy of paying men and women "equal pay for equal work."

pay grade (military) A level of employment, as designated by the military. There are nine enlisted pay grades and ten officer pay grades through which personnel can progress during their career. Pay grade and length of service determine a service member's pay. *See also* **enlisted pay grades** and **officer pay grades.**

"pay or play" health insurance A proposal that would provide a health insurance pool run by the Federal Government for people who have jobs which do not provide health insurance and for individuals who are unemployed. Employers who do not provide health insurance for their employees would be taxed by the Government to pay for insurance.

pay plan In the Federal civil service system, the pay system or schedule under which an employee's rate of basic pay is determined. Examples: the General Schedule and the Federal Wage System.

pay rate determinant In the Federal civil service system, a designation of the special factors, if any, that have been used in determining an employee's salary.

pay retention entitlement In the Federal civil service system, the right of an employee to retain, under certain circumstances, a rate of basic pay that is higher than the maximum rate of the grade for the position which the person occupies.

pay scale The graduated wage rates that have been established by a business or because of a collective bargaining agreement, and that determine the amount paid to employees.

pay, severance Money paid to employees separated by a reduction in force and not eligible for retirement. Federal employees can receive basic severance pay, which is one week's pay for each year of civilian service up to ten years and two weeks' pay for each year served over ten years. Federal employees may also qualify for an age adjustment allowance, which is ten percent of the basic severance pay for each year over age 40.

payola The illegal payment to an individual to use the person's influence to promote a product or service. *Example:* a disk jockey who praises and plays recorded music to receive money from the producers of the recordings.

payroll clerk An individual who maintains records and computes earnings, vacation time, and sick leave balances due to employees. *See also* the OOH and **timekeeping clerk.**

payroll deductions Money subtracted from an employee's pay. Social Security (FICA) and income tax withholdings are required by law, but the employee may authorize payroll deductions, such as insurance premiums, pension contributions, and union dues.

payroll specialist (military) In the Army, Navy, Air Force, Marine Corps, or Coast Guard, an individual who computes basic pay and allowances, bonuses, and other payments; computes Social Security, income tax, insurance, and other deductions; and prepares pay and travel vouchers, earnings and deductions statements, and financial accounts and reports. *See also* the *Military Careers* guide.

PBGC An abbreviation of *Pension Benefit Guaranty Corporation. See also* **Pension Benefit Guaranty Corporation.**

PBX An abbreviation of *private branch exchange*, a switchboard used by a particular business or organization to handle telephone calls.

PBX installer An individual who installs complex telephone systems, such as PBX systems for customers with special communication requirements for the transmission of voice and data.

PBX operator An individual who operates PBX switchboards for large corporations, hospitals, and hotels, and connects interoffice and house calls.

PBX repairer An individual who locates and repairs problems in complex telephone systems, such as PBX, CENTREX, or KEY installations.

Peace Corps A Federal Government agency that trains and sends volunteers to primarily underdeveloped countries to aid people in such areas as education, health and nutrition, community development, and agriculture.

pediatric dentist A dentist who specializes in the care of children's teeth.

pedicurist An individual who cleans, shapes, and polishes a customer's toenails.

penetration tester An individual who attempts to penetrate computer systems to detect possible security problems.

Pension Benefit Guaranty Corporation (PBGC) A self-financing, wholly owned Federal Government corporation that guarantees payment of a covered plan's nonforfeitable pension benefits if that plan terminates without sufficient assets to pay those guaranteed benefits or if the plan is insolvent.

people skills *Informal:* abilities necessary to work with or supervise other people successfully. *See also* **interpersonal skills.**

perform To carry out, fulfill, accomplish, or do.

performance **1)** The act of accomplishing some action, assignment, or work. **2)** A musical or dramatic entertainment.

performance appraisal A comparison, under a performance appraisal system, of an employee's actual performance against the performance standards previously established for the position.

performance contracts A legal agreement between a business, organization, or governmental unit and a provider of services, which specifies the work to be done (performed) and when it should be finished. In many cases, a fine must be paid if the work is not done according to the contract or by the specified time.

performance elements In the Federal civil service system, the major duties or responsibilities that are important for success in a position. These elements should be position-based and reflect the actual work assigned to an employee.

Performance Management and Recognition System In the Federal civil service system, the pay system established to replace the Merit Pay System for General Schedule employees in grades GS-13 through GS-15 who are in supervisory, managerial, or management official positions.

performance review An evaluation of the job performance of an individual usually on a regular basis.

performance standards In the Federal civil service system, the measure of the level of accomplishment of an individual's major duties and responsibilities.

periodic increase A salary increase provided in certain Federal Government pay plans based on time-in-grade and acceptable or satisfactory work performance.

periodic review *See* **performance review.**

periodic step increase In the United States Postal Service, an advancement from one step to the next within a specific grade of a position.

periodontist A dentist who specializes in the treatment of gum diseases.

peripheral equipment operator, electronic data processing *See* **computer and peripheral equipment operator.**

perk *Informal:* a short form of the word *perquisite*, used to indicate some bonus, special privilege, or fringe benefit given to an employee over and above the usual salary or expected benefits. *Examples:* a company car, day care for children, or a discount on merchandise.

permanent arbitrator An individual selected to serve for the life of an agreement or a stipulated term and authorized to hear all disputes that arise during this period. *See also* **arbitrator, conciliator,** and **arbitration.**

permissive intervenor An individual who may be permitted to participate in a proceeding if it will affect the participant directly and if intervention is otherwise appropriate under law. *See also* **intervenor** and **intervenors as a matter of right.**

personal attendant An individual who assists elderly, handicapped, or convalescent persons by performing various personal services. A personal attendant is also referred to as a companion.

personal contact Direct communication with friends and acquaintances to secure information on duties of a particular job, individuals to contact, availability of positions, and job leads. *See also* **job lead, networking,** and **contact person.**

personal secretary *See* **social secretary.**

personality psychologist A psychologist who specializes in the study of human nature, individual differences, and the ways in which those differences develop.

personnel action The process necessary to appoint, separate, reinstate, or make other changes affecting an employee.

personnel clerk An individual who keeps personnel records in order and up-to-date, helps new employees with required forms, and explains benefits. *See also* the OOH.

personnel consultant *See* **employment interviewer.**

personnel department The part of a company that deals with hiring and firing employees and keeping records pertaining to employees.

personnel investigation In the Federal civil service system, an investigation, including background investigation, covering reputation, suitability, loyalty, qualifications, and other pertinent factors, conducted by personal contact, written inquiry, letter, or electronic linkage with the sources of information.

personnel jacket *See* **official personnel folder.**

personnel management The management of human resources to accomplish a mission and provide individual job satisfaction.

personnel manager The individual in charge of the personnel department and responsible for employment, compensation, benefits, education, and training. *See also* the OOH.

personnel manager (military) In the Army,

Navy, Air Force, Marine Corps, or Coast Guard, an individual who plans recruiting activities to interest qualified young people in the military, directs testing and career counseling for military personnel, and classifies personnel according to job aptitude and interest and service need. *See also* the *Military Careers* guide.

personnel office identifier In the Federal civil service system, a numerical code number assigned to a Federal civilian personnel office and which identifies the office authorized to appoint and separate the employee, and, to the extent such functions have been delegated, to prepare personnel actions, maintain official personnel records, and administer programs for staff compensation, training and development, benefits and awards, and employee/labor relations.

personnel recruiter An individual who finds promising job applicants. Duties may include interviewing applicants, administering tests, and checking references.

personnel specialist (military) In the Army, Navy, Air Force, Marine Corps, or Coast Guard, an individual who organizes, maintains, and reviews personnel records; uses a computer terminal to enter and retrieve personnel information; and assigns personnel to jobs. *See also* the *Military Careers* guide.

personnel training specialist An individual who plans, organizes, and directs educational activities to develop employee skills and enhance productivity.

pest controller An individual who sprays chemical solutions, releases toxic gases, or sets traps to kill pests or vermin.

pet store caretaker An individual who provides daily care for and maintains animals available for purchase.

petition for appeal In the Federal civil service system, a request filed by an appellant with a Merit Systems Protection Board (MSPB) regional office for review of a Federal agency's action.

petition for review In the Federal civil service system, the request filed for review of an initial decision of a presiding Federal official.

petroleum engineer An individual who plans and supervises the exploration and drilling for oil and gas. *See also* the OOH.

petroleum pump systems operator An individual who operates and controls manifold and pumping systems to circulate liquids through a petroleum refinery.

petroleum supply specialist (military) In the Army, Navy, Air Force, Marine Corps, or Coast Guard, an individual who connects hoses and valves and operates pumps to load petroleum products into tanker trucks, airplanes, ships, and railroad cars; tests oils and fuels for pollutants; and repairs pipeline systems, hoses, valves, and pumps. *See also* the *Military Careers* guide.

petroleum technician An individual who measures and records physical and geologic conditions in oil or gas wells.

petty officer An individual in the Navy who has an advanced rating (E-4 through E-9) but is not a commissioned officer.

pharmacist An individual who dispenses drugs and medicines that have been prescribed by physicians and may also advise the public on the proper selection and use of medicines. *See also* the OOH.

pharmacist (military) An Army, Navy, or Air Force officer who manages pharmacy technicians who prepare, label, and dispense orders for drugs and medicines; advises doctors and patients on the proper use and side effects of drugs and medicines; and trains medical, nursing, and pharmacy staffs on the use of drugs. *See also* the *Military Careers* guide.

pharmacy assistant An individual who mixes pharmaceutical preparations under the direction of a pharmacist, labels and stores supplies, and cleans equipment.

pharmacy technician (military) In the Army, Navy, Air Force, or Coast Guard, an individual who reads doctors' prescriptions to determine the type and amount of drugs to prepare, weighs and measures drugs and chemicals, and mixes ingredients in order to produce prescription medications. *See also* the *Military Careers* guide.

phased retirement The practice of keeping older

workers on the payroll for a specified length of time.

phlebotomist An individual who collects, types, and prepares blood and its components for transfusions. Phlebotomists are also referred to as blood bank technologists.

photoengraving worker *See* **lithographic and photoengraving worker.**

photofinishing laboratory worker An individual who develops photographic film, makes prints and slides, and enlarges or retouches photographs.

photogrammetrist An individual who prepares maps and drawings by using mathematical formulas and analytical processes to measure and interpret aerial photographs. *See also* **surveyor, mapping scientist, cartographer, geodetic surveyor,** and **geophysical prospecting surveyor.**

photographer (military) In the Army, Navy, Air Force, Marine Corps, or Coast Guard, an individual who selects camera, film, and other equipment needed for photo assignments; determines camera angles, lighting, and any special effects needed; and takes still photos of people, events, military equipment, land areas, and other subjects. *See also* the *Military Careers* guide.

photographer and camera operator An individual who uses various types of cameras to portray people, places, and events accurately and artistically. *See also* the OOH.

photographic equipment repairer An individual who repairs and adjusts cameras and photographic equipment.

photographic equipment repairer (military) In the Army, Navy, Air Force, or Marine Corps, an individual who adjusts and repairs camera shutter mechanisms, focus controls, and flash units; maintains and repairs aerial cameras mounted in airplanes; and maintains aerial sensors that detect foreign military activities. *See also* the *Military Careers* guide.

photographic process worker An individual who develops and prints photographic film either by hand or by using automatic processing equipment. *See also* the OOH; **color film operator; developer, film; printer operator; airbrush artist; photographic retoucher; colorist; photographic spotter; color laboratory technician; color-printer operator; automatic print developer; takedown sorter;** and **automatic mounter.**

photographic retoucher An individual who alters photographic negatives and prints to accentuate the desired features of a subject or to remove undesirable ones.

photographic spotter An individual who covers or spots out imperfections on photographic prints.

photojournalist An individual who photographs newsworthy events, places, and people for newspapers and magazines in which photographs are the dominant feature.

photoprocessing specialist (military) In the Army, Navy, or Air Force, an individual who uses a series of chemical and water baths to develop film negatives; produces prints from negatives; and operates developing machines that make prints from film. *See also* the *Military Careers* guide.

physical and corrective therapy assistant/aide An individual who prepares patients and administers physical therapy treatment, such as massage; heat, light, and sound treatments; and traction.

physical chemist A chemist who studies the physical characteristics of atoms and molecules and investigates how chemical reactions work.

physical geographer An individual who studies the distribution of climates, vegetation, soil, and land forms.

physical metallurgist An individual who studies the nature, structure, and physical properties of metals and their alloys, as well as the methods of converting refined metals into final products.

physical meteorologist An individual who studies the atmosphere's chemical and physical properties; the transmission of light, sound, and radio waves; the transfer of energy in the atmosphere; and factors affecting the formation of clouds, rain, snow, and other weather phenomena.

physical oceanographer An individual who studies the physical aspects of oceans, such as currents and the interaction of the surface of the sea with the atmosphere.

physical science Sciences such as physics, chemistry, geology, and astronomy, used to analyze the nature and properties of energy and nonliving matter.

physical therapist An individual who works to improve the mobility, relieve the pain, or prevent or limit the permanent disability of patients suffering from injuries or disease. *See also* the OOH.

physical therapist (military) An Army, Navy, or Air Force officer who tests and interviews patients to determine the extent of their disabilities, consults with doctors to discuss and evaluate patients' progress, and plans individual physical therapy programs. *See also* the *Military Careers* guide.

physical therapy specialist (military) In the Army, Navy, Air Force, or Coast Guard, an individual who assists physical therapists in planning therapy programs for patients, gives patients massages and heat treatments, and helps patients improve their mobility through special exercises. *See also* the *Military Careers* guide.

physician An individual who performs medical examinations, diagnoses illnesses, and treats people suffering from injury or disease. *See also* the OOH and various medical specialties.

physician assistant (PA) An individual who works under the supervision of a physician and whose duties may include taking medical histories, performing physical examinations, ordering laboratory tests, and making preliminary diagnoses. *See also* the OOH and **surgeon's assistant.**

physician assistant (military) An Army, Navy, Air Force, or Coast Guard officer who records medical histories, examines patients, and makes initial diagnoses; treats common illnesses or injuries, calling in supervising physicians for serious health problems; performs routine physical examinations; and collects specimens for laboratory tests. *See also* the *Military Careers* guide.

physician/surgeon (military) An Army, Navy, or Air Force officer who examines patients to detect abnormalities in pulse, breathing, or other body functions; determines presence and extent of illness or injury by reviewing medical histories, X rays, laboratory reports, and examination reports; and develops treatment plans that may include medication, therapy, or surgery. *See also* the *Military Careers* guide.

physicist An individual who attempts to discover basic principles governing the structure and behavior of matter, the generation and transfer of energy, and the interaction of matter and energy. *See also* the OOH.

physicist (military) An Army, Navy, Air Force or Coast Guard officer who plans and conducts experiments in aerodynamics, optics, geophysics, biophysics, and astrophysics; conducts research to improve methods of radiation detection and protection; and analyzes strength, flexibility, weight, and other properties of metals, plastics, and other materials. *See also* the *Military Careers* guide.

physiological psychologist An individual who studies the relationship of behavior to the biological and neurological functions of the body.

physiologist An individual who studies life functions of plants and animals under normal and abnormal conditions.

piano tuner An individual who adjusts piano strings to the proper pitch.

picker An individual who works in the logging industry and selects and places logs onto skidders and log blocks and onto conveyors to be sent to other machines for further processing.

piece rate 1) A method of payment in which the worker is paid according to the number of items produced. **2)** In the United States Postal Service, in transportation under contract, a basis of payment according to the number of pouches, sacks, or outside pieces. The rate may be determined by distance from origin to destination or by an amount per piece.

piece work The type of work in which the worker is paid according to the number of items produced. *See also* **piece rate.**

pigeonhole 1) *Informal:* to put aside or postpone until some future time or indefinitely. **2)** To classify with a category that is too neat. **3)** In the United States Postal Service, an opening or section in a distribution case.

pilot, aircraft An individual who flies various types of airplanes or helicopters. *See also* the OOH.

pink-collar worker *Informal:* an individual in an occupation that is usually held by women. *Examples:* cosmetologist or secretary. *See also* **white-collar worker, blue-collar worker,** and **cloth cap.**

pink slip *Informal:* a notice of termination of employment.

pipe-organ tuner and repairer An individual who tunes, repairs, and installs organs that make music by forcing air through flue pipes or reed pipes.

pipefitter An individual who installs and repairs pipe systems used in manufacturing, the heating and cooling of buildings, and the generation of electricity. *See also* the OOH.

pipefitter (military) *See* **plumber/pipefitter (military).**

pipelayer An individual who lays glazed or unglazed clay, concrete, plastic, or cast iron pipe for storm or sanitation sewers, drains, and water mains.

pipelaying fitter An individual who aligns pipeline sections preparatory to welding and signals tractor drivers in placing pipeline sections in proper alignment.

place of employment The actual site, such as an office, factory, or store, where an individual works.

placement In the Federal civil service system, putting employees into jobs. This may be done by reinstatement of former employees, appointment of someone new to Government, promotion, change to lower grade, reassignment, or transfer within an agency or from other agencies.

placement counselor An individual in a college or university who helps students and alumni plan careers and locate jobs.

placement service A service, usually operated by an educational institution, that attempts to find jobs for students or alumni.

plant breeder A scientist who specializes in the selection and breeding of plants to develop and improve their economic or aesthetic characteristics.

plasterer An individual who finishes interior walls and ceilings with plaster and other materials. *See also* the OOH.

plastics molding and casting machine operator *See* **plastics-working machine operator.**

plastics-working machine operator An individual who tends machines that produce a variety of consumer and industrial goods made from plastics. *See also* the OOH.

platemaker An individual employed in the lithography or offset printing industry who uses a photographic process to make printing plates.

plating and coating machine operator, metal and plastic An individual who runs machines that produce metal and plastic parts used in manufactured products. *See also* the OOH.

Platoon Leaders Class (PLC) Program A Marine Corps program for college freshman, sophomores, and juniors who have made the decision to pursue a Marine Corps officer commission. Applicants must be enrolled in a four-year accredited college and are eligible to receive $100 per month in financial assistance after successful completion of their first summer of training.

Platoon Leaders Class-Law A Marine Corps program that is a post-baccalaureate degree program for individuals attending law school. Active duty is postponed until a student obtains a law degree and passes the bar examination.

player *Informal:* an individual who is an active participant in some situation. Example: a new vice president who is going to be a player by leading a new ad campaign. *See also* **level playing field.**

PLC An abbreviation of Platoon Leaders Class. *See* **Platoon Leaders Class Program.**

pleadings In the Federal civil service system, the formal written allegations of the parties who set forth their respective claims and defenses in a Federal case.

plumber An individual who installs and repairs the water, waste disposal, drainage, and gas systems in homes and commercial buildings. *See also* the OOH.

plumber/pipefitter (military) In the Army, Navy, Air Force, Marine Corps, or Coast Guard, an individual who uses blueprints and drawings to plan layouts of pipe systems; bends, cuts, and threads pipes made of lead, copper, and plastic; and installs connections, fittings, and joints. *See also* the *Military Careers* guide.

plumbing inspector An individual who examines plumbing systems to ensure compliance with building codes and regulations, zoning requirements, and contract specifications.

podiatrist An individual who diagnoses and treats disorders and diseases of the foot and lower leg. *See also* the OOH.

podiatrist (military) An Army, Navy, or Air Force officer who examines feet to discover the causes of ailments; arranges for laboratory tests and diagnostic X rays; and treats foot ailments, such as fractures, muscle damage, and bunions. *See also* the *Military Careers* guide.

poissonier A chef whose main responsibility is the care and preparation of fish and seafood items.

police officer An individual who performs a variety of duties to enforce laws and investigate crimes. *See also* the OOH; **detective, public; special agent;** and **FBI special agent.**

policeman/policewoman The preferred nonsexist term is police officer. *See* **police officer.**

policy processing clerk, insurance An individual who processes new policies, modifications to existing policies, and claims.

political geographer A geographer concerned with the relationship of geography to political phenomena----local, national, and international.

political scientist An individual who investigates the ways in which political power is organized, distributed, and used.

polygraph test A test that is sometimes used by employers to screen job applicants or to gather information when problems occur.

population trends Changes in the number and composition of people that can have an important effect on jobs. Predictions for the next decade include a growing demand for health services as the population ages, continuing growth in the South and West while the Northeast and Midwest increase slightly or stay the same, and a decline in the number of young workers while the proportion of middle aged and older people increases.

portable machine cutter An individual who works in the apparel industry and cuts out various pieces of material, following the outline of a pattern.

portal-to-portal rate Wages that start when a worker, usually a miner, begins a descent at a mine entrance (portal) and end when the worker exits the portal at the end of the shift. This method of payment was put into union contracts because the area where a miner actually begins work may be a long way from the mine entrance.

position **1)** A type of employment. *Example:* a position as a business manager for a company. **2)** In the Federal civil service system, the duties and responsibilities assigned by competent authority for performance by an employee. **3)** A stand taken on a particular matter or an attitude toward something. *Example:* a foreman's view that there is no excuse for being late to work.

position change In the Federal civil service system, a move by an employee to another position during continuous service within the same agency. When the move establishes the employee's eligibility for grade retention, the Nature of Action for the move is called "Position Change." It is also called "Position Change" when an employee already entitled to grade retention moves to another position at or below the person's retained grade. Moves when the employee is not entitled to grade retention are called promotions, changes to lower grade, or reassignments.

position classification In the Federal civil service system, analysis of the kind of work, level of difficulty and responsibility, and qualification requirements of a position, and the placement of the position in a class and grade according to published standards.

position classification specialist/classifier In the Federal civil service system, an individual who is a specialist in job analysis and determines the titles, occupational groups, appropriate pay system, and grades of positions.

position description In the Federal civil service system, an official written statement of the major duties, responsibilities, and supervisory relationships of a position.

position management The process of designing positions to combine logical and consistent duties and responsibilities into an orderly, efficient, and productive organization to accomplish the agency's mission.

position risk level In the Federal civil service system, the degree of risk vested in a public trust position based on its relationship to efficiency of the service.

position sensitivity In the Federal civil service system, the degree of sensitivity vested in a national security position based on its risk relationship to the national security and efficiency of the service.

position survey A review by a Federal agency of positions to determine whether they are still needed and, if so, whether the classification and position description are correct.

position title The name of a position, such as secretary or civil engineer.

Position Wanted The heading used in the classified section of some newspapers to list ads from individuals seeking jobs. *See also* **classified ad, help wanted ad,** and **situations wanted ad.**

positions, "PL 313 Type" Positions in the Federal Government that were established under Public Law 80-313 or similar authorities. These positions are a small group of high-level professional and scientific positions generally in the competitive service but not filled through competitive examinations. Salaries for these positions are usually set between GS-12 and GS-18. *See also* **General Schedule.**

post-employment restrictions Limitations on the jobs an individual can take after leaving a particular position. *Example:* a Federal Government employee who can not represent a company the employee had regulated while working for the Federal Government.

post office jobs *See* **postmaster, mailhandler, postal clerk,** and **mail carrier.**

Postal Carrier Executive Service In the United States Postal Service, a staffing category designed to develop and maintain a group capable of filling key management positions and providing leadership within the United States Postal Service.

postal clerk A United States Postal Service employee who separates incoming and outgoing mail according to established schemes or serves the public at a postal facility window. *See also* the OOH.

postal director (military) An Army, Navy, Air Force, or Marine Corps officer who directs the operation of post offices and mail rooms on military bases and ships, works with the United States Postal Service to forward service mail, and keeps information on the location and mailing addresses of military personnel. *See also* the *Military Careers* guide.

postal exams Competitive examinations given periodically and open to individuals interested in working for the United States Postal Service.

postal inspector An individual who investigates criminal activities, such as theft and misuse of the mail, and conducts management or financial audits.

Postal Service *See* **United States Postal Service.**

Postal Service schedule The salary schedule applying to craft employees of the United States Postal Service.

postal specialist (military) In the Army, Navy, Air Force, Marine Corps, and Coast Guard, an individual who uses metering and stamp-canceling machines to process mail, weighs packages to determine postage due, and examines packages to ensure that they meet mailing standards. *See also* the *Military Careers* guide.

postmaster A United States Postal Service employee responsible for all aspects of postal management and personnel within a specific post office.

postsecondary education Education at a college, trade school, or vocational school that occurs after graduation from high school.

potential Something that is possible or capable of being but has not been achieved yet. Example: a student who has the potential to get straight A's but lacks motivation and has gotten only average grades.

poultry cutter *See* **butcher and meat, poultry, and fish cutter.**

poultry scientist An individual who conducts research on the selection, breeding, feeding, and management of poultry.

power dispatcher An individual who monitors

equipment and records readings dealing with the transmission of electricity.

power distributor An individual who controls the flow of electricity through transmission lines to users.

power generating plant operator An individual who controls the machinery that generates electricity.

power plant electrician (military) In the Army, Navy, Air Force, Marine Corps, or Coast Guard, an individual who maintains and repairs motors, generators, switchboards, and control equipment; maintains and repairs power and lighting circuits, electrical fixtures, and other electrical equipment; and detects and locates grounds, open circuits, and short circuits in power distribution cables. *See also* the *Military Careers* guide.

power plant operator (military) In the Army, Navy, Air Force, Marine Corps, or Coast Guard, an individual who monitors and operates control boards to regulate power plants, operates and maintains diesel generating units to produce electric power, and monitors and controls nuclear reactors that produce electricity and power ships and submarines. *See also* the *Military Careers* guide.

power reactor operator An individual licensed by the Nuclear Regulatory Commission to operate all equipment in a nuclear power plant.

power tool repairer, home appliance An individual who installs and services home appliances and power tools.

powerhouse mechanic (military) In the Army, Navy, Air Force, or Coast Guard, an individual who installs generating equipment, such as gasoline and diesel engines, turbines, and air compressors; repairs and maintains nuclear power plants; and inspects and services pumps, generators, batteries, and cables. *See also* the *Military Careers* guide.

powerline installer and repairer An individual who installs and repairs electric power lines, cable television lines, telephone lines, poles, and terminals.

practical nurse, licensed (L.P.N.) *See* **licensed practical nurse.**

practitioner An individual engaged in an occupation or profession. *Example:* a doctor who is a practitioner of one of the healing arts.

precision assembler An individual who puts together manufactured parts and performs tasks such as interpreting detailed specifications, assembling prototypes, and using precision measuring instruments. *See also* the OOH.

precision instrument repairer An individual who installs, tests, repairs, maintains, and adjusts precision instruments used to measure and control variables such as pressure, temperature, and flow.

precision instrument repairer (military) In the Army, Navy, Air Force, or Marine Corps, an individual who calibrates weather instruments, such as barometers and thermometers; repairs gyrocompasses; and adjusts and repairs weapon-aiming devices, such as range finders, telescopes, periscopes, and ballistic computers. *See also* the *Military Careers* guide.

preference In the Federal civil service system, the right to special advantage or preferential treatment in personnel actions under authority of veteran laws.

preference, compensable disability in the Federal civil service system, a ten-point preference awarded to a veteran separated under honorable conditions from active duty, who receives compensation of ten percent or more for a service-connected disability.

preference disability in the Federal civil service system, a ten-point preference in hiring given to a veteran separated under honorable conditions from active duty, and who has a service-connected disability or receives compensation, pension, or disability retirement from the Department of Veterans Affairs or a uniformed service.

preference, eligible In the Federal civil service system, preference given an ex-serviceman or ex-servicewoman who has an honorable or general discharge from a period of active service that includes wartime or a campaign for which a campaign badge is awarded or who has a service-connected disability. Spouses and mothers of ex-servicemen or ex- servicewomen may also be preference eligibles under certain conditions.

preference, husband in the Federal civil service system, a ten-point preference to which an ex-servicewoman's spouse may be entitled.

preference, mother In the Federal civil service system, a ten-point preference to which the mother of a deceased or disabled military veteran may be entitled.

preference, tentative In the Federal civil service system, a five-point preference tentatively awarded an eligible by the Area Office of Examiners. This tentative preference must be verified by the appointing officer.

preference, 30 percent or more disabled In the Federal civil service system, a disabled veteran whose disability is rated at 30 percent or more and who is entitled to special preference in appointment and during reduction in force. *See also* **reduction in force**

preference, veteran In the Federal civil service system, the statutory right to special advantage in appointments or separations based on a person's discharge under honorable conditions from the Armed Forces for a service-connected disability.

preference, widow or widower In the Federal civil service system, a ten-point preference to which a military veteran's widow or widower may be entitled.

preference, wife In the Federal civil service system, a ten- point preference to which an ex-serviceman's spouse may be entitled.

premium pay In the Federal civil service system, additional pay for overtime, night, Sunday, holiday, or standby work.

prep cook An individual who does the preliminary work in a restaurant kitchen, such as washing, cutting, and precooking vegetables; preparing fruits and vegetables for further processing; and making meat and fish stock.

prerequisite Something that is needed before something can be done. *Example:* Beginning Typing as a prerequisite for Advanced Typing.

preschool teacher An individual who teaches preschool pupils in public or private schools.

presentation skills The abilities and skills necessary to **1)** present successfully an idea for approval, or **2)** prepare, display, and serve food specially for the aesthetic enjoyment of diners.

president, corporate and other organizations *See* **general manager/top executives.**

Presidential Management Intern Program A Federal Government program open to U.S. citizens scheduled to receive a graduate degree who have been nominated by a college official and have a personal interest in a Government career. Appointments to the Presidential Management Intern Program are for two years. At the end of the two-year period, the internship is converted to a permanent Government position.

President's Committee on Employment of People with Disabilities A group that provides information on career planning, training, or public policy for individuals with disabilities. Address: 1331 F St. NW., 3rd Floor, Washington, DC 20004. Phone: (202) 376-6200.

presiding official A person designated to preside over a hearing, to make rulings, and to issue a decision.

press operator, printing An individual who prepares and operates the printing presses in a pressroom. *See also* the OOH.

presser An individual in a dry-cleaning establishment who presses freshly washed or dry-cleaned clothes by hand or by using steam-press machinery.

pressing machine operator, apparel An individual who works in the apparel industry and uses a pressing machine to press garments.

Prevailing Rate System A subsystem of the Federal Wage System used to determine an employee's pay in a particular wage area. The determination requires comparing the rate of pay with the private sector for similar duties and responsibilities. Included are Federal employees in recognized trade or craft or skilled mechanical crafts; in unskilled, semiskilled, or skilled manual labor occupations; and other persons, including foreman or supervisors in positions where trade, craft, or labor experience or knowledge is the main requirement.

previous retirement coverage In the Federal

civil service system, an indicator of whether an employee has, at the time for most recent appointment to the Federal service, previously been covered by the Civil Service Retirement System or Federal Employee's Retirement System.

priest, Roman Catholic *See* **Roman Catholic priest.**

prime-age workers Workers age 25 to 54.

principal, school An individual who oversees the operation of an elementary or secondary school.

principle A basic idea, truth, rule, or assumption.

print developer, photographic An individual who produces negatives as a first step in the production of photographic prints.

print shop stenographer An individual who takes dictation, uses a typewriter to transcribe the dictated material, and prepares metal printing plates to be used by addressing machines.

printer operator An individual who works in the photographic processing industry and is responsible for printing photographs from negatives.

printing press operator An individual who prepares and operates printing presses in a pressroom. *See also* the OOH.

printing specialist (military) In the Army, Navy, Air Force, or Marine Corps, an individual who uses offset or lithographic printing processes to reproduce printed matter; prepares photographic negatives and uses copy cameras and enlargers to transfer them to printing plates; and prepares layouts of artwork, photographs, and text for lithographic plates. *See also* the *Military Careers* guide.

printmaker An individual who creates printed images from designs cut, etched, or engraved in linoleum, wood, metal, or stone, or from computer-driven data.

prison guard An individual who maintains order, enforces rules and regulations, and escorts prisoners.

private detective/investigator *See* **detective, private.**

private duty nurse A nurse who provides nursing care to one patient either in the patient's home or in some medical facility. *See also* **registered nurse, school nurse, public health nurse,** and **office nurse.**

private employment agency A business that attempts to match an available position with a qualified applicant. A fee is charged for this service and is usually paid by the employer.

private household worker An individual who may perform a variety of household tasks, such as cleaning, laundering, caring for children, and cooking. *See also* the OOH.

private school A school operated and financed by private individuals instead of a governmental unit.

private sector The part of the economic system that is owned by private individuals and is not under the direct control of the government. *See also* **public sector.**

probation officer An individual who monitors and counsels people on probation to assist them in becoming productive members of society. *See also* the OOH.

probationary period **1)** A trial period during which employment may be terminated without the procedures that may be in place to protect nonprobationary employees. **2)** In the Federal civil service system, a trial period that the Office of Personnel Management regards as a final and highly significant step in the examining process. This period provides the final test, that of actual performance on the job, which no preliminary testing method can approach in validity. During this period an employee may be released without undue formality. **3)** In the United States Postal Service, the initial trial period of employment during which a career employee does not yet have access to the grievance or adverse action appeal system. For bargaining unit employees, the trial period is the first 90 calendar days; and for nonbargaining unit employees, the trial period is the first six months.

Processing Occupations One of the nine primary categories for grouping occupations in the *Dictionary of Occupational Titles. Examples:* plater, silver spray worker, and shot dropper.

procurement clerk An individual who compiles

information and records to draw up purchase orders for the procurement of materials.

producer An individual who selects plays or scripts; hires directors, cast members, and production crews; coordinates activities; and secures financing for a play, motion picture, or TV production. *See also* the OOH.

production bonus Extra money sometimes given to employees as a reward for achieving or exceeding some production quota.

production goal *See* **production quota.**

production, planning, and expediting clerk An individual who coordinates and expedites the flow of work and materials according to production schedules.

production quota An aim or objective set by management to increase the output of a factory. *Example:* a production quota of 10,000 units per week announced by a supervisor.

productivity The ability or power to produce goods and services. *Example:* factory workers who are able to increase productivity after they learn that the company has lost money.

profession A type of occupation that requires a high degree of education and usually some type of qualifying examination and certification. Occupations such as doctor and lawyer are recognized as professions.

professional association/organization An organization composed of individuals in the same occupation and formed for the purpose of protecting the interests of its members, keeping them up to date on issues affecting their profession, and publishing magazines or newsletters. *Example:* American Physicians Association publications that provide not only medical information but also news of pending laws which might affect the members.

professional athlete An athlete paid to use his or her athletic ability either as an individual or as part of a team.

professional magazine A publication that contains articles of interest to a specific profession. *Example:* the *New England Journal of Medicine. See also* **trade magazine.**

professional society *See* **professional association/organization.**

Professional, Technical, and Managerial Occupations One of the nine primary categories for grouping occupations in the *Dictionary of Occupational Titles. Examples:* **librarian, clergy,** and **railroad conductor.**

professor A teacher in a college or university who has achieved the highest academic status.

profit sharing The practice of distributing part of the profits of a business to the employees.

profitability The capability of having money or resources remaining after all business expenses have been deducted.

programmer-analyst An individual who programs and analyzes computer systems, usually for a small company.

programmer, computer *See* **computer programmer.**

programmer, tool *See* **tool programmer, numerical control.**

progressive discipline The practice of making penalties increasingly more severe as offenses are repeated or accumulated.

prohibited occupations Jobs that, in some cases, cannot be held by minors. Examples: logging and saw mill occupations, brick or tile making jobs, positions in establishments serving alcoholic beverages, and certain construction jobs.

promote To advance an individual to a better job.

promotion **1)** Advancement to a job with higher status, pay, or responsibility. **2)** In the Federal civil service, a change of an employee to a higher grade when both the old and new positions are under the same job classification system and pay schedule, or to a position with higher pay in a different job classification system and pay schedule.

promotion, career In the Federal civil service, the promotion of an employee without current competition when **1)** the individual had earlier been competitively selected from a register or under competitive promotion procedures for an assignment intended as a matter of record to be preparation for the position being filled, or **2)** the position is reconstituted at a higher grade because of additional duties and responsibilities.

promotion certificate In the Federal civil service system, a list of best-qualified candidates to be considered to fill a position under competitive promotion procedures.

promotion, competitive In the Federal civil service system, the selection of a current or former Federal civil service employee for a higher-grade position, using procedures that compare the candidates on merit.

proofreader and copy marker An individual who reads transcripts or proofs of type setup to detect and mark for correction any grammatical, typographical, or compositional errors.

property and real estate manager An individual who acts for the owner of a house, apartment, or office building by handling rentals, scheduling repairs, preparing leases, and collecting rents. *See also* the OOH.

proprietor The owner of a business and in many cases the manager as well.

proprietory schools Private technical institutes that offer a variety of courses and in some cases a two-year associate degree program.

prosthodontist A dentist who specializes in making artificial teeth and dentures.

protected individuals A U.S. Immigration and Naturalization Service term for individuals such as citizens or nationals of the United States, lawful permanent residents, temporary residents, and persons granted refugee or asylum status. The residence status of individuals affects their eligibility for employment in the U.S. *See also* **employment eligibility documents.**

Protestant minister *See* **minister, Protestant.**

prototype A model or original creation that may be used as the basis for future developments or improvements.

provision A part of a contract, regulation, policy statement, or law. *Example:* a provision of a collective bargaining agreement to win an argument with a foreman.

provisional appointment In the Federal civil service system, a temporary appointment to a continuing position when the agency intends later to convert the employee to a nontemporary appointment and has current authority for such conversion.

psychiatric aide An individual who helps with the care of mentally ill individuals confined to hospitals or other health facilities. *See also* the OOH.

psychiatric nursing assistant *See* **psychiatric aide.**

psychiatric social worker An individual who provides individual and group therapy for psychiatric patients in mental hospitals, community mental health centers, and substance abuse treatment facilities.

psychologist An individual who studies human behavior and mental processes to understand, explain, and change people's behavior. *See also* the OOH.

psychologist (military) An Army, Navy, or Air Force officer who conducts research on human and animal behavior, aptitude, and job performance; gives psychological tests; and interprets results to diagnose patients' problems. *See also* the *Military Careers* guide.

public affairs specialist An individual employed by the Government to keep the public informed about the activities of Government agencies and officials.

public defender A lawyer who represents people charged with a crime who are unable to hire a private attorney.

public employment Jobs associated with some governmental unit instead of private industry. *Examples:* highway maintenance workers, teachers, and police officers.

public health dentist A dentist who works in community dental health facilities.

public health nurse A nurse who cares for patients in various community settings, such as clinics and retirement homes. Services may include nutrition counseling, immunizations, blood pressure testing, and health screenings.

public information officer (military) An Army, Navy, Air Force, Marine Corps, or Coast Guard officer who supervises the preparation of reports and other releases to the public and the military; briefs military personnel before they meet with the public and the news media; and provides information to newspapers, TV and radio stations, and civic organizations. *See also* the *Military Careers* guide.

public librarian An individual who works in a public library and serves people of all ages.

public-oriented careers *See* **public employment.**

public relations Efforts to project a positive image and to gain the good will of special groups or the general public.

public relations manager An individual who supervises a staff of public relations specialists and directs publicity programs. *See also* the OOH.

public relations specialist An individual who helps businesses, governments, universities, and hospitals build and maintain positive relationships with the public. *See also* the OOH, **public relations manager,** and **information officer.**

public sector That part of the economic structure which is controlled by some governmental unit.

public works Construction or maintenance projects for a governmental unit, such as a county, town, village, state, or the Federal Government.

public works inspector An individual who ensures that various kinds of government construction projects conform to contract specifications.

pulp piler An individual who works in the logging industry and stacks pulpwood logs at landings near logging roads.

punch in To use a time clock to record the time an employee officially begins work.

punch out To use a time clock to record the time an employee finishes work.

purchase-and-sales clerk An individual who works at a brokerage office and matches orders to buy securities with orders to sell securities.

purchasing agent and manager An individual who purchases supplies, equipment, and services needed by businesses and organizations. *See also* the OOH.

purchasing/contracting manager (military) An Army, Navy, Air Force, Marine Corps, or Coast Guard officer who reviews requests for supplies and services to make sure they are complete and accurate; prepares bid invitations or requests for proposals for contracts with civilian firms, which specify the type, amount, price, and delivery date for supplies or services; and reviews bids or proposals and awards contracts. *See also* the *Military Careers* guide.

put in your papers *Informal:* begin the process of applying for retirement.

♦Qq♦

qualification requirements The education, experience, and other prerequisites for employment or placement in a position.

qualifications The abilities, skills, talents, or accomplishments that make a person fit for a job.

Qualifications Review Board A U.S. Office of Personnel Management panel that determines whether a candidate for career appointment in the Senior Executive Service meets the managerial and executive criteria established by law.

qualifications, service academies To be eligible for consideration for admission to one of the service academies, an applicant must be **1)** at least 17 years of age, **2)** a citizen of the United States, **3)** of good moral character, **4)** academically qualified, and **5)** physically qualified. *See also* **service academies.**

qualified handicapped person A handicapped person who can perform the essential functions of a Federal position without endangering the health and safety of the handicapped person or others, and meets **1)** the experience requirements of the position, or **2)** the criteria for appointment under one of the special appointing authorities for handicapped persons.

qualifying event, COBRA The action that may make an individual and the person's spouse and dependents eligible to continue health insurance coverage under the Comprehensive Omnibus Budget Reconciliation Act (COBRA). Qualifying events include the **1)** termination of employment, **2)** death of the employee, **3)** employee's divorce or legal separation, and **4)** maximum eligibility age for a dependent child. *See also* **Comprehensive Omnibus Budget Reconciliation Act.**

quality assurance In the United States Postal Service, the function within the procurement process that determines contractual compliance of goods and services, through inspections, tests, surveys, and audits of contractors' production and quality control systems.

quality assurance inspector *See* **quality control inspector.**

quality circle A group of factory workers who meet to discuss work-related procedures or problems and then make suggestions or recommendations to management.

quality control A system to detect and reduce errors or problems that detract from the consistent and uniform production of an item or the rendering of a service.

quality control inspector An individual who inspects products manufactured or processed by private companies for Government use to ensure compliance with contract specifications.

quality control supervisor An individual who ensures that standards which have been set for the production of an item are being met. Quality control may involve random inspection or testing of the product, or working with employees to eliminate or reduce errors.

quality graduate A college or university graduate who was a superior student and can be hired at a higher grade for a Federal job than the one to which the individual would otherwise be entitled.

quality (step) increase **1)** In the Federal civil service system, an additional within-grade increase granted to General Schedule employees for high-quality performance above that ordinarily found in the type of position concerned. **2)** In the United States Postal Service, a step increase within a salary grade granted before expiration of required waiting periods in recognition of extra competence and outstanding performance.

quartermaster and boat operator (military) In the Army, Navy, Air Force, or Coast Guard, an individual who directs the course and speed of boats; operates amphibious craft during troop landings, and pilots tugboats when towing and docking barges and large ships. *See also* the *Military Careers* guide.

quarters (military) A housing allowance given to military personnel who do not live on a military base.

quasi-judicial A term for the condition of not being official but resembling or being close to the administration of justice, courts, or judges.

quickie strike A spontaneous or unannounced strike that lasts only a short time.

quitting Leaving a job voluntarily.

rabbi An individual who is the spiritual leader of a Jewish congregation and a teacher and interpreter of Jewish law and tradition. *See also* the OOH; **clergy; minister, Protestant;** and **Roman Catholic priest.**

racial discrimination Bias or prejudice against individuals because of their race. Racial discrimination is illegal and is dealt with by the Equal Employment Opportunity Commission. *See* **Equal Employment Opportunity Commission.**

radar and sonar equipment repairer (military) In the Army, Navy, Air Force, Marine Corps, or Coast Guard, an individual who uses electronic and electrical test equipment to test radar systems; monitors the operation of air traffic control, missile tracking, air defense, and other radar systems to make sure that there are no problems; and repairs sonar and radar components. *See also* the *Military Careers* guide.

radar and sonar operator (military) In the Army, Navy, Air Force, Marine Corps, or Coast Guard, an individual who detects and tracks the position, direction, and speed of aircraft, ships, submarines, and missiles; plots and records data on status charts and plotting boards; and sets up and operates radar equipment to direct artillery fire. *See also* the *Military Careers* guide.

radiation therapy technologist An individual who prepares cancer patients for treatment and administers prescribed doses of ionizing radiation to specific body parts.

radio and television announcer (military) In the Army, Navy, Air Force, Marine Corps, or Coast Guard, an individual who investigates and writes news stories, chooses topics of special interest for broadcast, and narrates special-event broadcasts. *See also* the *Military Careers* guide.

radio and television announcer and newscaster An individual who broadcasts news stories on radio or television. *See also* the OOH, **news anchor,** and **sportscaster.**

radio and television service technician An individual who maintains and repairs electronic home entertainment equipment, such as radios, televisions, video recorders, and compact disc players.

radio equipment repairer (military) In the Army, Navy, Air Force, Marine Corps, or Coast Guard, an individual who maintains, tests, and repairs radio equipment in broadcasting and relay stations, tanks, ships, and aircraft; maintains, repairs, and replaces circuitry, frequency controls, and other radio parts; and adjusts, tunes, and gauges microwave, satellite, aircraft, and other radio equipment. *See also* the *Military Careers* guide.

radio intelligence operator (military) In the Army, Navy, Air Force, or Marine Corps, an individual who records radio signals coming from foreign ships, planes, and land forces; studies radio signals to understand the tactics used by foreign military forces; and uses electronic direction-finding equipment to locate the source of foreign radio signals. *See also* the *Military Careers* guide.

radio operator (military) In the Army, Navy, Air Force, Marine Corps, or Coast Guard, an individual who transmits, receives, and logs radio messages according to military procedures; encodes and decodes classified messages; and sets up and tunes field radio equipment. *See also* the *Military Careers* guide.

radio repairer and mechanic An individual who installs and repairs stationary and mobile radio transmitting and receiving equipment.

radiographer *See* **radiologic technologist.**

radiologic technician (military) In the Army,

Navy, Air Force, or Coast Guard, an individual who reads requests or instructions from doctors to determine each patient's X-ray needs, positions patients under radiologic equipment, and processes X-ray pictures. *See also* the *Military Careers* guide.

radiologic technologist An individual who prepares patients for radiologic examinations and takes X-ray pictures of all parts of the human body for use in diagnosing medical problems. *See also* the OOH, **radiation therapy technologist,** and **sonographer.**

radiopharmacist An individual who applies the principles and practices of pharmacy and radiochemistry to produce radioactive drugs for patient diagnosis and therapy.

rail transportation occupations *See* **locomotive engineer, railroad conductor, railroad brake operator,** and **rail yard engineer.**

rail transportation worker *See* **rail transportation occupations.**

rail yard engineer An individual who moves locomotive cars within rail yards to assemble or disassemble trains.

railroad brake operator An individual who works under the direction of conductors and does the physical work necessary for adding or removing cars at railroad stations and railroad yards.

railroad conductor An individual who is in charge of a railroad locomotive used either for passengers or freight.

railroad inspector An individual who verifies the compliance of railroad systems and equipment with Federal safety regulations and investigates accidents involving railroads.

Railroad Retirement Board A Federal Government board that administers retirement-survivor and unemployment-sickness benefit programs for U.S. railroad workers and their families.

range conservationist *See* **range manager.**

range ecologist *See* **range manager.**

range manager An individual who manages, improves, and protects rangelands to maximize their use without damaging the environment. *See also* the OOH.

range scientist *See* **range manager.**

ranger An individual who works at a national park and performs a variety of services, such as giving out information and answering questions for visitors, giving lectures, monitoring camp sites, and enforcing regulations.

"rare bird" position In the Federal civil service system, a position for which the Office of Personnel Management has determined that----because of the pay or duties of the position, or limited number of qualified persons----filling the position through open-competitive examination is not in the interest of good civil service administration.

rate The wages paid for a particular time period, such as by the hour or day.

rate of basic pay In the Federal civil service system, the rate of pay fixed by law or administrative action for the position held by an employee before any deductions (such as taxes) and exclusive of additional pay of any kind (such as overtime pay).

readable *See* **machine readable.**

real estate agent An individual who sells real estate. Tasks may include soliciting listings, showing properties to prospective buyers, and acting as an intermediary between buyer and seller. *See also* the OOH, **real estate appraiser,** and **real estate broker.**

real estate appraiser An individual who inspects properties and estimates their value. *See also* the OOH, **real estate agent,** and **real estate broker.**

real estate broker An individual who sells real estate either directly or through a commission-sharing arrangement with employees who are real estate agents. Brokers provide office space, telephone service, and advertising for real estate agents. *See also* the OOH, **real estate agent,** and **real estate appraiser.**

real estate clerk An individual who performs duties concerned with real estate, such as typing copies of listings, holding collateral in escrow, and checking notices on taxes.

real estate manager An individual who oversees rental properties for the owner. Duties may include collecting rents, preparing leases, arranging repairs, and showing the property to prospective tenants. *See also* the OOH.

realignment In the Federal civil service system, the movement of an employee and the person's position when **1)** a transfer of function or an organization change occurs, **2)** the employee stays in the same agency, and **3)** there is no change in the employee's position, grade, or pay.

Realtor A real estate agent or real estate broker who is a member of the National Association of Realtors and possibly also a state association of Realtors. *See* **real estate agent** and **real estate broker.**

reasoning ability The ability to think about a problem or situation; gather facts if necessary; and then make a logical, rational decision or judgment.

reassignment In the Federal civil service system, the change of an employee from one position to another without promotion or change to lower grade. Reassignment includes **1)** movement to a position in a new occupational series, or to another position in the same series; **2)** assignment to a position that has been redescribed because of the introduction of a new or revised classification or job grading standard; **3)** assignment to a position that has been redescribed as a result of position review; and **4)** change where a difference in salary is the result of different local prevailing wage rates (for example, a change from WG-5 in one location to WG-5 in another location where the per-hour salary rate is higher or lower).

recall To summon employees back to work, usually from a layoff or furlough. *See also* **lay off** and **furlough.**

recareering Starting a second career.

receive-and-deliver clerk An individual who works in a brokerage office and physically receives and delivers stock certificates. Securities are taken from the vault of the brokerage firm and delivered to customers, banks, and other brokerage firms.

receiving clerk An individual who determines that the employer's orders have been correctly filled, by verifying incoming shipments against the original order and the accompanying bill of lading or invoice, and then records the shipment and the condition of its contents.

receptionist An individual who greets customers or visitors, determines their needs, and refers callers to the person or department that can help them. *See also* the OOH.

recipient Someone or something that receives. *Example:* a worker who is the recipient of the employee-of-the-month award because of a fine record.

recognition An employer's acceptance of a labor organization as authorized to negotiate, usually for all members of a bargaining unit.

record check *See* **Standard Form 75.**

record clerk An individual who maintains and updates various kinds of records, such as personnel records, sales figures, and blood donor lists. *See also* the OOH.

recording engineer An individual who operates and maintains sound or video recording equipment at a radio or television station. *See also* **transmitter engineer/operator, maintenance technician, field engineer, chief engineer, transmission engineer,** and **broadcast field supervisor.**

recreation attendant An individual who works at a recreation facility and whose duties may include allocating equipment, collecting fees, and operating rides or concessions.

recreation worker An individual who plans, organizes, and directs activities that help people enjoy and benefit from leisure time. *See also* the OOH.

recreational therapist An individual who uses various kinds of activities to treat mentally, physically, or emotionally disabled individuals and attempts to minimize symptoms and improve the well-being of patients. *See also* the OOH.

recruit An individual who has been accepted by the military and has taken the oath of enlistment.

recruit training (military) The first type of training for military personnel that includes being assigned to training groups and instructors; receiving uniforms and equipment; moving into quarters; receiving instruction in health, first aid, and military skills; and becoming oriented to military life. Recruit training is known also as *basic training*. The two components of military training that follow recruit training are job training and continuing education.

recruiter, military *See* **recruiting specialist.**

recruiter, personnel An individual who searches for promising job applicants. A recruiter's duties may include interviewing applicants, administering tests, checking references, and outlining benefits. *See also* **headhunter.**

recruiting manager (military) A Navy, Air Force, Marine Corps, or Coast Guard officer who plans programs to inform young people about military careers; directs staff in local recruiting offices who carry out programs to inform the public about military careers; and speaks at local civic groups and schools and with parents and young people about military careers. *See also* the *Military Careers* guide.

recruiting specialist (military) In the Army, Navy, Air Force, Marine Corps, or Coast Guard, an individual who interviews civilians interested in military careers, describes military careers to groups of high school students, and explains the purpose of the ASVAB (Armed Services Vocational Aptitude Battery) and test results to students and counselors. *See also* the *Military Careers* guide and **Armed Services Vocational Aptitude Battery.**

recruitment The process of attracting a supply of qualified eligibles for employment consideration.

recruitment bonus In the Federal civil service system, a one-time payment of up to 25 percent of basic pay to an employee who is newly appointed to a hard-to-fill position.

redress To repair, correct, compensate, or reform. *Example:* a supervisor who tries to redress an error after he finds out that he was wrong.

reduced benefits, Social Security *See* **Social Security reduced benefits.**

reduction in force (RIF) **1)** A personnel action that reduces the number of employees and may be required because of a lack of work or funds. **2)** In the Federal civil service system, the separation of an employee from the person's competitive level, required by the agency because of a lack of work or funds, the abolition of a position or agency, or cuts in personnel authorizations.

reduction in grade In the Federal civil service system, a personnel action, possibly disciplinary, that lowers the grade of an employee. *See also* **grade, grade retention action,** and **grade restoration action.**

reduction in pay In the Federal civil service system, a personnel action that lowers the wages of an employee.

reemployed annuitant In the Federal civil service system, a person retired under the Civil Service or Federal Employees' Retirement System whose annuity continues after the individual is reemployed by the Federal Government.

reemployment priority list In the Federal civil service system, a list of career and career-conditional employees an agency has separated because of a **1)** reduction in force, or **2)** compensable injury or disability where recovery takes more than one year from the time the employee began receiving compensation. When a qualified person is available on this list, the agency may not fill a competitive position by the transfer or new appointment of any person except a ten-point preference eligible.

reemployment rights In the Federal civil service system, the rights of an employee to return to the individual's long-term career employment after assignment for a relatively short period of time to other civilian employment where the person can make maximum contribution to the national interest. This other employment may be with the Foreign Service, public international organizations, or other agencies in the executive branch or oversees. *See also* **restoration rights.**

reentrant An individual who is reentering the job market after an absence. *Example:* women as reentrants after their children start school or finish college.

references Persons listed on a resume or job application who know the job applicant and can be expected to verify, usually in writing, to a prospective employer the applicant's good qualities, abilities, and experience. Normally, three references are required and should not be relatives. An applicant should be prepared to furnish to the prospective employer the name, address, and telephone number of the people listed as references. Permission to use the name of an individual as a reference should be secured before listing it on an application.

refractory repairer A bricklayer who specializes in the installation of firebrick and refractory tile in high-temperature boilers, furnaces, cupolas, ladles, and soaking pits in industrial establishments.

refrigeration mechanic *See* **heating, air-conditioning, and refrigeration mechanic.**

refuse collector An individual who collects and removes trash and garbage from private residences or commercial establishments.

regional geographer An individual who studies the physical, climatic, economic, political, and cultural characteristics of a particular region or area.

regional offices of the Merit Systems Protection Board Located in eleven major cities, offices that are authorized to receive appeals concerning the actions of Federal agencies. *See also* **Merit Systems Protection Board.**

regional planner An individual who develops programs to provide for the growth and revitalization of a particular region. *See also* the OOH, **urban planner,** and **city planner.**

register **1)** In the Federal civil service system, a list of qualified applicants compiled in the order of their relative standing for referral to Federal jobs after competitive civil service examination. **2)** In the United States Postal Service, a list of applicants for positions to be filled in an installation.

register of eligibles *See* **register.**

registered apprentice (military) A designation that Marines may apply for if they are assigned to a military occupational specialty (MOS) that has comparable requirements needed for certification in civilian occupations.

registered dietician A dietician who has successfully completed the academic and clinical requirements of the American Dietetic Association.

registered nurse (R.N.) An individual who cares for sick persons and helps people stay well. Duties are numerous and varied and deal with the physical, mental, and emotional needs of the patient. *See also* the OOH, **hospital nurse, nursing home nurse, public health nurse, private duty nurse, office nurse, industrial nurse,** and **school nurse.**

registered nurse (military) An Army, Navy, or Air Force officer who helps physicians treat patients; gives injections of pain killers, antibiotics, and other medicines as prescribed by physicians; and assists physicians during surgery. *See also* the *Military Careers* guide.

registered occupational therapist An occupational therapist who has passed a national certification examination given by the American Occupational Therapy Certification Board.

registered representative, securities *See* **securities sales representative.**

registrar An individual who is in charge of the educational records of students in a college or university. The duties of a registrar can include the preparation of student transcripts, evaluation of academic records, and the analysis of registration statistics.

registration The act of registering an individual who has met specific requirements for certain occupations. *Examples:* registered nurse and registered dietician.

regular military compensation The total value of basic pay, allowances, and tax savings, which represents the amount of pay a civilian worker would need to earn to receive the same take home "pay" as a service member.

regulatory inspector An individual who ensures compliance with the laws and regulations that protect the public welfare. *See also* specific types of inspectors.

rehabilitation counselor An individual who helps people deal with the personal and vocational impact of their disabilities.

reimbursement account *See* **flexible spending account.**

reinforcing ironworker An individual who sets the bars in the forms that hold concrete, by following blueprints which show the location, size, and number of reinforcing bars. *See also* the OOH and **structural and reinforcing ironworker.**

reinstatement In the Federal civil service system, the noncompetitive reemployment---in the competitive service as a career or career-conditional employee---of a person formerly employed in the competitive service who had a competitive status or was serving probation when the employee was separated.

reinstatement rights The right of an employee under the Federal civil service system to reclaim a job under certain conditions.

religious discrimination Bias or prejudice based on religion. Job discrimination based on religion is illegal. *See* **Equal Employment Opportunity Commission.**

religious education and activities director An individual who directs and coordinates activities of a religious group to meet the spiritual needs of students, and plans, organizes, and directs religious school programs designed to promote religious education.

religious program specialist (military) In the Army, Navy, or Air Force, an individual who assists chaplains in planning and preparing religious programs and activities, assists chaplains in conducting religious services, and organizes charitable and public service volunteer programs. *See also* the *Military Careers* guide.

relocation The act of settling in another city, state, or country.

relocation bonus In the Federal civil service system, a one-time payment of up to 25 percent of basic pay to a current employee who relocates to take a hard-to-fill position.

remote work Work, usually of a telecommunication or computer type, that does not require the individual to be in a specific place, such as an office, during regular office hours. *See also* **computer commuter** and **satellite office.**

removable partial denture technician An individual who works in a dental laboratory and makes and repairs contoured metal frames and retainers for teeth used in removable partial dentures.

removal In the Federal civil service system, a disciplinary separation action, other than for inefficiency or unacceptable performance, initiated by the agency, Office of Personnel Management, or Merit Systems Protection Board, where the employee is at fault.

remuneration Anything of value, including food and lodging, given in exchange for labor or services by an employee.

rent-a-cop *Informal:* a private security guard. *See* **guard.**

rental clerk An individual who answers questions, takes orders, receives payments, and accepts returns in establishments offering services such as dry cleaning, video rentals, and car rentals. *See also* the OOH.

repairman The preferred nonsexist term is *repairer* or *repair technician*. *See* specific types of repair services.

replacement workers The individuals who fill job openings that occur as people leave occupations to take a better job, return to school, retire, or change careers.

repo man *Informal:* a repossessor. *See* **repossessor.**

report **1)** A written statement that describes an event, presents research results, or indicates the actions of a meeting. **2)** The act of meeting a supervisor or manager, especially at the beginning of a new job or assignment. *Example:* reporting to the manager on the first day of work.

reporter/correspondent An individual who gathers information and prepares stories that inform readers, radio listeners, or TV viewers about local, state, national, and international events, or presents points of view on current issues. *See also* the OOH, **columnist,** and **editor.**

reporter/newswriter (military) In the Army, Navy, Air Force, Marine Corps, or Coast Guard, an individual who gathers information for military news programs and publications, writes radio and TV scripts, and arranges and conducts interviews. *See also* the *Military Careers* guide.

repossessor An individual who recovers or repossesses vehicles whose owners have failed to pay their loans.

representation The actions and rights of a labor organization to consult and negotiate with management on behalf of the bargaining unit and to represent employees in the unit.

representation election An election conducted to determine whether the employees in a unit desire a labor organization to act as their exclusive representative.

representative, political An elected official who makes laws and amends existing laws to meet the needs of constituents for an effective and efficient government.

reprimand A rebuke of an employee that can be either official and written or informal and oral.

research The act of investigating a subject carefully, using scientific methods to prove or disprove an idea, discover a new principle, or coordinate theories.

research assistantship An individual, usually a graduate student, who is employed to help with research projects being conducted at a college or university.

research dietician A dietician who uses established research methods and analytical techniques to conduct studies in areas that range from basic science to practical applications.

reservation agent An individual who usually works in a large central office answering customer telephone inquires and booking reservations often by computer. *See also* the OOH, **travel clerk,** and **travel agent.**

reservationist *See* **reservation agent.**

Reserve Officers' Training Corps (ROTC) A program of the Army, Navy, Air Force, and Marine Corps in which undergraduate students in public or private colleges or universities may receive training to become military officers. ROTC members sometimes receive a monthly allowance and scholarships for tuition, books, fees, and uniforms.

reservist A member of the Reserve forces of the Army, Navy, Air Force, Marine Corps, or Coast Guard. Reservists are highly trained by the services, usually while on active duty; drill regularly; and can be called to serve on active duty in times of national emergency.

residence counselor An individual who lives in residential care facilities, such as halfway houses for criminal offenders or group homes for children, the aged, and the disabled, and tries to advise and assist the residents with personal and social problems.

residency requirement A stipulation that an employee must live within a certain geographic area. *Example:* a city requiring that police officers and firefighters live within the city limits.

resident manager An individual who lives in a hotel, is on call 24 hours a day to resolve any problems or emergencies, and oversees the day-to-day operations of the hotel.

resignation A separation, prior to retirement, at an employee's request. A resignation is a voluntary expression of the employee's desire to leave the company or organization.

resolution The act of solving a problem.

resorts Large hotels that offer many types of sports facilities and entertainment areas for the enjoyment, rest, and relaxation of guests. *See also* spa.

respiratory care practitioner *See* **respiratory therapist.**

respiratory therapist An individual who specializes in the evaluation, treatment, and care of patients with breathing disorders. *See also* the OOH.

respiratory therapist (military) In the Army, Navy, or Air Force, an individual who assists in reviving patients who are no longer breathing or whose hearts have stopped, operates and monitors respiratory therapy equipment during treatment, and observes and records patient response to respiratory therapy. *See also* the *Military Careers* guide.

restaurant and food service manager An individual in charge of the operation of a food establishment and whose duties may include selecting and pricing menu items, using food and other supplies efficiently, achieving consistent quality in food preparation and service, recruiting and training personnel, and supervising their work. *See also* the OOH.

restaurant chef/cook *See* **chef, cook, kosher cook, and sous chef.**

restoration rights In the Federal civil service

system, the rights of an employee who enters military service or sustains a compensable job-related injury or disability to be restored to the same or greater employment status held before the individual's absence.

restructuring Changing the organization of a business or organization, usually to improve efficiency or reduce the number of employees.

resume A summary of an individual's qualifications and employment history, usually provided by a job applicant to a prospective employer. A resume should include **1)** the individual's name, address, and telephone number; **2)** the type of work or specific job being sought; **3)** education, including names and addresses of schools, dates of attendance, curricula, and highest grade completed or degree(s) awarded; **4)** experience, either paid or volunteer, including job titles, names and addresses of employers, job duties, and dates of employment; and **5)** special skills or knowledge and honors. The resume might conclude with the statement "References are available on request."

resume services Businesses that prepare resumes for job applicants for a fee. *See also* **resume.**

retail buyer *See* **wholesale and retail buyer.**

retail sales worker An individual who sells merchandise in various types of retail establishments. Duties may include demonstrating the use of a product; answering questions; making out sales checks; receiving cash, checks, or charge payments; giving change and receipts; and accepting returns. *See also* the OOH.

retained rate In the Federal civil service system, a rate of pay above the maximum rate of the employee's grade, which an employee is allowed to keep in special situations instead of reducing the individual's rate of basic pay.

retention The act of keeping or retaining an employee. *See also* **retention register, retention allowance,** and **retention preference.**

retention allowance In the Federal civil service system, the annual total dollar amount (up to 25 percent of basic pay) paid to an essential employee with unusually high qualifications or special skills in those cases where the agency determines that the employee would be likely to leave Federal employment if no allowance were paid.

retention preference In the Federal civil service system, the relative right of an employee to be retained in a position when similar positions are being abolished and employees in them are being separated or furloughed.

retention register In the Federal civil service system, a record of all employees occupying positions in a competitive level arranged by tenure groups and subgroups, and by service dates within the subgroup. The retention register is used in a reduction in force to determine which employees are retained and which are separated or reassigned.

retiree job bank *See* **job bank.**

retirement **1)** The practice of leaving a job when the age and length of service requirements have been met to qualify for any pension and Social Security benefits. **2)** In the Federal civil service system, the separation from the service when an employee is eligible to obtain annuity benefits. *See also* **phased retirement; early retirement; window; deferred retirement; disability retirement; retirement, discontinued service;** and **optional retirement.**

retirement age, Social Security *See* **Social Security retirement age.**

retirement benefits (military) After 20 years of active duty service, officers may retire and receive a monthly payment equal to 40 percent of their average basic pay for their last five years of active duty, medical care, and commissary/exchange privileges. Higher pay is paid to officers with more than 20 years of active service.

retirement deferred In the Federal civil service system, the retirement of a person age 62 or older with at least 5 years of civilian service who was formerly employed under the Civil Service Retirement System and then left Federal service or transferred to a position not under the retirement system.

retirement, discontinued service In the Federal civil service system, a retirement based on involuntary separation against the will or without the consent of the employee, other than on charges of misconduct or delinquency. An employee who does not meet the age and service requirements for optional retirement at the time of separation may retire on discontinued service if the individual is age 50 with 20 years of creditable service, or at any age with 25 years of creditable service including 5 years of civilian service.

retirement-in lieu of involuntary action (ILIA) In the Federal civil service system, retirement initiated by the employee under the optional retirement provisions of the Civil Service Retirement System in lieu of involuntary separation.

retirement incentive plans Benefits offered to employees to encourage them to retire. Incentives may be payments of money, increased pension credits, and continued health benefits.

retirement, optional In the Federal civil service system, the separation of an employee after the individual has become eligible for retirement on the basis of a combination of age and service. The minimum combinations of age and service making an employee eligible for optional retirement are age 62 with 20 years of creditable service, and age 55 with 30 years of creditable service. Employees covered by the Federal Employees' Retirement System can also retire with a reduced annuity at the Federal Employees' Retirement System minimum retirement age (55 to 57 depending on birth date) with 10 years of creditable service.

retroactive pay Wages for work done in the past but not paid at that time, usually because of a contract dispute or negotiations involving wages.

return to duty In the Federal civil service system, the placement of an employee back in pay and duty status after absence for furlough, suspension, or leave without pay.

revenue officer An individual who investigates delinquent tax returns and liabilities, discusses the resolution of tax problems with taxpayers, and recommends penalties and prosecution when necessary.

reverification The process of determining that an employee is still eligible for employment. A new U.S. Immigration and Naturalization Form I-9 must be filled out to complete the reverification. *See* **Form I-9.**

reverse discrimination Bias or prejudice against a group usually considered immune from discrimination, such as white males. *See also* **Bakke case.**

review, classification In the Federal civil service system, an official written request for reclassification of a position. Previously called a **classification appeal.**

revolving door policy The frequent changing of employees in a position.

RIF An acronym for *r*eduction *in* *f*orce. *See* **reduction in force.**

rigger An individual who sets up or repairs rigging for ships and shipyards, manufacturing plants, logging yards, and construction projects.

rigger (military) In the Navy, Air Force, Marine Corps, or Coast Guard, an individual who splices wire and rope cables to make slings and block-and-tackle devices; assembles rigging devices such as cranes and winches; and selects the correct cables, ropes, pulleys, and winches for the size and weight of loads. *See also* the *Military Careers* guide.

rigging slinger An individual who works in the logging industry and determines the sequence of logs to be yarded by the cable yarding system.

rights Things that are due individuals because of legal guarantees, moral principles, and rightful claims. *Example:* the provisions in the Bill of Rights that guarantee free speech and freedom of the press and religion.

rightsizing *Informal: See* **downsizing.**

river An individual who works in the logging industry and uses sledgehammers, mallets, wedges, and froes (cleaving tools) to split logs to form posts, pickets, shakes, and other objects.

R.N. An abbreviation of *registered nurse. See* **registered nurse.**

road conductor An individual who is in charge of train and yard crews and may be responsible for collecting tickets and fares, assisting passengers, and signaling the engineer.

roadie An individual who goes on tour with an entertainment group and performs a variety of tasks associated with the preparation and dismantling of the stage, lighting, and sound equipment.

roasting, baking, and drying machine operator/tender An individual who operates or tends roasting, baking, or drying equipment, such as hearth ovens, kiln driers, roasters, char kilns, steam ovens, and vacuum drying equipment to reduce the moisture content of food or tobacco products, to bake bread or other bakery products, or to process food preparatory to canning.

robot A machine designed to perform some of the tasks usually done by people.

robotics The industry that deals with the development and production of robots. *See also* **robot.**

rock splitter, quarry An individual who separates blocks of rough-dimension stone from a quarry mass, using a jackhammer and wedges.

role model An individual who displays good characteristics, qualities, or personality traits for others to imitate. Example: teachers who, by words and actions, are good role models for their students.

roller An individual who works in the steel industry and operates equipment that rolls steel ingots into semifinished shapes. The quality of the product and the speed at which the ingot is rolled depend on the skill of the roller.

Roman Catholic priest An individual who attends to the spiritual, pastoral, moral, and educational needs of the members of a Roman Catholic church. Duties may include delivering sermons, administering the sacraments, and presiding at functions such as funeral services. Similar duties are performed by Episcopal priests, Greek Orthodox priests, and Russian Orthodox priests for their congregations. *See also* the OOH; **clergy; minister, Protestant;** and **rabbi.**

roofer An individual who uses various types of roofing materials to repair or install roofs. *See also* the OOH.

ROTC An abbreviation of *Reserve Officers' Training Corps*. *See* **Reserve Officers' Training Corps.**

roustabout An individual who works in and around oil fields and pipeline operations and does routine physical labor and maintenance, such as digging ditches, loading or unloading trucks or boats, and mixing concrete. *See also* the OOH.

route driver An individual who delivers a firm's products, such as bread, meats, milk, and snacks, to stores. Additional duties may include trying to increase sales, arranging displays, and introducing new products to the store manager.

run The routes and distances traveled by trucks and may last from less than a day to several weeks. *See also* **turnarounds** and **sleeper run.**

rust belt *Informal:* areas of the country that have been highly industrialized for many years but whose industries have been forced to cut production severely or have ceased operation because of foreign competition or lack of automation.

sabbatical **1)** A leave granted to an employee, usually from an educational institution, to pursue research, to study, or to travel. **2)** In the Federal civil service, an absence from duty, without charge to pay or leave, that an agency may grant to a Senior Executive Service career appointee to engage in study or uncompensated work experience.

sacked *Informal:* fired.

saddlemaker A leather worker who specializes in making saddles, which are then dyed and decorated.

safety net *Informal:* any action, law, or situation that prevents unfortunate things from happening to individuals. *Example:* unemployment compensation as a safety net for the jobless worker.

salary A fixed amount of money paid to an employee as compensation for services. *See also* **wages.**

salary negotiations The process of bargaining for additional compensation.

salary range The variation between the minimum and maximum salary for a position.

salary review The policy or contractual requirement to examine the salary of an employee periodically to determine whether an increase should be given.

sales Pertaining to the selling of goods or services.

sales and stock specialist (military) In the Army, Navy, Air Force, Marine Corps, or Coast Guard, an individual who operates snack bars, laundries, and dry-cleaning facilities; orders and receives merchandise and food for retail sales; and records and accounts for money received and prepares bank deposits. *See also* the *Military Careers* guide.

sales associate A sales clerk. *See* **retail sales worker.**

sales engineer *See* **industrial sales worker.**

sales manager *See* **marketing manager.**

sales representative *See* **wholesale sales representative.**

salesman An individual who sells goods or services. The preferred nonsexist term is *salesclerk*, *sales representative*, or *salesperson*. *See also* **manufacturers' sales representative, wholesale sales representative,** and **retail sales worker.**

same period last year The accounting period or other period of comparative information for the preceding year.

sanction To give permission, approval, or support. *Example:* a union asked to sanction a new retirement policy.

sanitarian *See* **environmental health inspector.**

satellite office Located outside a metropolitan area, an office with computers and other communication equipment that employees may use without having to go to a central location in the city.

saucier A chef responsible for the preparation of soups and sauces.

scanner operator, offset printing An individual who uses computerized equipment to create film negatives or positives of photographs or art and uses the scanner to reproduce the colors and prepare printing plates.

Schedule A In the Federal civil service system, one of the categories of positions that is excepted from the competitive service and involves positions other than confidential or policy determining, and for which an examination is not practical.

Schedule B In the Federal civil service system, one of the categories of positions that is excepted from the competitive service and involves positions other than confidential or policy determining, and for which a *competitive* examination is not practical.

Schedule C In the Federal civil service system, one of the categories of positions that is excepted from the competitive service and involves positions of a confidential or policy-determining character.

schematic A diagram or drawing.

scholarship Money or other aid given to a student to enable the individual to attend an educational institution.

school career center A facility that may contain computers, books, magazines, or counselors to enable students to get part-time jobs.

school counselor An individual who uses interviews, counseling sessions, tests, or other tools to help students understand their abilities, interests, talents, and personality characteristics, and then helps students explore career options. *See also* **college career planning and placement counselor.**

school crossing guard *See* **crossing guard.**

school librarian A librarian who teaches students how to use the school library/media center; helps with assignments and projects; selects, orders, and organizes library materials; develops curricula; and teaches library/research skills. *See also* **library media specialist.**

school monitor An individual who performs a variety of duties in a school, such as supervising students in the cafeteria, halls, and playground or assisting teachers in the classroom, library, cafeteria, and halls.

school nurse A nurse who works in a school and whose duties may include handling minor injuries, scheduling athletic physicals, contacting parents, and verifying immunizations.

school principal *See* **principal, school.**

school psychologist A psychologist who works with teachers, parents, and administrators to resolve students' learning and behavior problems.

school secretary An individual who handles secretarial duties in elementary and secondary schools, prepares bulletins and reports, keeps track of money for school supplies and student activities, and maintains a calendar of school events.

school social worker An individual who helps students who are having difficulties and tries to find and arrange needed services.

school superintendent *See* **general manager/top executive.**

school teacher *See* **teacher.**

science manager An individual who oversees activities in agricultural science, chemistry, biology, geology, meteorology, or physics; manages research and development projects; and directs and coordinates testing, quality control, and production activities in industrial plants. *See also* the OOH.

science technician An individual who uses the principles of science and mathematics to solve problems in research and development, production, and oil and gas exploration. *See also* the OOH, **agricultural technician, biological technician, chemical technician, nuclear technician,** and **petroleum technician.**

scientific illustrator An individual who combines artistic skills with knowledge of the biological sciences and draws illustrations of parts of the human body, animals, and plants.

SCORE An acronym for Service Corps of Retired Executives. *See* **Service Corps of Retired Executives.**

scraper operator *See* **grader, dozer, and scraper operator.**

screen printing setter and setup operator An individual who sets up and operates screen printing machines to print designs onto articles and materials, such as glass or plastic ware or containers, cloth, and paper.

sculptor An artist who specializes in creating three-dimensional art works. *See also* the OOH.

seaman *See* **deckhand.**

seaman (military) In the Army, Navy, Air Force, or Coast Guard, an individual who operates hoists, cranes, and winches to load cargo or set gangplanks; supervises fire fighting and damage control exercises; and stands watch for security, navigation, or communications. *See also* the *Military Careers* guide.

seamstress A woman who makes clothing to the specifications of clients, and remodels, repairs, and hems garments.

seasonal employee **1)** In the Federal civil service, an employee who works on an annual recurring basis for periods of less than 12 months (2080 hours) each year. **2)** An individual who works only during certain seasons of the year. *Examples:* ski resort employees, summer resort employees, and harvest workers.

second career A new occupation usually in a different field. *See also* **career changer, career hop,** and **career switching.**

secondary school teacher An individual who teaches students in the upper grades, usually 9th grade through 12th grade. *See also* the OOH, **kindergarten teacher, elementary teacher, adult education teacher, library media specialist,** and **vocational education teacher.**

Secret Service A Federal Government agency that is responsible for protecting the President and Vice President, their families, and other important individuals; enforcing laws pertaining to the counterfeiting of currency; and investigating fraud or forgery involving Government securities.

Secret Service agent An individual who works for the Secret Service; protects the President, Vice President, their immediate families, and other important persons; and investigates counterfeiting, forgery of Government checks or bonds, and fraudulent use of credit cards.

secretary An individual who may perform a variety of tasks in an office, such as scheduling appointments, taking dictation, and typing. *See also* the OOH, **legal secretary, administrative secretary, medical secretary, technical secretary, social secretary, membership secretary,** and **school secretary.**

securities director An individual who implements regulations concerning securities, investigates applications for registration of securities sales and complaints of irregular securities transactions, and recommends necessary legal actions.

securities sales representative An individual who buys and sells various financial products, such as stocks, bonds, and annuities. *See also* the OOH.

securities trader *See* **securities sales representative.**

security clearance The possible result of investigating the background of an individual who is applying for a job that involves matters which, if revealed, could harm the security of the U.S. *Example:* an individual who has to have a security clearance when she applies for a job with the Central Intelligence Agency (CIA).

security guard An individual who protects government, commercial, and industrial property against theft, vandalism, illegal entry, and fire.

security officer (military) An Army, Navy, Air Force, Marine Corps, or Coast Guard officer who plans for the security of military bases and office buildings; directs security procedures, such as issuing passes, fingerprinting, recordkeeping, and patrolling; and works with investigators to solve possible security problems. *See also* the *Military Careers* guide.

seismologist An individual who interprets data from seismographs and other instruments to locate earthquakes and earthquake faults.

selectman An elected official who makes laws and amends existing laws to improve conditions for the people who elected the individual.

self-assessment The process of evaluating one's abilities, talents, and personality traits.

self-concept The idea or picture individuals form of themselves.

self-confidence A feeling of strong belief in one's abilities, talents, and potential for success.

self-employment The practice of earning a living by working for oneself instead of working for another individual or business. *Examples:* writer, plumber, and electrician.

self-esteem Good and positive feelings about oneself.

self-image The way an individual sees oneself as a person. *Example:* an individual having a positive self-image and feeling worthwhile, compared to an individual having a negative self-image and feeling inadequate. *See also* **image consultant.**

self-insured Protected by benefits paid from funds set aside by an employer or an organization for this purpose instead of being covered by insurance from an insurance company.

self-motivation The ability of an individual to act without being forced to do so by some outside force.

self-promotion techniques Methods that can be used by an individual to enhance the person's image, improve career chances, and get a job.

semiconductor processor *See* **electronic semiconductor processor.**

senator An elected official who makes or amends laws to improve conditions for the people who elected the individual.

Senior Executive Service (SES) In the Federal civil service system, a separate personnel system for persons who set policy and administer programs at the top levels of the Federal Government. These persons are classified above GS-15 of the General Schedule or in level IV or V of the Executive Schedule or an equivalent position, which is not required to be filled by an appointment by the President by and with the advice and consent of the Senate, and in which an employee directs, monitors, and manages the work of an organizational unit or exercises other executive functions.

senior level (SL) positions Positions established under the Federal Employees Pay Comparability Act of 1990 to replace positions at grades GS-16, GS-17, and GS-18 of the General Schedule. Senior level positions are classified above GS-15 of the General Schedule and are ungraded.

senior management Individuals in management positions who have the greatest responsibility and highest status and salaries.

sense of humor The ability to recognize and participate in amusing situations; enjoy books, skits, and plays of a comical nature; and understand jokes and puns. A sense of humor is regarded by many employers as a valuable asset in dealing with other employees, business problems, and stress.

separating and still machine operator/tender An individual who operates and tends machines such as filter presses, shaker screens, centrifuges, condensor tubes, precipitator tanks, and fermenting tanks to extract, sort, or separate liquids, gases, or solid materials from other materials in order to recover a refined product or material.

separation In the Federal civil service system, a personnel action that takes an employee off the agency's rolls. Separations include retirements, resignations, terminations, removals, discharges, and deaths.

series In the Federal civil service system, classes of positions similar in specialized line of work but differing in difficulty or responsibility of work or qualifications requirements, and therefore differing in grade and pay range.

service The act of supplying a needed activity.

service academies (military) Army: United States Military Academy at West Point, New York; Navy and Marine Corps: United States Naval Academy at Annapolis, Maryland; Air Force: United States Air Force Academy at Colorado Springs, Colorado; and Coast Guard: United States Coast Guard Academy at New London, Connecticut.

service classifier (military) An information specialist in the military who helps applicants select a military occupational field by matching aptitudes and interests with job training openings and by entering ASVAB scores into a computerized reservation system. *See also* **Armed Services Vocational Aptitude Battery** and **recruiting specialist.**

service computation date-leave In the Federal civil service system, the date that is used to determine leave accrual rate, length of service for retirement, or retention standing for reduction in force. For an employee with no prior civilian or military service, the service computation date is the effective date of the employee's first Federal civilian appointment. For an employee with prior service, the service computation date is constructed by totaling the days, months, and years of the employee's creditable civilian and military service and subtracting that total from the effective date of the employee's most recent appointment. *Example:* an employee is appointed on 10/12/88 and has 4 years, 3 months, and 3 days of prior service that is creditable. The service computation date would be 88-10-12 (year-month-day of appointment) minus 4 years, 3 months, 3 days (prior service), or July 9, 1984, shown as follows:

Year-month-day of appointment:	88-10-12
Creditable prior service:	--04-03-03
Service computation date:	84-07-09

service-connected disability A disability incurred while the individual was a member of the Armed Forces.

service control file In the Federal civil service system, a central file of service record cards that may be maintained by a personnel office for all employees to whom it provides service. The cards or records are usually filed by organization and, for each organization, by job series and grade of employees.

Service Corps of Retired Executives (SCORE) An organization that uses the business experience of its members to help new and small businesses by giving advice and other assistance.

service day A calendar day, usually 12:01 a.m. to midnight.

Service Members Opportunity Colleges (SOC) A group of colleges and universities that help enlisted personnel satisfy the requirements for college degrees. Participating educational institutions might assist enlisted personnel by accepting credits earned at other schools or awarding credit for some military training courses.

service obligation (military) The length of time an enlisted member agrees to serve in one of the branches of the Armed Forces. The service obligation is part of the enlistment agreement.

Service Occupations One of the nine primary categories for grouping occupations in the *Dictionary of Occupational Titles. Examples:* **bartender, manicurist,** and **embalmer.**

Service Occupations (military) One of the broad categories used by the Armed Forces to group occupations for enlisted and officer personnel.

service-producing industries Industries that offer services rather than produced goods. *Examples:* health care, business equipment servicing, sales, communications, insurance, finance, education, and transportation.

Service Record Card (Standard Form 7 or SF 7 card) In the Federal civil service system, a card or a comparable agency record that may be used to summarize an employee's work history with the agency and may be retained for reference purposes when the employee leaves the agency.

service station attendant An individual who fills fuel tanks, washes windshields, changes oil, repairs tires, and sells motor vehicle accessories.

service technician *See* **electronic home entertainment equipment repairer** and **home appliance and power tool repairer.**

services sales representative An individual who sells a wide variety of services in a number of different businesses. *See also* the OOH.

SES An abbreviation of *Senior Executive Service. See* **Senior Executive Service.**

set designer An individual who designs movie, television, and theater sets after studying scripts, conferring with directors, and conducting research to determine appropriate architectural styles.

setter and setup operator, metalworking and plastics-working machine An individual who prepares metalworking and plastics-working machines prior to production or a new job and makes adjustments to them during production.

setter and setup operator, soldering and brazing machine An individual who sets up and operates soldering or brazing machines to bronze, solder, heat-treat, or spot-weld fabricated metal products or components as specified by work orders, blueprints, and layout specifications.

setter and setup operator, textile machine *See* **textile machine setter/setup operator.**

7:01 rule In the United States Postal Service, the rule by which a city letter carrier who actually works more than seven hours but less than eight hours of a regular scheduled day and who is officially excused from the completion of the eight-hour tour is credited with eight hours of work time for pay purposes.

severance The separation, severing, or breaking off of something.

severance arrangements Items provided to a worker when leaving a job. *Examples:* extra salary and job placement services.

severance pay **1)** Money paid to an employee who is being terminated, usually because of a reduction in force, and who is not eligible for retirement. **2)** In the Federal civil service system, the sum of money, based on last salary, length of service, and age, that an employee may be paid when separated involuntarily from an agency, such as during a reduction in force. An employee is ineligible for severance pay if the separation results from misconduct or if the individual is eligible to retire on an immediate annuity.

sewage treatment plant operator *See* **water and wastewater treatment plant operator.**

sewer and sewing machine operator, apparel An individual who operates a sewing machine in a garment factory. *See also* **garment sewing machine operator** and **nongarment sewing machine operator.**

sexual discrimination The practice of excluding individuals from jobs or promotions because of their sex. *See also* **glass ceiling.**

sexual harassment The practice of verbal abuse, pressure for sexual activity, sexual remarks, or display of sexually explicit material directed at a coworker of the opposite sex.

SF-171 *See* **Standard Form 171.**

shadowing An educational technique in which a student accompanies a worker in an occupation that interests the student. This experience in the actual workplace can be helpful as the student explores career choices.

shake-up A drastic change in a business or organization that usually results in personnel changes, such as dismissals or reassignments.

shared decision making The practice of having employees participate with management in making judgments affecting the business or organization. *See also* **empower.**

sheet metal worker An individual who makes, installs, and maintains air-conditioning, heating, ventilating, and pollution-control-duct systems, plus various other building parts and products made from metal sheets. *See also* the OOH.

sheet metal worker (military) In the Navy, Air Force, Marine Corps, or Coast Guard, an individual who reads blueprints and lays out work on sheet metal; uses shears or tin snips to cut metal; and solders, welds, rivets, or screws sheet metal parts together. *See also* the *Military Careers* guide.

Sheetrocker *See* **drywall installer.**

sheriff A law enforcement official, usually of a county, who may also be responsible for the collection of taxes and other governmental services.

shift A period of time, usually eight hours, worked by employees of a factory or a governmental service that is required 24 hours per day. *Examples:* police service and fire service.

shift differential Extra wages paid to an individual because of the shift worked. *See also* **night differential.**

ship captain *See* **captain.**

ship electrician (military) In the Navy or Coast Guard, an individual who installs wiring for lights and equipment, uses test meters to troubleshoot electrical wiring and equipment, and inspects and maintains devices that distribute electricity throughout ships. *See also* the *Military Careers* guide.

ship engineer *See* **marine engineer.**

ship engineer (military) An Army, Navy, or Coast Guard officer who directs engine room operations in nuclear or diesel-powered vessels; directs crews that inspect and maintain the electrical generators which supply power for lights, weapons, and equipment; and directs crews that inspect and maintain ship transmission and propulsion systems. *See also* the *Military Careers* guide.

ship/submarine officer An Army, Navy, or Coast Guard officer who commands vessels of all sizes at sea or in coastal waters; plans and manages the operating departments under the captain's direction; and directs search and rescue missions. *See also* the *Military Careers* guide.

shipfitter An individual who lays out and fabricates metal structural parts, such as plates, bulkheads, and frames; braces them in position within a hull or a ship for riveting or welding; and prepares molds and templates for fabrication of nonstandard parts.

shipfitter (military) In the Army, Navy, or Coast Guard, an individual who inspects hulls, hatches, and decks for leaks; welds or rivets metal plates onto hulls and decks to repair damage; and repairs the walls that separate ship compartments. *See also* the *Military Careers* guide.

shipping and receiving clerk An individual who keeps records of all goods shipped and received. *See also* the OOH.

shipping and receiving specialist (military) In the Army, Navy, Air Force, Marine Corps, or Coast Guard, an individual who prepares shipping papers for goods to be shipped; chooses the kind of transport and route; and calculates shipping costs based on the shipping rates of commercial carriers. *See also* the *Military Careers* guide.

shoe and leather worker An individual who creates leather products, such as shoes, luggage, and saddles. *See also* the OOH.

shoe repairer An individual who repairs shoes and sometimes other leather articles, such as handbags. *See also* the OOH.

shoe sewing machine operator and tender An individual who operates or tends single, double, or multiple-needle stitching machines to join or decorate shoe parts, reinforce shoe parts, or attach buckles.

short order cook An individual who prepares food to order in restaurants and coffee shops that provide fast service. *See also* the OOH.

shorthand reporter A stenographer with special training who records all statements made in an official proceeding. *See also* **court reporter.**

sick days The number of days allotted to an employee that can be used when the employee is ill and for which there will be no reduction in salary.

signal or track switch maintainer An individual who installs electric gate crossings, signals, track switches, and intercommunication systems in a railroad network.

silvering applicator An individual who sprays silver, tin, and copper solutions on glass in the manufacture of mirrors.

silversmith An individual who uses artistic and metalworking skills to make silver jewelry and items for the home.

singer An individual who uses knowledge of voice production, melody, and harmony to interpret music. Singers are classified according to their voice range----soprano, contralto, tenor, baritone, or bass----or by the type of music they sing, such as opera, rock, folk, or country and western.

site The area where something is or will be located.

situations wanted ad A classified newspaper ad that lists information about an individual who is looking for a job. *See also* **help wanted ad** and **blind ad.**

skill The ability to do something well.

skills enhancement program A program, usually sponsored by businesses, whose aim is to improve and expand the abilities of a group of workers.

SL An abbreviation of *senior level. See* **senior level (SL) positions.**

sleeper run A trucker's trip that usually involves two drivers so that one driver can sleep in a berth behind the truck cab while the other trucker drives. A sleeper run may last for days or weeks.

slowdown A deliberate reduction of output or services without an actual strike in order to force concessions from an employer. *See also* **job action** and **work-to-rule.**

Small Business Administration An agency of the Federal Government responsible for aiding, counseling, and assisting small businesses. Assistance might involve helping to obtain loans after some disaster, preparing bids and obtaining Federal contracts, and assisting with production problems.

small-engine mechanic An individual who adjusts, cleans, lubricates, and----when necessary----replaces worn or defective parts for small engines used for chain saws, lawn mowers, and garden tractors. *See also* the OOH.

SOC *See* **Service Members Opportunity Colleges.**

social psychologist A psychologist who examines people's interactions with others and with the social environment. Areas of study might include group behavior, leadership, attitudes, and interpersonal perception.

social scientist An individual who studies all aspects of human society. *See also* the OOH, **anthropologist, economist, geographer, historian, political scientist, psychologist, sociologist,** and **urban/regional planner.**

social secretary An individual who arranges social functions, answers personal correspondence, and keeps the employer informed about social activities.

Social Security benefits Money paid to eligible individuals as part of the Social Security system. Benefits are determined largely by an individual's earnings, date of birth, and type of benefit.

Social Security death benefit A one-time benefit of $225 payable to certain members of the family of the deceased.

Social Security disability benefit A benefit available to employees who have the required number of Social Security credits to qualify for disability and have a physical or mental impairment that is expected to keep them from doing any substantial work (less than $500 per month) for at least a year or have a condition that is expected to result in death. Dependents who qualify for benefits on the wage earner's work record do not need work credits. The number of work credits needed for disability benefits depends on the age of the employee when the individual becomes disabled.

Social Security payroll tax The percentage of an employee's wages that is deducted on account of the Federal Insurance Contribution Act. *See also* **FICA.**

Social Security records Some of the documents, such as a Social Security card, birth certificate, or

W-2 form, that an individual may need when signing up for Social Security benefits.

Social Security reduced benefits Eligible individuals may start receiving Social Security benefits at age 62 but only 80 percent of the benefits rather than 100 percent.

Social Security retirement age Eligible individuals born before 1938 can retire at age 65; but beginning in the year 2000, the age for full benefits will increase in gradual steps from age 65 to 67.

Social Security Supplemental Security Income (SSI) *See* **Supplemental Security Income.**

Social Security survivors benefits Benefits to which certain members of a family of an individual covered by Social Security may be eligible if the family breadwinner dies. Family members who may be eligible for Social Security benefits are spouses age 60 or older, a spouse 50 years or older and disabled, a spouse at any age if the person is caring for a child under 16 or a disabled child. Children can receive benefits if unmarried and under 18, or under 19 if they are full-time students, or 18 or older and severely disabled.

Social Security work credits Units earned by workers covered by Social Security during their working years (about four credits per year) that may qualify the individuals for Social Security benefits. The number of credits needed varies with the benefit and age, but most people need forty credits to qualify for benefits.

social service technician *See* **human services worker.**

social work assistant An individual who handles eligibility determination for social welfare programs, such as food stamps, Medicaid, and other welfare programs.

social worker An individual who helps individuals, families, or groups cope with social problems, such as unemployment, homelessness, illness, and handicapping conditions. *See also* the OOH, **psychiatric social worker, medical social worker,** and **school social worker.**

social worker (military) An Army, Navy, or Air Force officer who counsels military personnel and their family members, supervises counselors and caseworkers, and plans social action programs to rehabilitate personnel with problems. *See also* the *Military Careers* guide.

sociologist An individual who studies human society and social behavior by examining the groups and social institutions that people form, such as families, tribes, communities, and governments. *See also* the OOH.

software documentation writer An individual who produces the written instructions, explanations, and glossaries that accompany computer software programs, so that the buyer can learn to use the program.

SOICC An abbreviation of *State Occupational Information Coordinating Committee. See* **State Occupational Information Coordinating Committees.**

soil conservationist An individual who provides technical assistance to farmers, ranchers, and others concerned with the conservation of soil, water, and related natural resources.

soil scientist An individual who studies soil characteristics; maps soil types; determines the best types of crops for each soil; and studies the chemical and physical characteristics of soils and their responses to fertilizer, tillage practices, and crop rotation.

solderer and brazer An individual who uses hand soldering and brazing equipment to join together metal parts or components of metal products, or to fill holes, indentations, and seams of fabricated metal products, as specified by work orders, work layout specifications, or blueprints.

soldering and brazing machine operator/tender An individual who operates or tends soldering and brazing machines that braze, solder, or spot-weld fabricated metal products or components, as specified by work orders, layout specifications, or blueprints.

soldering and brazing machine setter and setup operator An individual who sets up and operates soldering or brazing machines to bronze, solder, heat-treat, or spot-weld fabricated metal products or components, as specified by work orders, layout specifications, or blueprints.

sonar operator (military) *See* **radar and sonar operator (military).**

sonographer An individual who uses nonionizing equipment to transmit sound waves at high frequencies into a patient's body and then collects reflected echoes to form an image that is used to locate medical problems.

sous chef The individual who assists the executive chef in a large restaurant by assuming responsibility for the preparation and production of food.

spa A hotel that offers various types of facilities for guests. Originally the term was used for a hotel near a mineral spring so that guests could improve their health by drinking or bathing in the mineral water. Now the term is used for any hotel or resort that tries to improve the health or appearance of guests by providing programs which emphasize weight reduction, fitness, and mental relaxation.

space operations officer (military) A Navy or Air Force officer who manages activities of the flight control facility; manages operation of guidance, navigation, and propulsion systems for ground and space vehicles; and plans space stations. *See also* the *Military Careers* guide.

space science The various scientific disciplines that deal with the study of space and space flight.

space systems specialist (military) In the Navy or Air Force, an individual who uses aerospace ground equipment to transmit and verify spacecraft commands; monitors computers and telemetry display systems; and analyzes data to determine spacecraft operational status. *See also* the *Military Careers* guide.

special agent A collective term for individuals who operate as plainclothes investigators for agencies such as the Federal Bureau of Investigation; U.S. Customs Service; Bureau of Alcohol, Tobacco, and Firearms; U.S. Secret Service; and Internal Revenue Service. *See also* specific types of agents.

special agent (military) An Army, Air Force, Marine Corps, or Coast Guard officer who plans investigations of suspected treason, sabotage, espionage, and other security violations; performs counterterrorism and counterintelligence investigations with other law enforcement agencies; and assists detectives to conduct homicide, arson, burglary, and other criminal investigations.

special Government employee In the Federal civil service system, an employee who is appointed to work for a period not to exceed 130 days during any period of 365 days. The standards of employee conduct for a special Government employee are not the same as for other Government employees.

special librarian An individual who works in information centers or libraries maintained by government agencies, corporations, law firms, advertising agencies, medical centers, and research laboratories.

special operations forces (military) In the Army, Navy, Air Force, and Marine Corps, individuals who are specially trained to conduct offensive raids, demolitions, intelligence, and search and rescue missions.

special pay Money paid to members of the military for certain types of hazardous duty, such as parachute jumping, flight deck duty, and explosives demolition. Special pay is also given for sea duty, diving duty, and special duty in certain foreign areas or areas subject to hostile fire.

special pay adjustment for law enforcement officers In the Federal civil service system, an additional payment made to a law enforcement officer whose official duty station is in one of eight special pay areas defined in the Federal Employees Pay Comparability Act of 1990.

special salary rates In the Federal civil service system, salary rates that are higher than the regular statutory schedule. They are established for occupations in which private enterprise pays substantially more than the regular Federal schedule and this pay gap significantly handicaps the Federal Government's recruitment or retention of well-qualified persons.

specialty fast-food cook An individual who prepares a limited selection of menu items in a fast-food restaurant.

specifications The descriptions of the various components and materials needed to complete a building or project.

speech-language pathologist An individual who identifies, assesses, and treats persons with speech and language disorders. *See also* the OOH.

speech pathologist *See* **speech-language pathologist.**

speech therapist (military) An Army, Navy, or Air Force officer who identifies speaking and language problems, evaluates examination and test data to determine the type and amount of hearing loss, and conducts programs to help patients improve their speaking skills. *See also* the *Military Careers* guide.

split shift The practice of having an employee work a few hours and then return later in the day to complete the shift. *Example:* fast-food restaurant employees who work during the morning and evening peak mealtimes but are free to go home midday.

spoils system *Informal:* the hiring or removal of an individual for political reasons instead of merit.

spook *Informal:* a spy, especially an agent of the Central Intelligence Agency (CIA).

sports medicine A collective term for the health professionals, such as doctors and physical therapists, who have special training that enables them to deal with injuries suffered by athletes.

sportscaster A news writer who specializes in reporting on sports events, athletes, and teams for a radio or television station.

spray-machine operator An individual who uses equipment with spray guns to coat metal, wood, ceramic, fabric, and paper with paint and other coating solutions. *See also* the OOH.

spray painter An individual who uses spraying equipment to apply paints and coatings to manufactured items. *See also* the OOH.

spreader, apparel An individual who works in the garment industry and spreads out layers of material on the cutting table.

sprinklerfitter An individual who installs automatic fire sprinkler systems in buildings.

SSI An abbreviation of *Supplemental Security Income*. *See* **Supplemental Security income.**

stable staff **1)** Individuals who care for horses and perform tasks such as feeding and grooming the horses, cleaning stalls, and saddling and unsaddling horses. **2)** A staff that does not change frequently. *See also* **turnover rate.**

staff The employees of a particular establishment, educational facility, or hospital.

staffing The act of choosing the work force required to operate a business or organization.

staffing differential In the Federal civil service system, the annual total dollar amount (equal to 5 percent of basic pay) paid over and above basic pay to make it easier to hire and retain employees in selected General Schedule grades and occupational groups when authorized by the Office of Personnel Management.

Standard Form 7 *See* **Service Record Card.**

Standard Form 50 - Notification of Personnel Action In the Federal civil service system, a form completed by the personnel or administrative office to which appointing authority has been delegated. The form is used to notify the employee and the payroll office and to record the action in the employee's Official Personnel Folder/Merged Records Personnel Folder to provide a chronological file record of actions that have occurred.

Standard Form 52 - Request for Personnel Action In the Federal civil service system, a form used by operating officials or supervisors to request personnel actions and to secure internal agency clearance of requests for personnel action.

Standard Form 75 - Request for Preliminary Employment Data In the Federal civil service system, a form used to obtain information about the Government employment of an applicant who is currently employed by another agency or whose Official Personnel Folder/Merged Records Personnel Folder is in the possession of another appointing officer. Standard Form 75 information is usually obtained before a firm offer of employment is made.

Standard Form 171 - Application for Federal Employment The application form for applying for most Federal positions.

Standard Occupational Classification Manual A Federal Government publication that provides a coding system for identifying and classifying occupations and includes descriptions of job duties for occupational groups.

standard of proof The amount of proof needed to establish a fact or prove a case.

standards **1)** Authoritative rules, specifications,

or principles that can be used to measure the physical characteristics or value of something. **2)** In the Federal civil service system, statements of significant requirements job applicants must meet (qualification standards) and guides against which duties and responsibilities of a position are measured (classification standards).

standards of conduct The Federal Government ethics regulations define general standards of conduct in which the employee must avoid any action that might result in or create the appearance of **1)** using public office for private gain, **2)** giving preferential treatment to anyone, **3)** impeding Government efficiency or economy, **4)** losing complete independence or impartiality, **5)** making a Government decision outside official channels, or **6)** affecting adversely the public's confidence in the integrity of the Government.

Standards of Conduct for Labor Organization A Federal sector code that governs internal democratic practices, fiscal responsibility, and procedures to which a labor organization must adhere to be eligible to receive any recognition.

standby A system that has employees "stand by" or be ready to work if regularly scheduled employees can not complete work on schedule or if an emergency is anticipated. *Example:* a telephone crew that is on standby in case an approaching hurricane causes a great deal of damage.

standby pay Extra wages paid to an employee who is on standby duty. *See also* **standby** and **premium pay.**

state employment service In coordination with the Labor Department's U.S. Employment Service, state offices operated in many U.S. cities to help job seekers locate employment and to help employers find qualified workers.

State Occupational Information Coordinating Committees (SOICC) These groups, located in every state, provide or help locate labor market and career information. A listing of the title of the individual in charge, address, and phone number can be found in the OOH.

state police officer *See* **highway patrol officer.**

state policeman *See* **highway patrol officer.**

state trooper *See* **highway patrol officer.**

statement clerk An individual who assembles and sends out customers' bank statements. *See also* the OOH.

stationary engineer An individual who operates and maintains equipment such as boilers, air-conditioning and refrigeration equipment, diesel engines, turbines, and pumps. *See also* the OOH.

statistical clerk An individual who compiles and computes data according to statistical formulas for use in statistical studies.

statistician An individual who designs, carries out, and interprets the numerical results of surveys and experiments. *See also* the OOH.

status The prestige, standing, or rank of an individual. *Example:* a company president, who has more status than an unskilled worker.

status employee In the Federal civil service system, an individual who has completed the probationary period under the career-conditional employment system. *See also* **career-conditional appointment.**

status quo employee In the Federal civil service system, an employee who failed to acquire competitive status when the position in which the individual was serving was placed in the competitive service by a statute, Executive order, or civil service rule that permitted the person's retention without acquisition of status.

steamfitter An individual who installs pipe systems that move liquid or gases under high pressure.

steelworker A collective term for individuals who operate and tend machinery that produces steel. *See also* the OOH, **stove tender, blower, keeper, melter, molding and casting machine operator, heater, roller,** and **manipulator operator.**

stenographer An individual who takes dictation and then transcribes notes on a typewriter or word processor. *See also* the OOH, **stenotype operator, technical stenographer, shorthand reporter, court reporter, transcribing machine operator, dictating-machine transcriber/typist,** and **print shop stenographer.**

stenotype operator An individual who uses a

stenotype machine to take dictation and then transcribes the notes on a typewriter or word processor.

step In the Federal civil service system, the step (level) or section of the pay plan under which an employee is paid. *See also* **General Schedule** and **wage grade system.**

step adjustment In the Federal civil service system, a change in the step of the grade at which an employee is serving but without a change in the employee's rate of basic pay.

step increase **1)** A salary increase provided in certain Federal Government pay plans based on time-in-grade and acceptable or satisfactory work performance. **2)** In the United States Postal Service, an advancement from one step to the next within a specific grade of a position, and dependent on performance and waiting-period criteria.

stevedore An individual who moves goods on loading docks and loads and unloads ships.

steward/stewardess The preferred nonsexist term is *flight attendant. See* **flight attendant.**

steward, union An individual who represents a union local in a plant or department. A union steward is appointed by the union members to adjust grievances, collect dues, solicit new members, and carry out other union duties.

stipend **1)** An amount of money paid for an occasional service, such as giving a lecture, leading a workshop, or speaking at a conference. **2)** A payment to a student especially for a scholarship or fellowship.

stipulation **1)** A point or condition agreed upon, as in a contract. **2)** In U.S. Merit Systems Protection Board appeals, an agreement between the appellant (person appealing) and the agency that a particular fact or set of facts is true.

stock and inventory specialist (military) In the Army, Navy, Air Force, Marine Corps, or Coast Guard, an individual who locates and catalogs stock; verifies the quantity and description of stock received; and gives special handling to medicine, ammunition, and other delicate supplies. *See also* the *Military Careers* guide.

stock bonus An employee bonus paid in the form of company stock instead of money.

stock boy The preferred nonsexist term for this job is *stock clerk. See* **stock clerk.**

stock broker *See* **securities sales representative.**

stock clerk An individual who receives, unpacks, checks, stores, and keeps track of merchandise or material. *See also* the OOH.

stock plan An arrangement by which employees may buy stock in the company sometimes at a reduced cost and through payroll deduction.

stock specialist *See* **sales and stock specialist.**

stocker *See* **stock clerk.**

stockroom clerk *See* **stock clerk.**

stonemason An individual who builds stone walls and sets stone exteriors and floors. *See also* the OOH.

store detective An individual who is hired by department stores and other commercial establishments to deal with shoplifters and other types of security problems.

store manager (military) An Army, Navy, Air Force, Marine Corps, or Coast Guard officer who directs personnel in purchasing, pricing, and selling food, supplies, and equipment; directs personnel in receiving, storing, and issuing supplies and equipment; and supervises the inspection, care, and testing of products before their use or sale. *See also* the *Military Careers* guide.

stove tender An individual in a steel mill who monitors the controls that indicate the temperature of the air inside the stoves which blow hot air into the bottom of the blast furnace.

straight time The time an employee works for which no overtime is paid.

stratigrapher An individual who studies the distribution and arrangement of sedimentary rock layers by examining their fossil and mineral content.

streetcar operator An individual who drives electric-powered streetcars to transport passengers, collects fares, and issues change and transfers.

strength The quality of being mentally or physically powerful.

stress management A plan to reduce and control feelings of emotional or mental pressure or distress.

strike Temporary stoppage of work by a group of

employees to express a grievance, enforce a demand for changes in conditions of employment, obtain recognition, or resolve a dispute with management. *See also* **wildcat strike, quickie strike, slowdown, walkout, blue flu,** and **work to rule.**

stripper **1)** An individual who cuts film to the required size and arranges and tapes the negatives onto "flats" or layout sheets, which are used by platemakers to make offset press plates. **2)** *Informal:* an individual who entertains by removing articles of clothing.

structural and reinforcing ironworker An individual who fabricates, assembles, and installs materials made from steel and iron. *See also* the OOH.

Structural Work Occupations One of the nine primary categories for grouping occupations in the *Dictionary of Occupational Titles. Examples:* hood maker, jig fitter, and **rigger.**

stucco mason An individual who applies stucco (a mixture of portland cement and sand) over cement, concrete, masonry, and lath.

Student Guide to Federal Financial Aid Programs A publication of the U.S. Department of Education that provides information on grants, loans, work-study programs, and other benefits to students. Copies are available from Federal Student Aid Programs, P.O. Box 84, Washington, DC 20044. Phone: toll-free (800) 433-3243.

student loan Money that can be borrowed from banks and credit unions by individuals who need funds for educational expenses.

submarine cable equipment technician An individual who repairs, adjusts, and maintains the machines and equipment used in submarine cable offices or stations to control cable traffic.

subordinate An individual who has a position that is inferior to others in the same organization.

subsidiaries Companies that are owned or controlled by larger companies.

subsistence (military) A food allowance issued to military personnel who live away from the military base.

substantially continuous service In the Federal civil service system, civilian service that continued without a break or interruption, and a period of service from which time off the agency's rolls was not deducted or subtracted from the employee's total period of service.

subway operator An individual who guides subway trains; starts, slows, or stops the subway train on signal; and makes announcements.

suggestion An idea or comment intended to correct a problem, increase efficiency or productivity, and save money. Some employers reward employees who submit particularly useful suggestions.

suit *Informal:* an executive or management-level employee who not only dresses in a suit for work but also displays a serious and businesslike outlook.

suitability An applicant's or employee's fitness for employment as indicated by character, reputation, and conduct.

summer youth programs Programs that provide summer jobs in city, county, and state government agencies for low-income youth. Students, school dropouts, or graduates entering the labor market who are from 16 through 21 years of age are eligible.

superior qualifications appointment In the Federal civil service system, the placement of a person in a hard-to-recruit-for position at General Schedule 11 or higher at a pay rate above the minimum. The appointment is justified by the applicant's unique or unusually high qualifications, a special Government need for the person's services, and the fact that the individual's present salary or salary offerings are higher than the minimum rate of the grade level to which the applicant can be appointed.

supersede To replace one thing with another. *Example:* a regional office that supersedes an agency and makes changes in some of the agency's jobs.

supervise To check, inspect, or oversee an activity in progress.

supervisor An individual who oversees the work of others and may be responsible for hiring, assigning, promoting, transferring, furloughing, and suspending workers.

supervisor, agricultural, forestry, fishing, and related occupations An individual who directly supervises and coordinates the activities of agricultural, forestry, fishing, and related workers.

supervisory differential In the Federal civil service system, the annual total dollar amount paid to a General Schedule supervisor who provides direct, technical supervision over the work of one or more civilian employees in other pay plans who receive a higher rate of total pay than does the supervisor.

supplemental benefits *See* **fringe benefits.**

supplemental qualifications statements Promotion or lateral transfer tests for Federal employees.

Supplemental Security Income (SSI) A Social Security benefit that provides monthly checks to people who **1)** are 65 or older, **2)** are citizens or living in the U.S. legally, **3)** are blind, **4)** are disabled, or **5)** have few assets or a low income. For SSI purposes, blind means either being totally blind or having very poor eyesight. Children as well as adults can get benefits because of blindness. For SSI purposes disabled means that there is a physical or mental problem that prevents an individual from working and is expected to last at least a year or result in death. Children as well as adults can get benefits because of disability. Income and assets qualifications include the consideration of wages, Social Security checks, pensions, and the spouse's income. SSI payments are the same nationwide, but some states provide additional money for SSI recipients.

supply/warehousing manager (military) An Army, Navy, Air Force, Marine Corps, or Coast Guard officer who analyzes the demand for supplies and forecasts future needs; directs personnel who receive, inventory, store, and issue supplies and equipment; and evaluates bids and proposals submitted by potential suppliers. *See also* the *Military Careers* guide.

support services Occupations that help sustain or uphold a particular operation. *Examples*: guidance counselor and school psychologist in an educational institution.

surgeon A physician who specializes in surgery.

surgeon (military) *See* **physician/surgeon.**

surgeon's assistant A physician assistant (PA) who specializes in surgery, provides pre- and post-operative care, and may work as first or second assistant in major surgery. *See also* the OOH and **physician assistant.**

surgical technician *See* **surgical technologist.**

surgical technologist An individual who works under the supervision of surgeons and registered nurses and whose duties may include setting up the operating room, preparing patients for surgery, and transporting patients to the operating room. *See also* the OOH.

survey classification An intensive study of all positions in an organization to ensure their correct classification.

survey technician An individual who operates surveying instruments, collects information, holds measuring tapes, compiles notes, and makes sketches. *See also* the OOH.

survey worker An individual who works for an information organization and conducts surveys of the public either by interviewing people or contacting them by telephone. Survey workers also review, classify, and sort the responses to the surveys.

surveying and mapping manager (miliitary) An Army, Navy, Air Force, Marine Corps, or Coast Guard officer who plans surveys and aerial photography missions; directs the activities of survey teams; and directs the calculation of latitude and longitude, slope, elevation, and other features of the land. *See also the Military Careers* guide.

surveying and mapping technician (military) In the Army, Navy, Air Force, Marine Corps, or Coast Guard, an individual who uses drafting tools such as easels, templates, and compasses to draw maps and charts; draws land elevations, distances between points, and locations of landmarks on maps; and builds scale models of land areas out of wood, clay, and paper that show hills, lakes, roads, and buildings. *See also* the *Military Careers* guide.

surveyor An individual who measures and maps

the earth's surface. *See also* the OOH, **land surveyor, survey technician, mapping scientist, cartographer, photogrammetrist, map editor, geodetic surveyor, geophysical prospecting surveyor,** and **marine surveyor.**

survival equipment specialist (military) In the Army, Navy, Air Force, Marine Corps, or Coast Guard, an individual who inspects parachutes for rips and tangled lines, packs parachutes for safe operation, and repairs life rafts and loads them with emergency provisions. *See also* the *Military Careers* guide.

suspension In the Federal civil service system, the placement of an employee in a temporary nonpay status and nonduty status (or absence from duty) for disciplinary reasons or other reasons pending an inquiry.

swing In the United States Postal Service, a short tour (hours of work) required to cover an absence.

swing time In the United States Postal Service, the period employees spend not directly engaged in work activities, such as at lunch or on coffee break.

switch operator A rail transportation employee who throws track switches to route railway cars to certain tracks if the cars are to be unloaded or to an outgoing train if their final destination is farther down the line.

switchboard operator **1)** An individual who operates a PBX or switchboard and connects interoffice or house calls, answers and relays outside calls, and assists company employees in making outgoing calls. **2)** An individual who works in an electric generating plant and controls the flow of electricity from a central point. *See also* the OOH.

synoptic meteorologist An individual who studies information on air pressure, temperature, humidity, and wind velocity and then applies physical and mathematical relationships to make short- and long-range weather forecasts.

systems analysis The act of determining what information is required, how it will be used, and what methods will achieve the objective so that a computer program can be written to fill the specific needs.

systems analyst, computer An individual who plans and develops new computer systems or devises ways to apply existing systems to processes still completed manually or by some less efficient method. *See also* the OOH.

systems operator *See* **electric power distributor and dispatcher.**

systems programmer An individual who maintains the software that controls the operation of a computer system. Duties may include changing the sets of instructions that determine how the central processing unit of the computer handles the various jobs it has been given and how it communicates with peripheral equipment, such as terminals, printers, and disk drives.

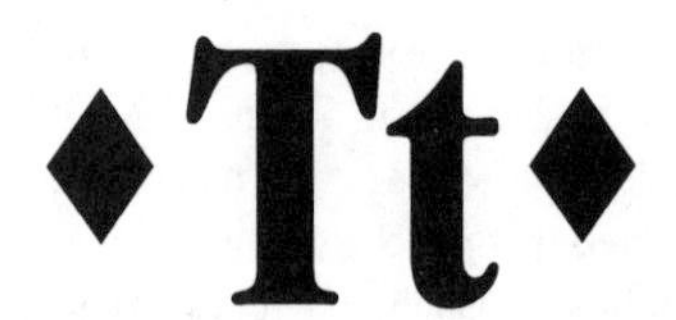

tailor An individual who makes clothing according to customers' requirements from the measuring process to the finished product. *See also* the OOH.

take *Informal:* an evaluation, appraisal, or opinion on a subject. *Example:* a person giving a take on a new project.

takedown sorter An individual who works in the photographic processing industry and sorts processed film.

takeover The act of gaining control over a company. *See also* **hostile takeover** and **friendly takeover.**

talk show host An individual on a radio or television program who interviews guests or members of the studio audience, gives an opinion on some topic, or talks with people who call in with comments or questions.

tank crew member In the Army or Marine Corps, an individual who drives tanks or amphibious assault vehicles, operates target-sighting equipment to aim guns, and loads and fires guns. *See also* the *Military Careers* guide.

tank officer An Army or Marine Corps officer who gathers and evaluates intelligence on enemy strength and positions; formulates battle plans; and coordinates actions with infantry, artillery, and air support units. *See also* the *Military Careers* guide.

TAPER *See* **appointment, TAPER.**

taper *See* **drywall finisher.**

task force A special group that is gathered to solve a specific problem or take a particular action.

taxi driver An individual who drives people in a taxi to their destinations, collects fares, and assists with luggage.

taxidermist An individual who prepares and preserves the skin of animals and then stuffs and mounts them so that they appear lifelike.

teacher An individual who teaches children or adults. *See also* the OOH, **adult education teacher, college/university faculty, kindergarten teacher, elementary school teacher, preschool teacher,** and **secondary school teacher.**

teacher aide An individual who helps classroom teachers by supervising students, recording grades, and setting up equipment. *See also* the OOH.

teacher/instructor (military) An Army, Navy, Air Force, Marine Corps, or Coast Guard officer who develops course content, training outlines, and lesson plans; prepares training aids, assignments, and demonstrations; and delivers lectures. *See also* the *Military Careers* guide.

teaching assistantship A plan that pays a graduate student for helping a university faculty member with a variety of teaching/education tasks.

technical education Training/educational programs that deal with courses of a practical nature.

technical institute An educational institution that offers intensive technical training but less theory and general education than junior and community colleges. Many offer two-year associate degree programs.

technical occupations *See* **Professional, Technical, and Managerial Occupations.**

technical secretary An individual who uses secretarial skills to assist engineers or scientists.

technical stenographer A stenographer who must know the technical terms used in a particular profession or field, such as medicine, law, engineering, or chemistry.

technical writer An individual who uses writing skills and knowledge of technology to write various documents for firms in industries such as manufacturing, chemicals, aerospace, telecommunications, and computers.

technician An individual who works in direct support of engineers, medical professionals, or scientists and solves practical problems related to these fields. Although the terms **technician** and **technologist** are sometimes used interchangeably, technologists are usually certified or registered, but technicians are not. *See also* **certification** and **registration.**

technological change The changes brought about by scientific or industrial discoveries and progress.

technologist An individual who applies the principles of science for commercial, industrial, or medical goals. Technologists are usually highly trained and certified or registered by some national organization. *See also* **certification, registration,** and specific types of technologists.

technology Knowledge that deals with applied science and engineering.

telecommunications industry The businesses involved with the technology of communications by electronics. *Examples:* radio, television, and cable.

telecommuting The practice of using telecommunication equipment to work at home or at electronic centers instead of commuting to a central office. See also **computer commuter.**

telefundraising The practice of raising money for charitable causes by using telephone solicitors or people monitoring banks of phones on television programs where the host tries to get viewers to pledge funds.

telegraph plant maintainer *See* **communications equipment mechanic.**

telemarketer An individual who contacts prospects by phone to try to persuade them to order items or to set up appointments with people selling services.

telemarketing The practice of trying to sell goods and services by phone instead of maintaining a store. *See also* **nonstore retailing.**

telemarketing representative An individual who works for an organization that develops information by conducting surveys of the public by phone.

telephone-answering-service operator An individual who manages a switchboard to provide answering services for such persons as doctors, dentists, entertainers, and small-business owners.

telephone installer An individual who assembles equipment, installs wiring, connects telephones, and tests the installations. *See also* the OOH.

telephone line installer/repairer *See* **line installer and cable splicer.**

telephone operator An individual who works in the central office of a telephone company and helps customers with calls that require assistance, person-to-person calls, mobile telephone calls, and collect calls. *See also* the OOH and **PBX operator.**

telephone operator (military) In the Army, Navy, Air Force, or Marine Corps, an individual who operates different types of telephone switchboards, installs and operates switchboards in the field, and receives and delivers messages or battle commands. *See also* the *Military Careers* guide.

telephone repairer An individual who makes repairs on telephones or changes existing wiring in homes and offices. *See also* the OOH.

telephone technician (military) In the Army, Navy, Air Force, Marine Corps, or Coast Guard, an individual who determines the cause of equipment failure, installs interior wiring and switching equipment, and repairs or replaces broken equipment. *See also* the *Military Careers* guide.

teletype installer An individual who installs, repairs, and maintains telegraphic equipment.

teletype operator (military) In the Army, Navy, Air Force, Marine Corps, or Coast Guard, an individual who prepares and sends messages through teletype and cryptographic machines; receives and decodes incoming messages, following security procedures; and categorizes and stamps messages with the proper security classification. *See also* the *Military Careers* guide.

teletype repairer (military) In the Army, Navy, Air Force, Marine Corps, or Coast Guard, an individual who tests and repairs communications equipment; monitors the operation of cryptographic (coded message) systems, terminals, and teletypewriters; and installs and repairs circuits and wiring. *See also* the *Military Careers* guide.

television announcer and newscaster An individual who works for a television station and may broadcast general news or specialize in weather or sports. *See also* the OOH, **weatherman, sportscaster,** and **news anchor.**

television camera operator An individual who works for a television station and uses a videotape camera to photograph either in studios or in the field.

television industry The businesses involved with the production and broadcasting of television programs.

television selling *See* **nonstore retailing.**

television service technician An individual who repairs home television equipment.

teller, bank An individual who cashes checks and processes deposits and withdrawals in a bank.

temp (temporary) *Informal:* an individual employed by an agency that places its employees in positions for a short period of time. Temps sometimes replace workers on leave or vacation or help during busy periods.

temporary appointment In the Federal civil service system, an appointment made for a limited period of time and with a specific not-to-exceed date determined by the authority under which the appointment is made.

temporary placement agencies Organizations that provide temporary workers to businesses. *See also* **temp.**

temporary work *See* **temp.**

ten-point preference *See* **preference, compensable disability; preference, disability; preference, mother; preference, wife;** and **preference, husband.**

tenant farmer An individual who farms land owned by another person and pays rent in cash or crops.

tender, chemical *See* **chemical equipment tender.**

tenure **1)** In the Federal civil service system, the period of time an employee may reasonably expect to serve under a current appointment. Tenure is granted and governed by the type of appointment under which an employee is currently serving, without regard to whether the individual has competitive status or whether the person's appointment is to a competitive position or an excepted position. **2)** In education, the granting of a position on a permanent basis from which an individual can be dismissed only with just cause.

tenure groups In the Federal civil service system, the categories of employees ranked in priority order for retention during reduction in force. Within each group, veterans are ranked above nonveterans.

Tenure Group 1
Competitive Service. Includes employees serving under career appointments who either have completed initial appointment probation or are not required to serve initial appointment probation.
Excepted Service. Includes permanent employees whose appointments carry no restriction or condition, such as conditional, indefinite, specific time limitation, or trial period.
Tenure Group 2
Competitive Service. Includes employees serving under career-conditional appointments, under career appointments, and under career appointments who are serving initial appointment probation.
Excepted Service. Includes employees who are serving trial periods or whose tenure is equivalent to career-conditional tenure in the competitive service in agencies which use that type of appointment system.
Tenure Group 3
Competitive Service. Includes indefinite employees, employees under temporary appointments pending establishment of registers; employees under term appointments, employees in status quo; employees under any other nonstatus, nontemporary appointments; and employees serving on provisional appointments.
Excepted Service. Includes employees whose appointment is indefinite, those whose appointments have specific time limitations of more than one year; employees who, though currently under appointments limited to one year or less, complete one year of current continuous employment; and employees serving on provisional appointments.

See also **reduction in force; career appointment; career-conditional appointment; excepted service;** and **appointment, temporary-limited.**

tenure subgroups In the Federal civil service system, the ranking of veterans above nonveterans in each tenure group, as follows:

Tenure Subgroups
Subgroup AD. Includes each preference eligible employee who has a compensable service-connected disability of 30 percent or more.
Subgroup A. Employees with veteran preference who are not in subgroup AD.
Subgroup B. Employees who have no veteran preference (nonveterans).

term appointment *See* **appointment, term.**

terminated Discharged from a job.

terminating event, COBRA A situation that would end health insurance coverage for an individual under the Comprehensive Omnibus Budget Reconciliation Act (COBRA). A terminating event might be reemployment, failure to pay premiums, remarriage of a spouse, or attainment of the time limit of 18 or 36 months.

termination 1) The act of dismissing an employee from a job. **2)** In the Federal civil service system, an agency-initiated action of separation where the employee is not at fault. A termination might be an action to move an employee from one agency to another; a separation that meets the *Federal Personnel Manual* definition of involuntary separation, a separation when the employee enters active military duty or fails to return from leave without pay, a separation because of an employee's mental or physical disability, a separation on the not-to-exceed date of a temporary appointment, or an action to document the separation of a dependent who leaves a job when the person's military sponsor is transferred to a new location.

terminology The specialized terms associated with a particular industry, science, or occupation. *See also* **jargon.**

terrazzo worker An individual who creates walkways, floors, and patios by exposing marble chips and other fine aggregates on the surface of finished concrete. See also the OOH and **concrete mason.**

test pilot A pilot who puts newly built or designed planes or helicopters through a series of maneuvers to determine whether the quality of the aircraft is satisfactory.

tester An individual who uses various types of equipment to test the quality of different kinds of products, such as foods or structural steel.

testing The process of determining the quality, safety, or content of a product or service.

testing services Companies that test various products for a fee.

textile bleaching and dyeing machine operator/tender *See* **bleaching and dyeing machine operator, textile.**

textile designer An individual who designs fabrics for garments, upholstery, rugs, and other products.

textile machine operator An individual who tends the machines that manufacture textile goods. *See also* the OOH.

textile machine setter/setup operator An individual who prepares machinery before a production run. Other tasks may include maintaining the equipment, adjusting the timing, and feeding patterns into the machine.

thanatologist An individual who is an expert in grief and death.

theatrical design The development of sketches, construction of models, and plan and arrangement of sets for a theatrical performance.

therapeutic recreational therapist *See* **recreational therapist.**

therapist *See* **occupational therapist, physical therapist, recreational therapist,** and **respiratory therapist.**

ticket agent An individual who sells tickets for travel by plane, train, ship, or bus. The person may have other responsibilities, such as checking luggage, examining visas, and making boarding announcements.

ticket clerk *See* **ticket agent.**

ticket seller *See* **ticket agent.**

tilesetter An individual who applies tile to floors, walls, and ceilings. *See also* the OOH.

timber cutting and logging occupations *See* **faller, bucker, choker setter, rigger, logging tractor operator, log handling equipment operator, log grader/scaler, cruiser, brush**

clearing laborer, tree trimmer, picker, log marker, river, rigging slinger, chaser, and **pulp piler.**

time-after-competitive restriction In the Federal civil service system, the provision that three months must elapse after an employee's latest nontemporary competitive appointment before the individual may be promoted; reassigned to a different line of work or to a different geographical area; or transferred to, or reinstated to, a higher grade or different line of work in the competitive service.

time-in-grade restriction In the Federal civil service system, that part of the civil service regulations which prevents agencies from making excessively rapid promotions from a competitive service position that is subject to the General Schedule. As a general rule, an employee being promoted to a position above GS-5 must have service for 52 weeks in grade at the next lowest grade, or 52 weeks in grade at the second lower grade if the job is graded at two-grade intervals.

time management The act of handling or controlling the time available to an individual. *Example:* a person whose ability to manage time and organize tasks earned a quick promotion.

timekeeping clerk An individual who distributes and collects time cards each pay period, and informs managers and other employees about new policies or procedural changes. *See also* the OOH.

timeliness In the Federal civil service system, the adherence to established, published time limits. Example: an employee who must appeal to the Merit Systems Protection Board within 20 calendar days of the effective date of an agency's action in order to meet the board's timeliness requirements.

tip A method of payment used mostly for service workers such as waiters, waitresses, bartenders, and cosmetologists. A tip is usually a percentage of the total bill and is given in recognition of good service.

tire building machine operator An individual who operates machinery to build pneumatic tires from rubber components.

tire repairer/changer An individual who repairs and replaces tires and related products on automobiles, buses, and trucks.

title abstractor An individual who summarizes pertinent legal or insurance details or sections of statutes or case law from reference books for the purpose of examination, proof, or ready reference, and may search out titles to determine whether the title deed is correct.

title examiner An individual who searches public records and examines titles to determine the legal status of property titles; copies or summarizes recorded documents, such as mortgages and trust deeds, that can affect the title to property; and prepares and issues policies that guarantee the legality of the title.

title searcher An individual who searches public and private records for real estate and title insurance companies to compile lists of mortgages, deeds, contracts, judgments, and other instruments pertaining to titles.

tobacco inspector *See* **alcohol, tobacco, and firearms inspector.**

tokenism The practice of making a symbolic effort rather than a genuine attempt. *Example:* employing a member of a minority group, such as a black or an Asian, just to appear unbiased and to avoid complaints or protests.

toll-free number As a telephone link to a business, organization, or agency, an 800 number that is billed as a local call for the caller.

tool allowance Extra money paid to workers as payment for supplying their own tools. Example: an auto shop mechanic who is paid a tool allowance for providing specialized and expensive tools.

tool-and-die maker An individual who produces tools, dies, and other devices used in machines that produce various products. See also the OOH.

tool programmer, numerical control An individual who plans and writes programs to operate numerically controlled machinery. See also the OOH.

top executive An individual who formulates the policies or directs the operation of a business or governmental agency. *See also* the OOH.

top management Individuals who occupy the

most important management positions in a business or organization. *Examples:* president, vice president, and treasurer.

total quality management A technique being used by some businesses, educational institutions, and organizations to reduce bureaucracy and encourage employees to become involved in making decisions, solving problems, and assuming responsibility. *See also* **quality circle.**

tour The time spent at a particular duty assignment by military personnel.

tour conductor/guide An individual whose duties may include showing visitors around an attraction or historical site while commenting on interesting features, history, or significance, or taking a group of people to a foreign country to visit places of interest and learn about the culture. Tours may vary from less than a hour to several weeks.

tour of duty **1)** In the Federal civil service system, the hours of a day (daily tour of duty) and the days of an administrative workweek (weekly tour of duty) that are scheduled in advance and during which an employee is required to perform work on a regularly recurring basis. **2)** In the United States Postal Service, an employee's scheduled duty hours during a workday or workweek. **3)** In the military, a period of obligated service. Also a type of duty tour, such as a "Mediterranean tour."

tow truck operator An individual who assists people by moving their cars that are disabled or have been in an accident and must be towed from the scene.

tower-crane operator An individual who operates various kinds of equipment used to lift and move materials, machinery, or other heavy objects.

track record *Informal:* the past incidents, employment situations, honors, and failures that might have some effect on the employment of an individual. *Example:* an employer who is reluctant to hire a prospective employee because of the applicant's poor track record.

trade **1)** The act of buying or selling goods. **2)** An occupation especially of a mechanical or skilled labor type.

trade adjustment assistance A Federal Government program that offers additional benefits, job training, and an allowance to seek employment in another area if the individual has become unemployed as a result of increased foreign imports. *See also* **foreign imports.**

trade and labor occupations *See* **job grading system for trades and labor occupations.**

trade association An organization whose main purpose is to promote the welfare of its members who belong to a particular industry or group. *Examples:* merchants or manufacturers.

trade magazine A publication that specializes in articles of interest to a particular trade or group.

traffic clerk An individual who maintains records on the destination, weight, and charges on incoming and outgoing freight. *See also* the OOH.

traffic controller, air An individual who keeps track of planes flying within their assigned area, directs airplanes to ensure that they take off and land safely, and minimizes delays. See also the OOH.

traffic inspector An individual who oversees the scheduled service of streetcar, bus, or railway systems and determines the need for additional vehicles, revised schedules, or other changes to improve service.

train To form or develop the skills necessary to accomplish some task.

trainee An individual who is learning skills necessary for an occupation.

trainer An individual who develops skills in people or animals so that they can accomplish some task.

trainer (military) In the Navy, Air Force, Marine Corps, or Coast Guard, an individual who prepares course outlines and materials to present during training, selects training materials such as textbooks and films, and teaches classes and gives lectures. *See also* the *Military Careers* guide.

training Formal instruction or planned exposure to learning.

training and education director (military) An Army, Navy, Air Force, Marine Corps, or Coast Guard officer who develops new training courses; reviews and approves course material and training outlines prepared by instructors; and assigns duties to instructors, curriculum planners, and training aids specialists. *See also* the *Military Careers* guide.

training manager An individual who supervises training programs to develop employee skills, enhance productivity, and build loyalty to the firm.

training, on-the-job *See* **on-the-job training.**

training program Organized instructional programs to improve employees' skills, teach new methods, and provide orientation. *See also* **skills enhancement program.**

training seminar An organized meeting for the purpose of training people.

training specialist An individual who plans, organizes, and directs a wide range of training activities.

transcribe To make a written or typewritten copy of dictated material. *See also* **stenographer** and **court reporter.**

transcribing machine operator An individual who listens to recordings and uses a typewriter or word processor to transcribe this information.

transcript **1)** An official record of a proceeding. **2)** The official record of a student's courses and grades.

transfer **1)** A change of an employee from one position to another within the same company or organization. **2)** In the Federal civil service system, a change of an employee, without a break in service of one full workday, from a position in one agency to a position in another agency that can be filled under the same appointing authority.

transfer clerk An individual who works in a brokerage office and examines stock certificates for adherence to banking regulations.

transfer of function In the Federal civil service system, the transfer, for reduction-in-force purposes, of the performance of a continuing function from one competitive area to another, or the movement of the competitive area in which the function is performed to another local commuting area.

transferable skills Abilities used in a job or profession that can be used in another type of job. *Examples:* typing skills and computer literacy.

transit clerk An individual who sorts, records, proofs, and prepares transit items for mailing to or from out-of-city banks to ensure correct routing and prompt collection.

translator An individual who can understand more than one language and can translate written or spoken information from one language to another.

translator (military) *See* **interpreter/translator.**

transmission engineer An individual who supervises technicians who operate and maintain broadcasting equipment.

transmitter engineer/operator An individual who monitors and logs outgoing radio and television signals and operates radio and television transmitters.

Transportation and Material Handling Occupations (military) One of the twelve broad categories used by the Armed Forces to group occupations for enlisted personnel.

transportation geographer An individual who studies cities and metropolitan areas.

transportation industry The businesses that deal with the transportation of people or goods. *Examples:* trains, planes, ships, and trucks.

transportation/maintenance manager (military) An Army, Navy, Air Force, Marine Corps, or Coast Guard officer who directs repair shop and garage operations; oversees the ordering and use of repair parts, equipment, and supplies; and plans and develops training programs for staff. *See also* the *Military Careers* guide.

transportation manager An individual who plans, organizes, directs, controls, or coordinates management activities relating to transportation facilities such as airports, harbors, and terminals.

transportation manager (military) An Army, Navy, Air Force, Marine Corps, or Coast Guard officer who determines the fastest and most economical way to transport cargo or personnel, directs the packing and crating of cargo, and oversees the handling of special items such as medicine and explosives. *See also* the *Military Careers* guide.

Transportation Occupations (military) One of the nine broad categories used by the Armed Forces to group occupations for officers.

transportation specialist (military) In the Army, Navy, Air Force, Marine Corps, or Coast Guard, an individual who arranges for passenger travel by plane, bus, train, or ship; prepares transportation requests and shipping documents; and serves as a military airplane flight attendant. *See also* the *Military Careers* guide.

transportation ticket agent An individual who sells tickets, answers inquiries, and checks baggage at transportation facilities such as airports, bus terminals, and train stations. *See also* the OOH.

trapper An individual who uses bait, traps, snares, cages, or nets to catch animals and birds. *See also* the OOH.

travel accommodations rater An individual who inspects hotels, motels, restaurants, campgrounds, and vacation resorts to evaluate travel and tourist accommodations for travel guide publishers and automobile clubs.

travel agent An individual who makes arrangements for transportation, hotels, and car rentals and provides information and advice to people traveling for business or pleasure. *See also* the OOH.

travel clerk An individual who works for an automobile club, hotel, business firm, or government agency and plans trips, offers travel suggestions, provides literature, makes reservations, and arranges for visas. *See also* the OOH.

treasurer An individual whose duties may include preparing financial reports, overseeing the financial management department, and developing economic policy. *See also* the OOH.

treatment plant operator, water and wastewater An individual who operates equipment used to process water and wastewater to render it harmless and reusable.

tree trimmer An individual who works in the logging industry and uses saws or pruning shears to prune treetops and branches.

trick In the United States Postal Service, an employee's scheduled duty hours during a workday or workweek.

trouble locator **1)** An individual who operates a testboard to determine the source of telephone problems. **2)** An individual who makes sure that a cable television subscriber's television set receives the proper signal.

troubleshoot To find and solve problems that are cause difficulties.

troubleshooter An individual who tries to identify and solve problems.

truck driver An individual who transports a variety of items by truck and while on the road is responsible for the routine maintenance of the truck. *See also* **run, sleeper run,** and **turnarounds.**

truck driver (military) In the Army, Navy, Air Force, Marine Corps, or Coast Guard, an individual who drives vehicles over all types of roads, traveling alone or in convoys; reads travel instruction to determine travel routes, arrival dates, and types of cargo; and makes sure that vehicles are loaded properly. *See also* the *Military Careers* guide and **truck driver.**

truck mechanic *See* **diesel mechanic.**

trucker *See* **truck driver.**

trust officer *See* **financial manager.**

tuition The required fee for a college course.

tuition reimbursement A benefit provided by some employers to employees who are taking college courses in addition to working. After the successful completion of the course, the employee is repaid the tuition expense.

tuition repayment *See* **tuition reimbursement.**

tumbling barrel painter An individual who deposits articles of porous materials in a barrel of paint, varnish, or other coating and then rotates the barrel to ensure thorough coverage.

tune-up mechanic An individual who adjusts ignition timing and valves, and adjusts or replaces spark plugs and other parts in motor vehicles to ensure efficient engine performance.

tuner, musical instruments An individual who adjusts the pitch on musical instruments. *See also* the OOH.

turnaround A short trip by a truck driver, usually to a nearby city to pick up a loaded trailer and drive it back to the home base the same day.

turnaround time The time needed to repair something or to complete an operation. *Example:* a mechanic who estimates a turnaround time of two days after a car is taken to the shop.

turnover rate The percentage of workers who must be replaced in a particular business, industry, or organization in a specific period of time.

tutor An individual who helps older children or adults with homework or assists them in learning a language or a specific subject.

TV repairer *See* **electronic home entertainment equipment repairer.**

201 file *See* **Official Personnel Folder.**

typesetter An individual who may use one or more of the various methods of setting type for printing. *See also* the OOH.

typist An individual who uses a typewriter to produce letters, reports, and memorandums. *See also* the OOH.

♦Uu♦

UAW An abbreviation of *United Auto Workers. See* **United Auto Workers.**

ultrasound technologist *See* **sonographer.**

unacceptable performance The actions of an employee that fail to meet established performance standards in one or more elements of the employee's position.

unassembled examination *See* **examination, unassembled.**

unauthorized alien *See* **undocumented alien.**

underemployment A situation in which an applicant considers or accepts a job whose requirements are less than the applicant's skills or education.

underground economy The practice of paying workers with wages that are not recorded in a company's accounting records. Income and Social Security taxes are not deducted from these wages, and they are not declared for tax purposes. *See also* **off-the-books** and **black economy.**

understaffed The condition of not having enough employees to accomplish required tasks.

underwriter An individual who works for an insurance company and whose responsibilities may include appraising and selecting the risks the company will insure and analyzing information in insurance applications, medical reports, and actuarial studies. *See also* the OOH.

undocumented alien An individual who does not have the proper documents or permission to work in the U.S. *See also* **employment eligibility documents.**

unemployed Without a job.

unemployment compensation **1)** The sums of money paid to workers who are unemployed, file a claim for unemployment compensation at a local unemployment office, and have worked long enough and earned enough to qualify. The amounts received and the number of weeks during which compensation is paid vary from state to state. **2)** In the Federal civil service system, income maintenance payments to former Federal employees who are unemployed, file a claim at a local employment office for unemployment compensation, and register for work assignment.

unemployment insurance The program that provides payments, under certain conditions, to unemployed workers. *See also* **unemployment compensation.**

unemployment rate A monthly Federal Government statistic that indicates the number of people who sought jobs but were unable to find employment.

unfair labor practices Management or labor organization actions prohibited by law.

unfunded plans Pension plans that rely on income to pay pension benefits instead of having sums of money invested for this purpose.

uniform allowance Additional money paid to an employee in a uniformed service for the purpose of purchasing or maintaining work uniforms. *Example:* a police officer or firefighter given a sum of money each year for the purchase or maintenance of a uniform.

uniformed military services A collective term for the Armed Forces----Army, Navy, Air Force, and Marine Corps.

union An organization of individuals employed in the same industry or in similar jobs, which is formed to improve salaries, working conditions, and benefits for its members.

union apprenticeship programs Apprentice training sponsored by various trade unions, usually in the construction trades. *See also* **apprentice, apprenticeship,** and **journeyman.**

union hiring hall Provided by a union, an assembly room where members report early in the morning and signify their readiness to work at their trade if jobs are available. *See also* **business agent.**

union scale The wages an employer is required to pay according to a union contract.

union shop A business that operates under a trade union contract which requires that new employees join the union within a specified period of time. *See also* **closed shop.**

United Auto Workers (UAW) The labor organization that represents the majority of the workers who produce motor vehicles.

United States Civil Service Commission An agency that has been replaced by the Office of Personnel Management and the Merit Systems Protection Board. *See* **Office of Personnel Management** and **Merit Systems Protection Board.**

United States Employment Service A Federal agency that provides employment information and assistance and operates in coordination with state employment services. *See also* **state employment service.**

United States Government Manual Published annually, this official handbook of the United States Government lists the principal officials and provides useful information about the agencies in the legislative, judicial, and executive branches. For each agency, this manual gives a brief statement concerning the purpose of the agency, its major programs and activities, and its history. Some of the agencies whose work relates to occupations are identified in this book. *See* the names of individual agencies.

United States Postal Service Established July 1, 1971, the successor to the Post Office Department and now an independent agency within the executive branch.

United States service academies (military) *See* **service academies (military).**

university faculty A group of individuals who teach and advise students in colleges and universities. *See also* the OOH.

unmotivated Lacking the will or desire to take some action. *Example:* A job applicant who is so unmotivated that the interviewer did not even consider the individual for the vacancy. *See also* **motivated.**

unskilled jobs Jobs that require little or no education or training.

unwritten exam *Informal:* an indication that an applicant for a Federal Government job has not been required to take an examination for the job. Instead, after a review of the applicant's education and qualifications, the individual is given a rating and placed on a register.

upholsterer An individual who makes new furniture or reconditions or restores old furniture, which may require operations such as stripping furniture down to its frame and installing webbing, springs, padding, and new covering material. *See also* the OOH.

upwardly mobile The ability and interest of individuals in moving up the social scale by living better; trying new sports or activities; and associating with people with more money, prestige, and status.

urban geographer An individual who studies cities.

urban/regional planner An individual who devises comprehensive plans for industrial and public sites and develops programs for the use of land for the revitalization of cities or regions. *See also* the OOH.

used car salesman An individual who works for a car dealer and sells previously owned cars and trucks.

user friendly A term which originally meant that a computer program had been produced to be as easy and helpful as possible to the user. The term has now been extended to any program or device that is easy to use or displays a manufacturer's consideration of users' needs.

usher An individual who collects admission tickets at theaters or sporting events. Ushers may also hand out programs or help people find their seats.

utilities customer service representative An individual who works for a utility company and interviews applicants for water, gas, electric, or telephone service.

utilities meter reader An individual who works for a utility company and reads electric, gas, water, or steam meters and records the volume used by customers.

utilities operations manager An individual who plans, organizes, directs, controls, or coordinates management activities for a utility supplying gas, electricity, or water.

utility A company that provides public services, such as telephone, gas, water, or electricity.

utility carrier In the United States Postal Service, a full-time city delivery letter carrier who replaces scheduled absences within a group of routes.

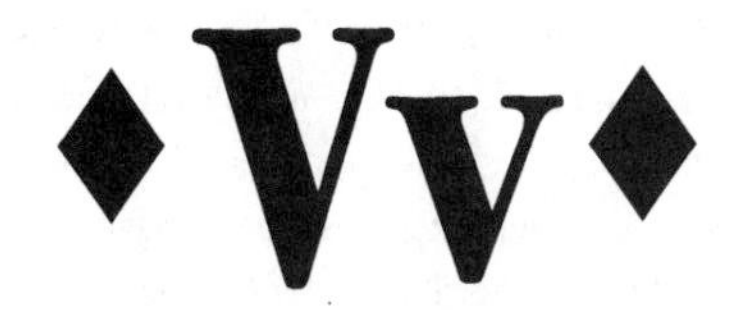

VA An abbreviation of Veterans Administration, a name still commonly used even though the Veterans Administration was changed to the Department of Veterans Affairs in 1989.

VA compensation *See* **Veterans Administration compensation.**

VA pension *See* **Veterans Administration pension.**

vacancy **1)** The state of being vacant or empty. **2)** An available job.

vacancy announcement A notice that a job is available. When a vacancy is announced for a job with the Federal Government, the vacancy announcement usually includes the job title, grade, closing date for application, location of job, area of consideration, duties, and qualifications.

vacation pay Wages paid to a worker for the time the individual is on vacation.

VCR repairer *See* **electronic home entertainment equipment repairer.**

Vehicle and Machinery Mechanic Occupations (military) One of the twelve broad categories used by the Armed Forces to group occupations for enlisted personnel.

vehicle washer An individual who cleans automobiles, buses, or trucks.

vending machine servicer and repairer An individual who installs, services, and stocks vending machines that dispense food and beverages. *See also* the OOH.

vendoring out The practice of having an outside vendor provide services that were formerly done by employees within the business. *Example:* having an outside company take care of the payroll.

venture capitalist An individual who has money and is willing to invest in new businesses.

verify To confirm, prove, or substantiate that something is true or correct.

vertical move A career change that is a move up the career ladder to a job with more money, responsibility, and status. *See also* **horizontal move.**

vestibule school A type of training facility in which shop conditions are duplicated for trainees before putting them on the shop floor.

vesting accumulating enough work time so that an employee is eligible for a pension at some future time.

veteran An individual who was separated from active duty in the Armed Forces with an honorable discharge or under honorable conditions.

Veterans Administration (VA) The former name for the U.S. Department of Veterans Affairs. *See* **Department of Veterans Affairs.**

Veterans Administration compensation Money paid by the Department of Veterans Affairs for service-connected disability of ten percent or more.

Veterans Administration pension Money paid by the Department of Veterans Affairs for disability that is not necessarily service connected.

veterans employment representative An individual at a state employment service center who works with veterans who are entitled to priority assistance.

veterans preference In the Federal civil service system, the right to special advantage in connection with appointments or separation based on a person's discharge under honorable conditions from the Armed Forces or for a service-connected disability, or for certain relatives of veterans. *See also* **preference, compensable disability; preference, 30 percent or more disabled; preference, disability; preference, mother; preference, wife; preference, tentative; preference, veteran;** and **preference, widow or widower.**

veterinarian An individual who diagnoses medical problems, prescribes and administers medicines, and performs surgery on animals. *See also* the OOH.

veterinarian (military) An Army or Air Force officer who inspects food to determine its condition and quality; plans measures to control contagious diseases that may be transmitted by food or animals; and treats sick or injured military guard dogs, horses, and other animals. *See also* the *Military Careers* guide.

veterinary assistant An individual who assists a veterinarian by feeding and bathing animals and administering prescribed medications. *See also* the OOH.

veterinary technician An individual who assists a veterinarian by keeping records, taking specimens, performing laboratory tests, and dressing wounds. *See also* the OOH.

vice president *See* **general manager/top executive.**

video-control engineer An individual who works for a television studio and regulates the quality, brightness, and contrast of television pictures. *See also* **broadcast technician, recording engineer, transmission engineer,** and **broadcast field supervisor.**

visibility **1)** The ability to be seen. **2)** In a career, the state of being noticed, obvious, or prominent, which can become a career asset. *Example:* a new public relations job that gives the worker a lot of good visibility.

visual artist An individual who uses artistic talent and various techniques and materials to communicate ideas or feelings. *See also* the OOH, **graphic artist, fine artist, cartoonist, animator, sculptor,** and **commercial artist.**

vita A written description of important information about a person. In the employment field, this term has largely been replaced by resume. *See also* **resume.**

vo-tech *See* **vocational-technical high schools.**

vocational counselor *See* **counselor.**

vocational education Educational courses that train people to enter specific trades or occupations, such as mechanic or cosmetologist.

vocational education teacher An individual who teaches in a vocational school that prepares students for occupations not requiring a college education, such as welding, dental assisting, and cosmetology. *See also* the OOH.

vocational exploration A program designed to

expose participants to the operations and types of jobs available in private industry. Exploration experiences may include observation, instruction, practical experience, and shadowing. *See also* **shadowing.**

vocational guidance The process of helping individuals choose a suitable career, prepare for it, and search for a specific job.

vocational nurse, licensed *See* **licensed practical nurse.**

vocational rehabilitation counselor *See* **counselor.**

vocational-technical high schools Secondary schools that prepare students for skilled trades jobs. Similar education is available through private technical and vocational schools.

vocational training *See* **vocational education.**

volunteer service Work without payment for some worthwhile project or program.

voucher In the Federal civil service system, a formal inquiry to employers, references, professors, and others who presumably know a job applicant well enough to describe the individual's job qualifications and personal character.

VP An abbreviation of *vice president.*

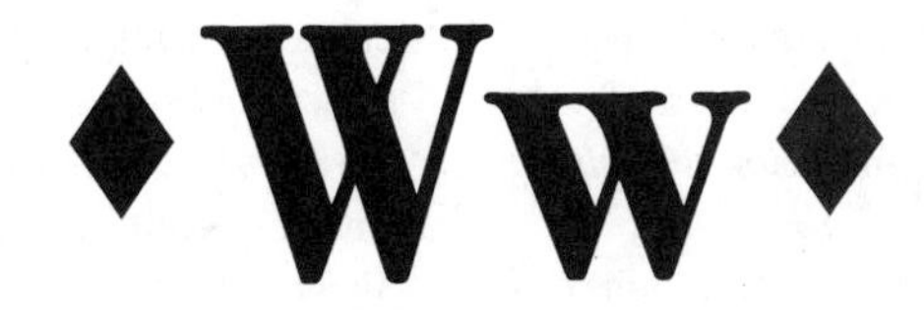

W-2 wage and tax statement The form issued yearly by an employer to show the employee's earnings and the amount of income taxes and FICA withheld. *See also* **FICA.**

wage area In the Federal civil service system, a geographical area defined by the Office of Personnel Management within which a single set of wage schedules is applied uniformly by Federal installations to the occupations covered by the Federal Wage System.

wage earner An individual who works for wages.

wage employees In the Federal civil service system, those employees in trades, crafts, or labor occupations covered by the Federal Wage System and whose pay is fixed and adjusted periodically in accordance with prevailing rates. *See also* **Federal Wage System.**

wage grade system The pay scale established by the Federal Government for blue-collar workers. The range is from the entry-level WG-1 (trainee) to WG-9 to WG-12 for a journeyman.

wage-hour compliance inspector An individual who inspects employers' time, payroll, and personnel records to ensure compliance with Federal laws on such matters as minimum wages, overtime, pay, and employment of minors.

wage indexation system A system that ties wages to some index which causes automatic adjustments in wages as the index changes. *See also* **cost-of-living index** and **cost-of-living adjustments/allowance.**

wage-price freeze Government regulations that limit increases in both wages and prices for a particular period of time, usually in an effort to control inflation.

wage restraint Pressure or efforts to limit wage increases.

wage scale The different or graduated rates paid to employees in a business or factory.

wage statement A form that accompanies an employee's pay and generally shows the hours worked, rates paid, gross and net wages, and deductions.

wage worker *See* **wage earner.**

wages Usually compensation to a blue-collar worker who is paid hourly or daily. *Salary* is usually used for compensation to white-collar workers.

wait staff The group of individuals in a restaurant, such as waiters and waitresses, who serve or "wait on" the customers.

waiter/waitress An individual who takes a customer's order, serves food and beverages, prepares checks, and sometimes accepts payment. *See also* the OOH.

walkout A strike that may or may not be authorized by the union.

Wall Street A collective term for the financial services businesses and brokerage houses. The term originated from the fact that many years ago most of these businesses began operations in the area around Wall Street in New York City.

Wall Street Journal A publication that specializes in news about business and finance, and whose classified ad section is used by individuals and businesses for employment ads relating to jobs in those fields. *See also* ***National Business Employment Weekly.***

want ads Advertisements that appear in the classified ads section of a newspaper or magazine and give information about available jobs. Some ads give information about the job requirements, salary, and duties, while other ads list only things like the job title and a box number for a response. *See also* **blind ad, situations wanted ad,** and **help wanted ad.**

ward attendant *See* **psychiatric aide.**

warden An individual who oversees the day-to-day operations of a correctional institution, such as a prison.

warehouse clerk *See* **stock clerk.**

warehousing manager (military) *See* **supply/warehousing manager.**

WARN An acronym for *W*orker *R*eadjustment *a*nd *R*etraining *N*otification Act. *See* **Worker Readjustment and Retraining Notification Act.**

washer, vehicle An individual who cleans motor vehicles.

wastewater treatment plant operator *See* **water** and **wastewater treatment plant operator.**

watchmaker An individual who repairs, cleans, and adjusts watches and clocks.

water and sewage treatment plant operator (military) In the Army, Navy, Air Force, Marine Corps, or Coast Guard, an individual who operates pumps to transfer water from reservoirs and storage tanks to treatment plants; adds chemicals and operates machinery that purifies water for drinking or cleans it for safe disposal; and tests water for chlorine content, acidity, oxygen demand, and impurities. *See also* the *Military Careers* guide.

water and wastewater treatment plant operator An individual who operates equipment that treats water to make it safe to drink or treats wastewater to remove harmful pollution. *See also* the *Military Careers* guide.

water transportation occupations *See* **captain, marine engineer, deckhand, master,** and **marine oiler.**

weakness Inadequacy, frailty, or a lack of strength or firmness. *Example:* an employer who considers indecisiveness a serious weakness.

weather observer (military) In the Army, Navy, Air Force, Marine Corps, or Coast Guard, an individual who launches weather balloons to record wind speed and direction, identifies the types of clouds present and estimates cloud height and the amount of cloud cover, and forecasts weather based on readings and observations. *See also* the *Military Careers* guide.

weathercaster An individual who broadcasts weather information for a radio or television station.

weatherman *See* **weathercaster.**

weekend pay Wages paid over and above the regular rate as compensation for working on Saturday or Sunday.

weigher An individual who weighs materials, supplies, or equipment for the purpose of keeping necessary records.

welder (military) In the Army, Navy, Air Force, Marine Corps, or Coast Guard, an individual who welds, brazes, or solders metal parts together; forges and repairs small items and tools; and operates automatic welding machines to connect metal parts. *See also* the *Military Careers* guide.

welder, cutter, and welding machine operator An individual who joins metal parts. The work is done by a skilled craftsman using welding equipment or by the use of welding machines. *See also* the OOH.

welding machine operator *See* **welder, cutter, and welding machine operator.**

welfare eligibility worker and interviewer An individual who determines who can receive welfare or other types of assistance. *See also* the OOH and **social worker.**

welfare fund/plan An employee benefit program to which an employer typically contributes a set amount of money for each employee. Trustees for the fund decide how the money will be dispensed for the benefit of the members. Money that goes into a welfare fund is not taxed to the employee and can be used for such items as dental, optical, disability, or accidental death and dismemberment insurance, or for payment of the health insurance deductible.

well driller (military) In the Army or Navy, an individual who selects drilling sites, erects and positions derricks, and uses drilling rigs to drill wells. *See also* the *Military Careers* guide.

wellness programs Activities provided by employers to benefit the health and fitness of their employees. Programs might include gym facilities, blood pressure or cholesterol testing, health fairs, and smoking clinics.

WG An abbreviation of *wage grade* system. *See* **wage grade system.**

whistle blower *Informal:* a present or former employee who discloses information that the individual reasonably believes is evidence of a violation of a law, rule, or regulation; mismanagement; a waste of funds; an abuse of authority; or a danger to public health or safety.

white-collar worker *Informal:* a person whose job is clerical or managerial and is done in an office instead of a factory. *See also* **blue-collar worker, pink-collar worker,** and **cloth cap.**

white knight *Informal:* an individual or a company that comes to the aid of another company threatened by a leveraged buyout. The white knight usually offers better financial arrangements or nonfinancial incentives to the company to be acquired. *See also* **hostile takeover** and **friendly takeover.**

wholesale and retail buyer An individual who buys various types of merchandise to resell. Wholesale buyers purchase goods directly from the manufacturer or other wholesale firms for resale to retail firms, commercial establishments, and institutions. Retail buyers purchase goods from wholesale firms or directly from the manufacturer for resale to the public. See also the OOH.

wholesale bakery driver-sales worker An individual who delivers and arranges bread, cakes, rolls, and other baked goods on display racks in grocery stores; estimates the amount and variety of baked goods that will be sold; and solicits new business.

wholesale sales representative An individual who visits prospective buyers, shows samples or catalogs, and tries to persuade the prospects to order items being offered for sale. *See also* the OOH.

wildcat strike A strike not sanctioned by a union and which may violate a collective bargaining agreement. *See also* **strike, quickie strike,** and **slowdown.**

winch operator *See* **hoist** and **winch operator.**

window A term used by the employees of some companies, such as IBM, for special retirement plans or incentives that are available for a limited time.

within-grade denial In the Federal civil service system, an agency decision that an employee's performance is not of an acceptable level of competence and, therefore, that the employee will not be granted a within-grade salary increase.

within-grade increase In the Federal civil service system, a periodic increase in an employee's rate of basic pay by advancement from one step of the individual's grade to the next after the employee meets requirements for length of service and performance.

without compensation In the Federal civil service system and under certain circumstances, an agency may be authorized to appoint an employee to provide services to the Government without pay.

wood machine operator An individual who cuts logs into planks, timbers, or boards; cuts veneer sheets; or makes furniture parts such as legs, drawers, and rails. *See also* the OOH.

wood machinist An individual who works with

other skilled woodworkers to produce customized, one-of-a-kind items.

woodworker, precision An individual who cuts, shapes, and assembles complex wood parts into a finished product.

woodworking occupations *See* **cabinetmaker; wood machinist; furniture and wood finisher; wood machine operator;** and **woodworker, precision.**

word processing The use of word processing equipment to record, manipulate, and transcribe data.

word processing machine operator *See* **word processor.**

word processor An individual who uses word processing equipment to record, edit, store, and revise text information for reports and correspondence. *See also* the OOH.

work environment The surroundings, atmosphere, influences, and conditions that affect an employee's workplace.

work ethic A collective term for the values that encourage a worker to be responsible, reliable, honest, industrious, ambitious, and thrifty.

work experience A collective term for all of the jobs----either paid or unpaid----that an individual has had which might qualify the person for a new job.

work-family issues The factors involving a worker's family life that affect the workplace and may become issues in the collective bargaining process. Examples: maternity leave, parental leave, employee assistance programs, and child care. *See also* **maternity leave, parental leave, employee assistance program,** and **child care.**

work force **1)** All of the workers who are available for a particular project. **2)** The total number of workers available for employment throughout the nation.

work force reduction The elimination of jobs. *See also* **downsizing** and **reduction in force.**

work order A written instruction that may accompany a job.

work programs Plans that provide jobs for students so that they can work part-time while completing their education. Work programs are usually sponsored by the Federal Government or educational institutions.

work satisfaction A sense of fulfillment, contentment, or pleasure an employee feels about the work the person is doing.

work schedule In the Federal civil service system, the time basis on which an employee is paid. A work schedule may be full-time, part-time, or intermittent.

work-study program **1)** In the Federal civil service system, a program in which a student alternates periods of education and Federal employment under terms of an agreement between the individual's school and a Government agency. Co-op agreements normally provide for the student's permanent employment in the agency on satisfactory completion of the education and work assignments required by the agreement. **2)** A program for students that permits them to alternate formal study with employment to gain practical experience.

work-to-rule A tactic used by workers to try to persuade employers to yield to some demand. In work-to-rule, the employees do only those duties that are required by contract, rules, and regulations. *Example:* teachers who go home at the time specified in their contract instead of staying to help students, attend committee meetings, or work with colleagues.

workaholic *Informal:* an individual who appears to get pleasure from working and spends an excessive amount of time at the person's place of work.

Worker Readjustment and Retraining Notification Act (WARN) A law that requires larger businesses to provide a 60-day advance notice to employees if a plant is to be closed or mass layoffs are planned. *See* **mass layoff.**

workers' compensation programs *See* **workmen's compensation.**

workhorse *Informal:* an individual who works unusually hard, especially at some difficult task.

working capital The money available to a business to carry on its operations.

working class The group of individuals whose income is from wages rather than from investments or the ownership of a business.

ments or the ownership of a business.

working conditions The circumstances or situations that make up the surroundings for a worker. Collective bargaining agreements and Government regulations affect the working conditions in many industries. *Example:* inspectors from OSHA finding in a factory a number of health and safety violations that were having an impact on the working conditions.

working papers Forms that must be filed by job seekers who are under 18 years of age. Working papers are in most cases required to avoid violation of child labor laws.

working relationships The involvement or association of people as they work together. In a good working relationship, people understand each other, respect each other's abilities, and enjoy working together.

workingman An individual who works for wages rather than a salary.

workload The amount of work an employee is expected to complete in a given period of time.

workman An individual who does some type of labor.

workmanlike The quality of being well done by a skilled worker.

workmanship The quality of work produced by a skilled worker.

workmen's compensation An insurance plan that provides compensation for workers injured on the job or to their families if the worker is killed in a job-related accident. The preferred nonsexist term is *workers' compensation*.

workplace The office, factory, or institution where an individual works.

workroom A place where work is done, especially the work of fashion designers, apparel manufacturers, and jewelry repairers.

workshop **1)** A room where work is done----especially mechanical work. **2)** A meeting of a group of individuals for the purpose of learning about and discussing some problem, situation, or new idea.

workstation The specific place where an employee works. *Examples:* a desk, counter, or workbench.

worktable A table, usually with drawers for tools and materials, that is used for some kind of work.

workweek The number of days or hours normally worked per week.

writ An official order from a governmental unit which specifies that an individual should do or refrain from doing some specific act.

writer An individual who produces original fiction or nonfiction for books, magazines, newspapers, radio, or TV. *See also* the OOH, **editor,** and **columnist.**

writer, technical An individual who writes about scientific and technical subjects.

X-ray technician An individual who takes X-rays of various parts of the body for use in diagnosing medical problems. *See also* the OOH.

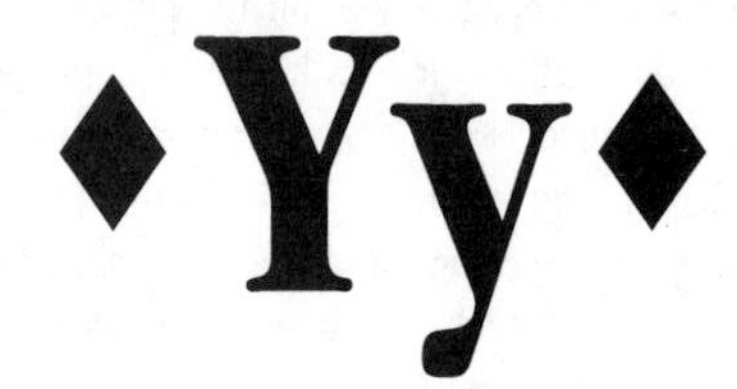

yard clerk *See* **stock clerk.**

yard conductor *See* **road conductor.**

Yellow Pages The section of the phone book that lists companies according to the type of service or product they offer. This section can be useful to job seekers interested in employment in a particular type of business. *Example:* a waitress who uses the Restaurants heading in the *Yellow Pages* to phone restaurants to inquire about any openings.

young adult librarian An individual who helps junior and senior high school students select and use books and other materials, organizes programs of interest to young adults, and coordinates the library's work with school programs.

youth labor force Workers from age 16 through age 24.

yuppies *Informal:* young, upwardly mobile, urban professionals. This group resulted from the baby boom generation. With large disposable incomes, yuppies became an important economic factor during the 1980s. *See also* **baby boomers.**

♦Zz♦

zoning enforcement officer An individual who enforces the zoning rules and regulations of a governmental unit. *Example:* a builder who is told that zoning regulations prevent him from constructing an office building in a residential neighborhood.

zookeeper An individual who feeds and cares for animals in zoos.

zoologist An individual who studies the origin, behavior, diseases, and life processes of animals.

Works Consulted

America's Federal Jobs. Indianapolis: JIST Works, Inc., 1991.

U.S. Department of Defense. *Military Career Guide*. Washington, D.C: U.S. Department of Defense, 1989.

_______. *Military Careers: A Guide to Military Occupations and Selected Military Career Paths 1992-1994*. Washington, D.C.: U.S. Government Printing Office, 1992.

U.S. Department of Labor. *Dictionary of Occupational Titles*. Fourth Edition. Washington, D.C.: U.S. Government Printing Office, 1991.

_______. *Occupational Outlook Handbook*. 1988-89 Edition. Washington, D.C.: U.S. Government Printing Office, 1988.

_______. *Occupational Outlook Handbook*. 1990-91 Edition. Washington, D.C.: U.S. Government Printing Office, 1990.

_______. *Occupational Outlook Handbook*. 1992-93 Edition. Washington, D.C.: U.S. Government Printing Office, 1992.

U.S. Government Manual. 1991-92 Edition. Lanham, MD: Bernan Press, 1991.

U.S. Office of Personnel Management. *Federal Personnel Manual Supplement 296-33*. Washington, D.C.: U.S. Office of Personnel Management, 1992.

U.S. Postal Service. *Glossary of Postal Terms*. Washington, D.C.: U.S. Postal Service, 1988.

Overview of Categories and Occupations in the Index of Occupational Terms

This overview section lists in alphabetical order all the categories and occupations in the following Index of Occupational Terms. Included are listings that are cross-referenced to direct you to the headings of lists of related terms defined in the *Dictionary*. Suppose that you want to look up job-related terms for the Air Travel industry. For "Air Travel," this section refers you to the heading "Transportation." When you look up this heading in the following Index of Occupational Term, you see in the list some terms related to air travel. These are the terms to look up in the *Dictionary*.

Q

R

S

T

U

V

W

Index of Occupational Terms Grouped by Occupation or Category

This extensive index groups *Dictionary* entries under major categories or occupations so that you may find related terms quickly. For example, if you are interested in terms related to "Banking," this index refers you to the index heading "Finance/Financial Services/Banking," where you find a list of *Dictionary* terms related to the topic. Similar lists for such headings as "Automotive," "Books/Publications," and "Business" are provided throughtout the index.

(EEOC) *See* at location.
Federal student aid programs *See* ***Student Guide to Federal Financial Aid Programs.***
Handbook of Accredited Private Trade and Technical Schools *See* at location.
Handbook of Occupational Groups and Series *See* at location.
Handbook X-118 *See* at location
Handbook X-118C *See* at location.
Hispanic worker *See* at location.
Job Grading System for Trades and Labor Occupations *See* at location.
Job Opportunities for the Blind Program *See* **minorities,** *Blind.*
National Apprenticeship Program and Apprenticeship Information *See* at location.
minorities *See* at location.
National Association for Hispanic Elderly *See* **Hispanic worker** and **minorities,** *Older workers.*
National Association for the Advancement of Colored People (NAACP) *See* **minorities,** *Minorities.*
National Association of Older Workers Employment Services *See* **minorities,** *Older workers.*
National Caucus/Center on Black Aged, Inc. *See* **minorities,** *Older workers.*
National Council on the Aging *See* **minorities,** *Older workers.*
National Home Study Council *See* at location.
National Urban League, Employment Dept. *See* **minorities,** *Minorities.*
National Urban League, Washington Operations *See* **minorities,** *Minorities.*
President's Committee on Employment of People with Disabilities *See* **minorities,** *Disabled*, and at location.
Student Guide to Federal Financial Aid Programs *See* at location.
U.S. Department of labor, Women's Bureau *See* **minorities,** *Women.*
Wider Opportunities for Women *See* **minorities,** *Women.*
women *See* **minorities,** *Women.*

Administrative/Management

account executive
ad hoc arbitrator
administrative assistant
administrative secretary
administrative services manager
administrative support specialist (military)
administrative workweek
administratively uncontrolled overtime (AUO)
administrator, education
administrator, health services
advertising manager
agency
air traffic control manager (military)
apartment manager
arbitration
arbitrator
art director
assistant
assistant principal
athletic director
attache (military)
bank manager
banquet chef
binding award
blue-collar worker supervisor
board of directors
board of governors
brainstorming
chief executive, government
chief executive officer (CEO)
city manager
city planner
clerical supervisor/manager
collective bargaining
collective bargaining agreement
communications manager (military)
compensation manager
conciliation
conciliator
conciliator, labor relations
construction manager
consultant, management
contract
convention services manager
credit manager
data processing manager
director
director of admissions
director of student services
director, religious education and activities
education administrator

education and training manager
emergency management officer (military)
employee-benefits and welfare manager
engineering manager
executive
executive chef
farm manager
federal labor relations authority
federal mediation and conciliation service
financial manager
financial manager (military)
first-line supervisor
food and beverage manager
food service manager
food service manager (military)
foreman/forewoman
front office manager
funeral director
general manager/top executive
government chief executive and legislator
grievance
grievance interview
grievance procedure
health services administrator (military)
health services manager
historic site director
hospital administrator
hotel manager/assistant
impasse procedures
industrial production manager
industrial relations
interviewer
job enrichment
job evaluation
job fair
job freeze
job interview
job opening
job performance
job rotation
labor-management relations
labor relations
labor relations manager
law enforcement director (military)
lockout
loss prevention manager
maintenance administrator
maintenance manager (military)
mall manager
manage
management
management analyst (military)
management analyst/consultant
management consultant
management dietician
management effectiveness
management official
management rights
management trainee
manager
managerial
mapping manager
marketing manager
mediation
mediator
medical records administrator
middle manager
National Labor Relations Board (NLRB)
negotiability
negotiated agreement
negotiated contract
negotiated grievance procedure
negotiations
nursing home administrator
office manager
permanent arbitrator
personnel management
personnel manager
personnel manager (military)
president, corporate and other organizations
Presidential Management Intern Program
presiding official
property and real estate manager
public relations manager
purchasing agent and manager
purchasing/contracting manager (military)
range manager
real estate manager
recruiting manager (military)
registrar
resident manager
restaurant and food service manager
sales manager
science manager
securities director
Senior Executive Service
senior level positions
senior management

shared decision making
store manager
supervisor
supply/warehousing manager (military)
surveying and mapping manager (military)
top executive
top management
total quality management
training manager
transportation/maintenance manager (military)
transportation manager
transportation manager (military)
trust officer
unfair labor practices
vice president
warehousing manager (military)

Advertising
Advertising clerk
advertising copywriter
advertising manager
art director

Agriculture/Forestry/Animal Breeding
agribusiness
agricultural commodity grader
agricultural commodity inspector
agricultural equipment mechanic
agricultural quarantine inspector
agricultural scientist
agricultural technician
agronomist
animal breeder
animal scientist
apiculturist
conservation scientist
conservationist
dairy scientist
farm and home management advisor
farm equipment mechanic
farm labor contractor
farm manager
farm operator
farm worker
forest and conservation worker
forester
horticulturist
migrant worker
plant breeder
poultry scientist
range conservationist
range ecologist
range manager
range scientist
soil conservationist
soil scientist
tenant farmer

Air Travel *See* **Transportation.**

Aircraft/Airplane-related
aeronautical drafter
air crew member (military)
Air Force Reserve (military)
Air National Guard (military)
air safety inspector
air traffic control manager (military)
air traffic controller
air traffic controller (military)
aircraft electrician (military)
aircraft launch and recovery specialist (military)
aircraft mechanic (military)
aircraft mechanic and engine specialist
aircraft pilot
aircraft technician
airplane navigator (military)
airplane pilot (military)
avionics technician
controller, air traffic
flight engineer
flight engineer (military)
flight instructor
flight operations specialist (military)
helicopter pilot
helicopter pilot (military)
pilot, aircraft
test pilot

Airplanes *See* **Aircraft/Airplane-related.**

Animals
animal attendant
animal breeder
animal caretaker, except farm
animal control officer
animal health technician
animal scientist
animal technician
animal trainer
dog catcher

dog control officer
dog warden
euthanasia technician
harnessmaker
laboratory animal technician
laboratory animal technologist
pet store caretaker
taxidermist
veterinarian
veterinarian (military)
veterinary assistant
veterinary technician
zookeeper

Apparel
apparel worker
custom tailor
cutter, apparel
dressmaker
fashion designer
garment sewing machine operator
garment worker
hand cutter
hand presser
hand sewer
hand trimmer
layout worker, apparel
leather worker
marker, apparel
patternmaker, apparel
pressing machine operator, apparel
seamstress
sewer and sewing machine operator, apparel
shoe and leather worker
shoe sewing machine operator and tender
tailor
textile designer

Artists----Visual/Performing
actor
airbrush artist
animator
art director
artisan
artist
caricaturist
cartoonist
choreographer
commercial artist
dancer
designer
editorial artist
fashion artist/illustrator
fashion designer
fine artist
floral designer
graphic artist
graphic designer
graphic designer and illustrator (military)
illustrator
industrial designer
interior designer
medical illustrator
package designer
painter, visual artist
printmaker
producer
scientific illustrator
sculptor
set designer
silversmith
textile designer
theatrical design
visual artist

Automotive
air-conditioning mechanic, automotive
auto body repairer
auto mechanic
automobile mechanic (military)
automotive air-conditioning mechanic
automotive body repairer
automotive body repairer (military)
automotive mechanic
automotive painter
automotive-radiator mechanic
automotive service technician
front-end mechanic
motor vehicle body repairer
motor vehicle inspector
motor vehicle repairer
parts manager
tire repairer/changer
tow truck operator
truck mechanic
tune-up mechanic

B

Banking *See* **Finance/Financial**

Services.

Benefits
accidental death and dismemberment
benefit
break
cafeteria plan
childcare
coffee break
coinsurance
commissary/exchange (military store) privilege
community resources
company car
contributory plan
co-pay
copayment
credit union
cross placement
death benefit
disability benefits
disabled veteran
discount
Employee Assistance Program (EAP)
employee benefits
employee benefits and welfare manager
employee development
employment benefits (military)
enlistment agreement/enlistment contract
entitlement
flexible benefits plan
flexible spending account
flexible workplace employment
flexitime
flextime
fringe benefits
gain-sharing plan
merchandise discount
noncontributory plan
nonmonetary perks
parental leave
perk
reduced benefits, Social Security
reimbursement account
retirement incentive plans
self-insured
service computation date-leave
severance arrangements
severance pay
shared decision making
sick days
skills enhancement program
Social Security benefits
Social Security death benefit
Social Security disability benefit
Social Security reduced benefits
Social Security survivors benefits
supplemental benefits
Supplemental Security Income (SSI)
trade adjustment assistance
tuition reimbursement
tuition repayment
welfare fund/plan
wellness programs

Beverages *See* **Food/Beverage.**

Binding *See* **Printing/Binding.**

Books/Publications
Civil Service Commission Classifications Standards
Civil Service Commission Handbook X-118
Dictionary of Occupational Titles (DOT)
Directory of Accredited Home Study Schools
Directory of Educational Institutions
Dress for Success
Encyclopedia of Associations
Federal Personnel Manual (FPM)
Federal Personnel Manual Bulletin
Federal Personnel Manual Letter
Federal Personnel Manual Supplements
Handbook of Accredited Private Trade and Technical Schools
Handbook of Occupational Groups and Series
Handbook X-118
Handbook X-118C
Job Bank series
Job Grading System for Trades and Labor Occupations
Military Career Guide, 1989
Military Careers: A Guide to Military Occupations and Selected Military Career Paths, 1992-1994
National Apprenticeship Program and Apprenticeship Information
National Business Employment Weekly
Occupational Outlook Handbook (OOH)
One Hundred Best Companies to Work for in America
Standard Occupational Classification Manual
Student Guide to Federal Financial Aid

Programs Trade Magazine
United States Government Manual
Wall Street Journal
Yellow Pages

Business

agribusiness
annual report
answering service
centralization
chairman
chairperson
chamber of commerce
cleaning services
commerce
consulting firm
corporate goals
corporate image
corporate planning
cost-conscious
cost sharing
costing techniques
credit manager
customer service
customer service representative
dealer compliance representative
decentralization
director
ecotourism
employment agencies
Encyclopedia of Associations
entrepreneur
executive search firm
expediter
fiscal year (FY)
florist
foreign imports
Fortune 500 company
franchise
franchisee
franchiser
franchising
free enterprise system
friendly takeover
goods-producing industries
gross domestic product
gross national product (GNP)
hostile takeover
hot line
in-house
inside collector
intermediary
job fair
lodging
mail order business
mall manager
market
Master of Business Administration (MBA)
merger
middleman
minimalizing
newsletter
no layoff policy
nondurable goods
nonprofit sector
organizational chart
outsourcing
overstaffing
partner
partnership
"pay or play" health insurance
personnel department
presentation skills
private sector
production goal
proprietor
quality circle
quality control
restructuring
resume services
rightsizing
rust belt
same period last year
Service Corps of Retired Executives (SCORE)
service-producing industries
shake-up
Small Business Administration
stable staff
staff
staffing
subordinate
subsidiaries
supervise
supervisor
takeover
task force
technological change
temporary placement agencies
testing services

top executive
top management
trade
trade association
troubleshoot
troubleshooter
turnaround time
turnover rate
understaffed
vendoring out
venture capitalist
Wall Street
white knight
Worker Readjustment and Retraining Notification Act (WARN)
working capital
Yellow Pages

C

Civil Rights

affirmative action
affirmative action coordinator
age bias
age discrimination
ageism
Bakke case
ceiling, glass
Commission on Civil Rights
employment discrimination lawsuits
Equal Employment Opportunity Law
Equal Employment Opportunity Commission (EEOC)
Equal Employment Opportunity counselor/representative
Equal Opportunity Employer (EOE)
glass ceiling
minorities
minorities, blind
minorities, disabled
minorities, older workers
minorities, women
racial discrimination
religious discrimination
reverse discrimination
sexual discrimination
sexual harassment

Civil Service

abandonment of position
absence (or absent) without leave (AWOL)
acceptable level of competence
accession
adjusted basic pay
administrative law judge
administrative workweek
admonishment
adverse action
agency
annual leave
annuitant
annuity
appeal
application forms
appointee
appointing officer
appointment
appointment, noncompetitive
appointment, provisional
appointment, superior qualifications
appointment, TAPER
appointment, temporary limited
appointment, term
area of consideration
area offices of the Office of Personnel Management
Armed Services experience
background check/investigation
break in service
candidate list
canvass
career appointment
career-conditional appointment
career reserved position
certificate
certification
certification, selective
certification, top of the register
change in duty station
change of appointing office
change to lower grade
civil service
civil service announcements
Civil Service Commission
Civil Service Commission Classification Standards
Civil Service Commission Handbook X-118
civil service eligibility
Civil Service Reform Act
civilian retiree

class of positions
classification appeal
classification review
classified service
classify
competitive area
competitive level
competitive position
competitive service
competitive status
consultant
consultant, management
consultant position
continuance
conversion
creditable military service
creditable service
critical element
denial of within-grade increase
detail
differentials
direct hiring authority
disability retirement
disability retirement pay (uniformed service)
discharge
discharge during probation/trial period
dismissal with prejudice
dismissal without prejudice
dual compensation
duty station
effective date
eligible
eligible list
entry on duty
entry on duty date
examination, assembled
examination, fitness-for-duty
examination, unassembled
excepted position
Excepted Service
Excepted Service agencies
executive inventory
executive resources board
executive schedule
expert
expert position
Federal Government service
Federal Merit System
Federal Personnel Manual (FPM)
Federal Personnel Manual Bulletin
Federal Personnel Manual Letter
Federal Personnel Manual Supplements
Federal Wage System
50
52
flexible workplace employment
frozen service
full-time work schedule
furlough
furlough without pay
general position
General Schedule (GS)
grade
grade restoration action
grade retention action
grade retention entitlement
hearing
hearing examiner
hearing officer
incentive awards
indefinite appointment/tenure
induction
injury compensation
interim geographic adjustment
intermittent work schedule
intervenor
intervenors as a matter of right
involuntary separation
lead agency
leave, annual
leave, court
leave, military
leave, sick
leave with pay
leave without pay
legal authority suffix
level of difficulty
limited appointment
locality adjustment
mass transfer
merged records personnel folder
merit pay system
merit promotion program
merit raise
merit staffing program
merit system
Merit Systems Protection Board
mobilization

national agency check and inquiries
nominating officer
nonappropriated fund employees
noncareer appointment
noncompetitive actions
Office of Personnel Management (OPM)
Official Personnel Folder (OPF)
OPF
part-time service
part-time work schedule
pass over
pay adjustment
pay cap
pay plan
pay rate determinant
pay retention entitlement
pay, severance
performance elements
Performance Management and Recognition System
performance review
performance standards
permissive intervenor
personnel investigation
personnel jacket
personnel office identifier
petition for appeal
petition for review
placement
pleadings
position
position change
position classification
position classification specialist/classifier
position description
position management
position risk level
position sensitivity
position survey
positions, "PL 313 Type"
post-employment restrictions
preference
preference, compensable disability
preference disability
preference, eligible
preference, husband
preference, mother
preference, tentative
preference, 30 percent or more disabled
preference, veteran
preference, widow or widower
preference, wife
previous retirement coverage
probationary period
promotion
promotion, career
promotion certificate
promotion, competititve
provisional appointment
Qualifications Review Board
qualified handicapped person
quality graduate
quality (step) increase
"rare bird" position
rate of basic pay
realignment
reassignment
record clerk
recruitment bonus
reduction in force (RIF)
reduction in grade
reduction in pay
reemployed annuitant
reemployment priority list
reemployment rights
regional offices of the Merit Systems Protection Board
register
reinstatement
reinstatement rights
relocation bonus
removal
restoration rights
retained rate
retention allowance
retention preference
retention register
retirement
retirement deferred
retirement, discontinued service
retirement-in lieu of involuntary action (ILIA)
retirement, optional
return to duty
review, classification
sabbatical
Schedule A
Schedule B
Schedule C

seasonal employee
security clearance
Senior Executive Service (SES)
senior level (SL) positions
separation
series
service computation date-leave
service control file
Service Record Card (Standard Form 7)
special Government employee
special pay adjustment for law enforcement officers
special salary rates
staffing differential
Standard Form 7 - Service Record Card
Standard Form 50 - Notification of Personnel Action
Standard Form 52 - Request for Personnel Action
Standard Form 75 - Request for Preliminary Employment Data
Standard Form 171 - Application for Federal Employment
standard of proof
standards
status employee
status quo employee
step
step adjustment
step increase
stipulation
substantially continuous service
superior qualifications appointment
supervisory differential
supplemental qualifications statements
survey classification
suspension
temporary appointment
tenure
tenure groups
tenure subgroups
term appointment
termination
time-after-competitive restriction
time-in-grade restriction
timeliness
tour of duty
transfer
transfer of function
unassembled examination
United States Civil Service Commission
unwritten exam
veterans preference
voucher
wage area
wage employees
within-grade denial
within-grade increase
without compensation
work schedule
work-study program

Cleaning *See* **Maintenance/Cleaning.**

Clergy *See* **Religion/Clergy.**

Clerical/Administrative Support

account collector
accounting clerk
accounting specialist (military)
adjuster
adjustment clerk
administrative secretary
administrative support specialist (military)
admitting clerk
advertising clerk
auditing clerk
bank teller
bill collector
billing clerk
bookkeeping, accounting, and auditing clerks
bordereau clerk
brokerage clerk
cashier
charge account clerk
claim clerk
clerical supervisor/manager
clerk
clerk-typist
correspondence clerk
counter clerk
court clerk
court reporter
court reporter (military)
credit authorizer
credit clerk
data entry keyer
dictating-machine transcriber/typist
dividend clerk
duplicating machine operator

field technician
hot line
information clerk
information officer
interpreter/translator (military)
journalist
linguist
maintenance administrator
maintenance technician
nonverbal communication/cues
office electrician
PBX
PBX installer
PBX operator
PBX repairer
public affairs specialist
public information officer (military)
public relations
public relations manager
public relations specialist
radio intelligence operator (military)
radio operator (military)
recording engineer
sonar operator (military)
switchboard operator
technical writer
telecommunications industry
telecommuting
telegraph plant maintainer
telephone installer
telephone line installer/repairer
telephone operator
telephone operator (military)
telephone repairer
telephone technician (military)
teletype installer
teletype operator (military)
teletype repairer (military)
toll-free number
translator
translator (military)
transmission engineer
transmitter engineer/operator
trouble locator
video-control engineer
writer
writer, technical

Compensation *See* **Money.**

Computer/Technology
applications programmer
artificial intelligence
bar code
common business oriented language (COBOL)
computer-aided design (CAD)
computer-aided engineering (CAE)
computer-aided instruction (CAI)
computer and office machine repairer
computer and peripheral equipment operator
computer-assisted instruction (CAI)
computer commuter
computer-integrated manufacturing (CIM)
computer operator (military)
computer programmer
computer programmer (military)
computer science
computer service technician
computer systems analyst
computer systems analyst (military)
computer systems development officer (military)
computer systems engineer (military)
data entry specialist (military)
data processing
data processing equipment repairer
data processing manager
data typist
electronic cottage
field engineer
field technician
information scientist
keypunch operator
machine readable
machine-tool operator, numerical control
neighborhood work center
numerical-control machine-tool operator
numerical-control tool programmer
penetration tester
programmer-analyst
programmer, computer
programmer, tool
readable
remote work
satellite office
semiconductor processor
software documentation writer
systems analysis
systems analyst, computer

systems programmer
telecommuting
tool programmer, numerical control
user friendly

Construction
applicator, drywall
bricklayer
bricklayer and concrete mason (military)
brickmason
building electrician (military)
bulldozer operator
carpenter
carpenter (military)
carpet installer
cement mason and terrazzo worker
concrete mason
concrete mason (military)
construction and building inspector
construction equipment mechanic
construction equipment operator
construction equipment operator (military)
construction inspector
construction laborer
construction machinery operator
construction manager
construction trades helper
construction unions
cost estimator
crane operator
cutter, welding
dozer operator
drywall finisher
drywall installer
electrician
elevator constructor
elevator installer/repairer
excavating and loading machine operator
floor covering installer
forklift operator
frame wirer
furnace installer
glazier
grader, dozer, and scraper operator
heating equipment technician
heavy equipment operator
heavy mobile equipment mechanic
helper, construction trades
hoist and winch operator
inspector, construction and building
insulation worker
ironworker
laborer
lather
marble setter
material moving equipment operator
mobile heavy equipment mechanic
painter
paving, surfacing, and tamping equipment operator
pipefitter
pipefitter (military)
pipelaying fitter
plasterer
plumber
plumber/pipefitter (military)
reinforcing ironworker
roofer
scraper operator
sheet metal worker
sheet metal worker (military)
Sheetrocker
ship electrician (military)
shipfitter
shipfitter (military)
sprinklerfitter
steamfitter
stonemason
structural and reinforcing ironworker
stucco mason
TAPER
terrazzo worker
tilesetter
tower-crane operator
welder (military)
welder, cutter, and welding machine operator
welding machine operator
winch operator

Corrections *See* **Law Enforcement/Corrections/Regulator.**

Counseling/Counselors
addiction counselor
AIDS counselor
camp counselor
career center
career counseling
career planning counselor
college career planning and placement counselor

director of student services
director, religious education and activities
distributive education
education administrator
education and training manager
educational assistant
educational psychologist
educational requirements
elementary school teacher
employee development
Employment and Training Administration
examination
examination, assembled
examination, unassembled
Federal Cooperative Education Program
fellowship
field trip
financial aid officer
grant
home study courses
instruct
instructor
instructor (military)
interest inventory tests
intern
job enrichment
job evaluation
job training
journeyman
journeyman (military)
journeyman level
junior college
kindergarten teacher
Lamaze instructor
liberal arts education
library media specialist
management trainee
Master of Business Administration (MBA)
media specialist
National Apprenticeship Program and
Apprenticeship Information
National Home Study Council
Naval Reserve Officers' Training Corps (NROTC)
night school
occupational education
occupational preparation
Officer Candidate School (OCS)
Officer Training School (OTS)
on-the-job-training
performance appraisal
Platoon Leaders Class (PLC) Program
Platoon Leaders Class-Law
polygraph test
postsecondary education
preschool teacher
Presidental Management Intern Program
principal, school
private school
professor
proprietory schools
recruit training (military)
registered apprentice (military)
registrar
research assistantship
Reserve Officers' Training Corps (ROTC)
sabbatical
scholarships
school crossing guard
school counselor
school librarian
school monitor
school nurse
school principal
school psychologist
school secretary
school social worker
school superintendent
school teacher
secondary school teacher
shadowing
stipend
student loan
teacher
teacher aide
teacher/instructor (military)
teaching assistantship
technical education
technical institute
tenure
testing
train
trainee
trainer
trainer (military)
training
training manager
training, on-the-job
training program

injury, traumatic
injury, work-related
intergovernmental personnel assignment
internal revenue agent
Job Corps
Job Grading System for Trades and Labor Occupations
Job Information Centers
level of difficulty
management official
Medicaid
Medicare
Merit Systems Protection Board (MSPB)
National Apprenticeship Program and Apprenticeship Information
National Credit Union Administration
National Labor Relations Board (NLRB)
National Mediation Board
National Security Agency
Nuclear Regulatory Commission
Occupational Outlook Handbook (OOH)
Occupational Safety and Health Administration (OSHA)
Office of Personnel Management (OPM)
PACE
"pay or play" health insurance
Peace Corps
Pension Benefit Guaranty Corporation (PBGC)
post-employment restrictions
Presidental Management Intern Program
President's Committee on Employment of People with Disabilities
protected individuals
public employment
public sector
public works
public works inspector
reverification
Secret Service
Secret Service agent
Small Business Administration
Standard Occupational Classification Manual
standards of conduct
state employment service
trade adjustment assistance
United States Government Manual
unwritten exam
VA compensation
VA pension
vacancy announcement
Veterans Administration
Veterans Administration compensation
Veterans Administration pension
W-2 wage and tax statement
wage grade system
wage-price freeze

Finance/Financial Services/Banking

accountant
accountant/auditor (military)
accounting
accounting auditor
accounting clerk
accounting specialist (military)
accrue
actuary
assets
audit supervisor
auditing
auditing clerk
auditor
auditor (military)
bank manager
bank teller
bookkeeper
bookkeeping, accounting, and auditing clerks
broker
broker, securities and financial services
brokerage clerk
brokers' floor representative
budget
budget analyst
certified public accountant
controller, financial
credit union
dividend clerk
financial manager
financial manager (military)
financial planner
financial records processor
financial services sales representative
fiscal year (FY)
loan officer and counselor
loan processing clerk
margin clerk
mortgage broker
mortgage loan officer
mortgage processor
mortgage underwriter

teller, bank
transfer clerk
treasurer
trust officer

Fitness *See* **Health/Medical/Fitness/Dental.**

Food/Beverage
baker
baker, manufacturing
banquet chef
bartender
bartender helper
bread baker
brewmaster
busboy
butcher and meat, poultry, and fish cutter
chef
chef de garde manger
convention services manager
cook
cooking machine operator and tender
counter attendent
dining room attendant
dishwasher
86
enrobing machine operator
executive chef
fast-food cook
fast-food worker
fish cleaner
fish cutter
food and beverage manager
food inspector
food service manager
food service manager (military)
food service specialist (military)
food technologist
host/hostess
institutional cook
kitchen worker
kosher cook
meatcutter
mixologist
pastry chef/baker
poissonier
poultry cutter
prep cook
presentation skills
restaurant and food service manager
saucier
short order cook
sous chef
specialty fast-food cook
wait staff
waiter/waitress
wholesale bakery driver-sales worker

H

Health/Medical/Fitness/Dental
acupuncturist
administrator, health services
aerobics instructor
ambulance driver/attendant
audiologist
cardiopulmonary/EEG technician (military)
child health associate
chiropractor
clinical dietician
clinical laboratory technician
clinical laboratory technologist
clinical nurse specialist
clinical perfusionist
community dietician
community health nurse
competitive medical plan
coroner
cosmetic surgeon
dental assistant
dental ceramist
dental hygienist
dental laboratory technician
dental laboratory technician (military)
dental specialist (military)
dentist
dentist (military)
dermatologist
dietician
dietician (military)
dispensing optician
doctor, chiropractic
doctor, medical
doctor, optometry
doctor, osteopathic
doctor, podiatric medicine
doctor, veterinary medicine
druggist
EKG

EKG technician
EEG
EEG technologist
electroneurodiagnostic technologist
emergency medical technician (EMT)
endocrinologist
endodontist
environmental health officer (military)
environmental health specialist (military)
fitness trainer
geriatric aide
gerontology aide
gynecologist
health benefit
Health Care Occupations
Health Diagnosing and Treating Practitioner Occupations
health inspector
health insurance
health maintenance organization (HMO)
health psychologist
health services administrator (military)
health services manager
HMO
home health aide
homemaker-home health aide
hospital administrator
hospital attendant
hospital nurse
hygienist, dental
immunology technologist
industrial nurse
laboratory technician, dental
laboratory worker, medical
licensed practical nurse (L.P.N.)
licensed vocational nurse (L.V.N.)
management dietician
manufacturing optician
massage therapist
maxillofacial surgeon
Medicaid
medical assistant
medical illustrator
medical laboratory technician
medical laboratory technician (military)
medical leave
medical microbiologist
medical records administrator
medical records clerk
medical records technician
medical records technician (military)
medical records transcriptionist
medical secretary
medical service technician (military)
medical social worker
medical technologist
Medicare
mental health assistant
mental health counselor
mental health technician
midwife
neonatologist
neurophysiologic technologist
nuclear medicine technologist
nuclear pharmacist
nurse
nurse anesthetist
nurse clinician
nurse midwife
nurse practitioner
nurse's aide
nursing
nursing aide
nursing home administrator
nursing home nurse
nursing technician (military)
nutrition adviser
nutrition counselor
nutritionist
obstetrician
occupational health nurse
Occupational Safety and Health Act (OSHA)
Occupational Safety and Health Administration (OSHA)
occupational safety and health inspector
Occupational Safety and Health Review Commission
occupational therapist
occupational therapist (military)
occupational therapy
occupational therapy aide/assistant
occupational therapy specialist (military)
office nurse
oncologist
operating room technician
operating room technician (military)
opthalmologist
oral pathologist

oral surgeon
orderly
orthodontist
osteopathic physician
paramedic
pathologist, speech-language
pediatric dentist
periodontist
pharmacist
pharmacist (military)
pharmacy assistant
pharmacy technician (military)
phlebotomist
physical and corrective therapy assistant/aide
physical therapist
physical therapist (military)
physical therapy specialist (military)
physician
physician assistant (PA)
physician assistant (military)
physician/surgeon (military)
podiatrist
podiatrist (military)
practical nurse, licensed (L.P.N.)
private duty nurse
prosthodontist
psychiatric aide
psychiatric nursing assistant
public health dentist
public health nurse
radiation therapy technologist
radiographer
radiologic technician (military)
radiologic technologist
radiopharmacist
recreational therapist
registered dietician
registered nurse (R.N.)
registered nurse (military)
research dietician
respiratory care practitioner
respiratory therapist
respiratory therapist (military)
sanitarian
sonographer
speech-language pathologist
speech pathologist
speech therapist (military)
sports medicine
surgeon
surgeon's assistant
surgical technician
surgical technologist
therapeutic recreational therapist
ultrasound technologist
vocational nurse, licensed
ward attendant
wellness programs
X-ray technician

Hospital Jobs *See* **Health/Medical/Fitness/Dental.**

Human Services *See* **Welfare/Human Services/Social Services.**

I

Informal Terms

back burner
ballpark figure
bargaining chip
bite the bullet
black economy
blue-collar worker
blue flu
bottom line
brain drain
breadwinner
brown bagging
brown drain
brownie points
brownnose
buddy system
bump
bumping
burnout
call the shots
can of worms
candy striper
canned
card-carrying
carry the can
close to the vest
cloth cap
company man
computer commuter
cop-out
cronyism
dead-end job

deep pockets
double dipper
86
eyeball
fast tracker
G-man
gatekeepers
Girl Friday
glass ceiling
go-between
golden parachute
green card
hard hat
headhunter
in-the-can
jack-of-all-trades
jargon
level playing field
moonlighting
new broom
off-the-books
on his/her/their watch
on-the-carpet
on-the-job
out-of-the-loop
people skills
perk
pigeonhole
pink-collar worker
pink slip
player
put in your papers
rent-a-cop
repo man
rightsizing
rust belt
sacked
safety net
spoils system
spook
stripper
suit
take
temp (temporary)
track record
unwritten exam
whistle blower
white-collar worker
white knight
workaholic
workhorse
yuppies

Inspectors
agricultural commodity inspector
agricultural quarantine inspector
air safety inspector
alcohol, tobacco, and firearms inspector
aviation safety inspector
building inspector
construction and building inspector
construction inspector
consumer safety inspector
customs inspector
electrical inspector
elevator inspector
environmental health inspector
fire inspector
firearms inspector
food inspector
health inspector
immigration inspector
industrial safety and health inspector
inspector and compliance officer, except construction
inspector, construction and building
inspector, tester, and grader
logging operations inspector
mechanical inspector
mine inspector
motor vehicle inspector
occupational safety and health inspector
plumbing inspector
postal inspector
public works inspector
quality assurance inspector
quality control inspector
railroad inspector
regulatory inspector
traffic inspector
wage-hour compliance inspector

Installer *See* **Repairer/Servicer/Installer/Operator/Specialist/Tender.**

Insurance
accidental death and dismemberment (AD&D)
adjuster

agent, insurance
bordereau clerk
broker, insurance
casualty insurance agent/broker
claim adjuster
claim clerk
claim examiner
claim interviewer
claim representative
COBRA
coinsurance
Comprehensive Omnibus Budget Reconciliation Act (COBRA)
contributory plan
co-pay
copayment
deductible
Federal Insurance Contribution Act (FICA)
FICA
health benefit
health insurance
health maintenance organization (HMO)
HMO
insurance adjuster
insurance agent
insurance examiner
insurance man
insurance processing clerk
insurance sales worker
life insurance agent
life underwriter
Medicaid
Medicare
Omnibus Budget Reconciliation Act of 1989 (OBRA)
out-of-pocket expense
"pay or play" health insurance
qualifying event, COBRA
terminating event, COBRA
underwriter
unemployment insurance
workmen's compensation

J

Job-related Terms

ad
alternative career
alternative patterns of work
applicant
application
application essay
application forms
appraisal interview
approach letter
aptitude testing
"at will" clause
avocation
blind ad
career
career assessment
career blueprint
career center
career changer
career exploration
career goals
career hop
career information delivery system (CIDS)
career ladder
career path
career planning
career planning counselor
career plateau
career research
career strategies
career switching
career values
careerism
careerist
ceiling, glass
ceiling, personnel
classified ad
cold calling
cold contact
contact person
contingent employees
cover letter
cutback
cyclical unemployment
dead-end job
dehire
demotion
discharge
disciplinary action
disciplinary interview
dismissed
displaced employee program
displaced homemaker
displaced worker

downgrading
downsizing
dress code
drug testing
dumbing down
employability
Employee Assistance Program (EAP)
employee orientation
employee relations
employee welfare manager
employment agencies
employment application
employment authorization expiration date
employment eligibility documents
employment eligibility verification requirements
employment interviewer
employment office
employment outlook
employment prospects
employment skills
Employment Standards Administration
Encyclopedia of Associations
Enlistment Options Program
entrance-level position
entry-level job
executive recruiter
executive search firm
Federal Job Information Centers
fired
firing
Form I-9
Forty Plus
free-lance
free-lancer
full field investigation
furlough
glass ceiling
headhunter
help wanted ad
Holland system
horizontal move
in the field
informational interview
intermittent employment/service
interview
interviewee
interviewer
job
job action
job ad
job analysis
job analyst
job application
job bank
job burnout
job classification
job club
Job Corps
job description
job evaluation
job fair
job freeze
job-growth areas
job hopper
job hunt
Job Information Centers
job interview
job lead
job market
job opening
job order
job outlook
job performance
job ready
job resume
job retention
job rotation
job satisfaction
job scams
job search
job security
job service
job sharing
job title
job training
Job Training Partnership Act (JTPA)
job vacancy announcement
jobless rate
Jobs Offered
Jobs Wanted
lay off
layoff
letter of commendation
letter of recommendation
lie detector test
life skills
maintenance review
manpower

manpower development specialist
manpower shortage
marketable skills
mass layoff
minimalizing
motion study
National Business Employment Weekly
networking
occupation
occupational analyst
occupational disease
occupational group
occupational hazard
occupational neurosis
occupational preparation
occupationally obsolete
odd jobs
office politics
office temp
open-ended questions
orientation
outplaced employee
outplacement
outplacement consultant
overseas jobs
part-time employment
personal contact
personnel action
personnel consultant
personnel department
personnel recruiter
personnel specialist (military)
personnel training specialist
place of employment
placement service
position
position title
Position Wanted
prime-age workers
private employment agency
profession
prohibited occupations
promotion
quality circle
quitting
recall
recareering
recruitment
reduction in force (RIF)
reentrant
references
replacement workers
residency requirement
resignation
resume
resume services
retention
revolving door policy
rightsizing
school career center
second career
self-employment
self-promotion techniques
sexual discrimination
sexual harassment
situations wanted ad
Social Security work credits
stable staff
staff
staffing
standby
state employment service
State Occupational Information Coordinating Committees (SOICC)
stress management
subordinate
suggestion
summer youth programs
supervise
supervisor
support services
survey classification
suspension
task force
temp (temporary)
temporary placement agencies
terminated
termination
terminology
trade
transfer
turnover rate
underemployment
undocumented alien
unemployed
unemployment compensation
unemployment insurance
unemployment rate

United States Employment Service
unskilled jobs
vacancy
vacancy announcement
visibility
vita
vocational counselor
vocational exploration
vocational guidance
vocational rehabilitation counselor
volunteer service
wage earner
wage worker
want ads
work environment
work ethic
work experience
work-family issues
work force
work force reduction
work order
work programs
work satisfaction
work-study program
workaholic
workhorse
working class
working conditions
working papers
working relationships
workingman
workload
workman
workmanlike
workplace
workroom
workshop
workstation
worktable
Yellow Pages
youth labor force

L

Labor Union *See* **Unions.**

Laboratory Jobs *See* **Health/Medical/ Fitness/Dental.**

Law Enforcement/Corrections/ Regulators

alcohol, tobacco, and firearms agent
animal control officer
aviation safety inspector
bailiff
border patrol officer
building inspector
compliance officer
consumer safety inspector
correction officer
correction specialist (military)
county sheriff
customs agent
deputy sheriff
detective (military)
detective, public
Equal Employment Opportunity Commission (EEOC)
FBI special agent
guard
guard, crossing
highway patrol officer
immigration inspector
jailer
law enforcement
law enforcement director (military)
Merit Systems Protection Board (MSPB)
military police (military)
mine inspector
National Labor Relations Board (NLRB)
National Mediation Board
occupational safety and health inspector
parole officer
police officer
policeman/policewoman
prison guard
revenue officer
Secret Service
Secret Service agent
security guard
security officer (military)
sheriff
special agent
special agent (military)
special pay adjustment for law enforcement officers
state police officer
state policeman
state trooper

store detective
warden
zoning enforcement officer

Law/Laws/Regulations

administrative law judge
admission
affidavit
affirmative action
affirmative action coordinator
allegation
Americans with Disabilities Act (ADA)
appeal
assemblyman
assemblywoman
attorney
Bakke case
barrister
character evidence
Civil Service Reform Act
class action
Comprehensive Omnibus Budget Reconciliation Act (COBRA)
constituents
continuance
contract
court clerk
deposition
document
elder law
Equal Employment Opportunity Law
Equal Employment Opportunity Commission (EEOC)
Executive order
Fair Labor Standards Act
grandfather clause
grievance
hearing
hearing examiner
hearing officer
injury, traumatic
injury, work-related
intervenor
intervenors as a matter of right
Job Training Partnership Act (JTPA)
judge
law
lawyer
lawyer (military)
legal assistant
legal authority suffix
legal secretary
legal technician (military)
legislator
medical examiner
Merit Systems Protection Board (MSPB)
National Mediation Board
notarized
notary public
Occupational Safety and Health Act (OSHA)
Occupational Safety and Health Review Commission
Older Workers Benefit Protection Act
Omnibus Budget Reconciliation Act of 1989 (OBRA)
paralegal
performance contracts
permissive intervenor
Platoon Leaders Class-Law
probation officer
provision
public defender
quasi-judicial
selectman
whistle blower
Worker Readjustment and Retraining Notification Act (WARN)
writ

Librarians/Libraries

academic librarian
acquisitions librarian
adult services librarian
bibliographer
bookmobile driver
bookmobile librarian
cataloger
children's librarian
classifier
community outreach librarian
librarian
library assistant
library binding worker
library media specialist
library technician
public librarian
school librarian
special librarian
young adult librarian

Lodging *See* **Travel/Lodging.**

Logging
brush cleaning laborer
chaser
choke setter
cruiser
faller
log grader/scaler
log handling equipment operator
log marker
logging equipment mechanic
logging operations inspector
logging tractor operator
picker
pulp piler
rigging slinger
river
tree trimmer
wood machine operator

M

Maintenance/Cleaning
building custodian
carpet cleaner
chimney sweep
cleaner
cleaner, vehicles and equipment
cleaning lady
cleaning services
custodian
day worker
equipment cleaner
general houseworker
greenskeeper
groundskeeper
highway maintenance worker
housekeeper
janitor
landscape gardener
landscape maintenance worker
laundromat attendant
laundry and drycleaning machine operator and tender
lawn service worker
maid
maintenance data analyst (military)
maintenance mechanic, general
private household worker
refuse collector
vehicle washer
washer, vehicle

Management *See* **Administrative/Management.**

Manufacturing/Production/Processing/Mining
assembler, electrical and electronic
assembler, machine
assembler, precision
baker, manufacturing
bleaching and dyeing machine operator, textile
blower
blue-collar worker
blue-collar worker supervisor
boilermaker
brazer
cabinetmaker
cannery worker
cementing and gluing machine operator and tender
coil winder, taper, and finisher
computer-integrated manufacturing (CIM)
continuous mining machine operator
cooking machine operator and tender
cost estimator
crushing, grinding, and polishing machine oerator
cutter, welding
cutting and slicing machine operator and tender
cutting and slicing machine setter and setup operator
dairy processing equipment operator and tender
die maker
dinkey operator
dipper
drier operator and tender
dyer
electrical and electronic assembler
electronic semiconductor processor
extruding and forming machine operator and tender
extruding and forming machine setter and setup operator
forming machine operator/tender
furniture and wood finisher
gauger
heater
keeper

kettle operator and tender
kiln operator and tender
machine assembler
machine feeder and offbearer
machine-tool operator/tender
machine-tool setter/setup operator
machinery mechanic, industrial
machinist
machinist (military)
manipulator operator
manufacturers' sales representative
manufacturing
material moving equipment operator
melter
millwright
mine cutting and channeling machine operator
mining engineer
mining equipment repairer
mining machine operator
molding and casting machine operator
nongarment sewing machine operator
painting and coating machine operator
painting, coating, and decorating worker, hand
paper coating machine operator
paper goods machine setting and setup operator
plastic molding and casting machine operator
plastics-working machine operator
plating and coating machine operator, metal
 and plastic
precision assembler
rock splitter, quarry
roller
roustabout
screen printing setter and setup operator
setter and setup operator, metalworking and
 plastics-working machines
setter and setup operator, soldering and
 brazing machines
silvering applicator
solderer and brazer
soldering and brazing machine operator/tender
soldering and brazing machine setter and setup
 operator
spray-machine operator
spray painter
steelworker
stove tender
textile bleaching and dyeing machine
 operator/tender
textile machine operator
textile machine setter/setup operator
tire building machine operator
tool-and-die maker
tool programmer, numerical control
tower-crane operator
tumbling barrel painter
wood machinist
woodworker, precision

Marine-related Occupations

able seaman
aquatic biologist
boat engine mechanic
boatswain
captain
deckhand
diver (military)
fisherman
marine biologist
marine engine mechanic (military)
marine engineer
marine engineer (military)
marine geologist
marine oiler
marine surveyor
master
mate
merchant marine
motorboat mechanic
rigger
rigger (military)
seaman
seaman (military)
ship captain
ship electrician (military)
ship engineer
ship engineer (military)
ship/submarine officer
shipfitter
stevedore

Mechanics

agricultural equipment mechanic
air-conditioning mechanic
air-conditioning mechanic, automotive
aircraft mechanic (military)
aircraft mechanic and engine specialist
auto mechanic
automatic transmission mechanic

automobile mechanic (military)
automotive air-conditioning mechanic
automotive mechanic
automotive-radiator mechanic
boat engine mechanic
bus mechanic
communications equipment mechanic
construction equipment mechanic
diesel mechanic
elevator mechanic
engine mechanic (military)
engine specialist
farm equipment mechanic
front-end mechanic
general maintenance mechanic
heating, air-conditioning, and refrigeration mechanic
heating and cooling mechanic (military)
heavy equipment mechanic (military)
heavy mobile equipment mechanic
lawn and garden equipment mechanic
logging equipment mechanic
machinery mechanic, industrial
maintenance mechanic, general
marine engine mechanic (military)
mobile heavy equipment mechanic
motorboat mechanic
motorcycle mechanic
optical mechanic
ordnance mechanic
powerhouse mechanic (military)
radio repairer and mechanic
refrigeration mechanic
small-engine mechanic
truck mechanic
tune-up mechanic

Media
anchorman
announcer
audio control engineer
audiovisual production director (military)
audiovisual production specialist (military)
biographer
broadcast news analyst
broadcast standards editor
censor
columnist
commentator
copy writer
correspondent
critic
director
disk jockey
editor
ghostwriter
in-the-can
journalist
motion picture projectionist
movie projectionist
network
news anchor
newscaster
newsman
newspaper reporter
newswriter
producer
radio and television announcer (military)
radio and television announcer and newscaster
reporter/correspondent
reporter/newswriter (military)
sportscaster
talk show host
television announcer and newscaster
television camera operator
television industry
weathercaster
weatherman

Medical *See* **Health/Medical/Fitness/Dental.**

Military/Coast Guard/Veterans
absence (or absent) without leave (AWOL)
accountant/auditor
accounting specialist
active duty
administrative support specialist
advanced degree program
advanced formal school
advanced individual training
advanced training
aerospace engineer
air crew member
Air Force
Air Force Reserve
Air National Guard
air traffic control manager
air traffic controller
aircraft electrician

aircraft launch and recovery specialist
aircraft mechanic
airplane navigator
airplane pilot
allowance
amnesty discharge
Armed Forces
Armed Forces experience
Armed Services Vocational Aptitude Battery
Army
Army Civilian Acquired Skills Program
artillery crew member
artillery officer
ASVAB
attache
audiovisual production director
audiovisual production specialist
auditor
automobile mechanic
automotive body repairer
AWOL
band manager
base
basic formal school
basic pay
basic training
blasting specialist
boiler technician
bricklayer and concrete mason
broadcast and recording technician
building electrician
cardiopulmonary/EEG technician
cargo specialist
carpenter
caseworker and counselor
chaplain
chemist
civil engineer
class A school
class B school
class C school
clemency discharge
clothing and fabric repairer
Coast Guard
combat engineer
commissioned
commissioned officer
communications manager
compressed gas technician
computer data entry specialist
computer equipment repairer
computer operator
computer programmer
computer systems analyst
computer systems development officer
computer systems engineer
computer systems manager
concrete mason
construction equipment operator
continuing education
correction specialist
court reporter
creditable service
Delayed Entry Program (DEP)
dental laboratory technician
dental specialist
dentist
DEP
Department of Veterans Affairs
detective
dietician
direct appointment
direct commission
disabled veteran
discharge under honorable conditions
dispatcher
diver
drafter
duty
duty assignment
electrical/electronics engineer
electrical products repairer
electronic instrument repairer
electronic weapons systems repairer
emergency management officer
emergency management specialist
engine mechanic
enlisted commissioning programs
enlisted member
enlisted pay grades
enlisted personnel
enlistee
enlistment agreement/contract
Enlistment Options Program
environmental health officer
environmental health specialist
financial manager
firefighter

welder
well driller

Mining *See* **Manufacturing/Production/Processing/Mining.**

Miscellaneous Services

advance man
antiques dealer
appraiser
appraiser, real estate
archery instructor
au pair
auctioneer
baby-sitter
baggage porter
bagger
barber
beautician
beauty operator
bellhop
bodyguard
butler
candy striper
caretaker
carpet cleaner
caterer
catering
cemetery worker
chauffeur
childcare worker
chimney sweep
coin dealer
collateral lender
companion
concierge
conservator
cosmetologist
counter clerk
crossing guard
curator
day worker
detective, private
dispatcher
electrologist
embalmer
ergonomist
esthetician
estimator
executive housekeeper
facialist
facilitator
family daycare provider
fashion model
firefighter
fishing guide
fitness trainer
floral designer
funeral attendant
funeral director
furniture upholsterer
gardener
gemologist
genealogist
governess
grinder and polisher, hand
grocery clerk
guide
gunsmith
hair colorist
hair stylist
hand packer/packager
handler
house detective
hunter
hunting guide
hypnotherapist
hypnotist
illusionist
image consultant
infant nurse
jeweler
lifeguard
literary agent
lobby attendant
lobbyist
locksmith
luggage maker
magician
makeup artist
manicurist
masseur
masseuse
material mover, hand
messenger
model
mortitian
museum curator
nail technician

nanny
ophthalmic dispenser
optical goods worker
optician, dispensing
panhandler
paper carrier
paperboy
paperhanger
paraprofessional
parking lot attendant
pedicurist
personal attendant
personal secretary
pest controller
presser
private detective/investigator
professional athlete
purchasing agent and manager
ranger
receptionist
repo man
repossessor
rigger
roadie
saddlemaker
service station attendant
stevedore
stock boy
stocker
stockroom clerk
survey worker
taxidermist
telemarketing representative
telephone-answering-service operator
tester
thanatologist
title abstractor
title examiner
title searcher
trapper
troubleshooter
upholsterer
usher
watchmaker
weigher

Money

administratively uncontrolled overtime (AUO)
advance
after-tax income
allowance (military)
automatic pay increases
back pay
base rate
basic pay (military)
basic rate
before-tax income
binding award
bonus
bonus plan
buyout
by-the-piece
commission
comparable worth
compensation
compensation manager
compensation specialist
consumer price index (CPI)
cost-of-living adjustments/allowance (cola)
cost-of-living index
cost sharing
CPI
cutback
deadheading pay
death benefit
deductible
deep pockets
denial of within-grade increase
differentials
disability retirement pay (uniformed service)
discretionary income
disposable personal income
draw
dual compensation
dues
early retirement incentive
earning potential
earnings
employee, exempt
enlisted pay grades (military)
enlistment agreement/contract (military)
environmental differential
equal pay for equal work
escalation clause
executive schedule
expense account
Federal Wage System
fellowship
financial aid officer

foundation
401(k) plan
403(b) plan
gain-sharing plan
General Schedule (GS)
grade retention entitlement
grant
gross pay
guaranteed pay
hazard pay (military)
holiday premium pay
hourly wage
housing allowance (military)
incentive and special pay (military)
incentive awards
incentive pay
interim geographic adjustment
jury duty pay
Keogh plan
kickback
locality adjustment
longevity pay
Merit Pay System
merit raise
mileage reinbursement
minimum wage
National Credit Union Administration
net/net pay
night differential
noncontributory plan
off-the-clock
officer pay grades (military)
overtime pay
pay adjustment
pay cap
pay equity
pay grade (military)
pay plan
pay rate determinant
pay retention entitlement
pay scale
pay, severance
payola
payroll clerk
payroll deductions
payroll specialist (military)
Performance Management and Recognition System
periodic increase
periodic step increase
piece rate
piece work
portal-to-portal rate
premium pay
Prevailing Rate System
production bonus
profit sharing
quarters (military)
rate
rate of basic pay
recruitment bonus
reduction in pay
relocation bonus
remuneration
retained rate
retention allowance
retroactive pay
salary
salary negotiations
salary range
salary review
scholarship
severance arrangements
severance pay
shift differential
Social Security payroll tax
Social Security Supplemental Security Income (SSI)
special pay
special pay adjustment for law enforcement officers
special salary rates
staffing differential
standby pay
step
step adjustment
step increase
stipend
stock bonus
stock plan
student loan
subsistence (military)
supervisory differential
telefundraising
tip
tool allowance
tuition
tuition reimbursement

tuition repayment
underground economy
unemployment compensation
uniform allowance
union scale
VA compensation
vacation pay
Veterans Administration compensation
Veterans Administration pension
W-2 wage and tax statement
wage area
wage employees
wage grade system
wage indexation system
wage-price freeze
wage restraint
wage scale
wage statement
wage worker
wages
weekend pay
within-grade denial
within-grade increase
without compensation
working capital

Motor Vehicles *See* **Automotive.**

Music
band manager (military)
choral director
composer
conductor, orchestra
instrumental musician
musical instrument repairer and tuner
musician
musician (military)
musicologist
orchestra conductor
piano tuner
pipe-organ tuner and repairer
singer
tuner, musical instruments

N

Natural Gas *See* **Power.**

Newspapers *See* **Media.**

Nuclear Power *See* **Power.**

Nurses *See* **Health/Medical/Fitness/Dental.**

O

Operator *See* **Repairer/Servicer/Installer/Operator/Specialist/Tender.**

P

Pay *See* **Money.**

Pension/Retirement/Social Security
annuitant
annuity
civilian retiree
contributory plan
credits, Social Security
death benefit
deferred retirement
disability retirement
disability retirement pay (uniformed service)
disability, Social Security
discontinued service retirement
double-dipper
early retirement
early retirement incentive
Employee Retirement Income Security Act (ERISA)
Federal Employees' Retirement System
Federal Retirement Thrift Investment Board
FICA
401(k) plan
403(b) plan
injury compensation
injury, traumatic
injury, work-related
Keogh plan
optional retirement
Pension Benefit Guaranty Corporation (PBGC)
phased retirement
previous retirement coverage
put in your papers
Railroad Retirement Board
reduced benefits, Social Security

reemployed annuitant
retiree job bank
retirement
retirement age, Social Security
retirement benefits (military)
retirement deferred
retirement, discontinued service
retirement-in lieu of involuntary action (ILIA)
retirement incentive plans
retirement, optional
Social Security benefits
Social Security death benefit
Social Security disability benefit
Social Security payroll tax
Social Security records
Social Security reduced benefits
Social Security retirement age
Social Security Supplemental Security Income (SSI)
Social Security survivors benefits
Social Security work credits
Supplemental Security Income (SSI)
unfunded plans
vesting
window

Personal Services *See* **Miscellaneous Services.**

Phone Numbers *See* **Addresses/Phone Numbers.**

Photography/Photographic Developing
automatic mounter
automatic print developer
camera operator
camera operator, offset printing
camera operator, television, video, and motion pictures
camera repairer
cameraman
cinematographer
color film operator
color laboratory technician
color-printer operator
colorist
darkroom technician
developer, film
film developer
film mounter, automatic
laboratory technician, film
motion picture camera operator
motion picture camera operator (military)
photofinishing laboratory worker
photographer (military)
photographer and camera operator
photographic equipment repairer
photographic equipment repairer (military)
photographic process worker
photographic retoucher
photographic spotter
photojournalist
photoprocessing specialist (military)
platemaker
print developer, photographic
printer operator
stripper
takedown sorter

Physical Fitness *See* **Health/Medical/Fitness/Dental.**

Physicians *See* **Health/Medical/Fitness/Dental.**

Police *See* **Law Enforcement/Corrections/Regulators.**

Postal Service
casual worker
Christmas casual
collect on delivery (COD)
Employee Involvement Program
flexi-employee
full-time regular employee
letter carrier
mail carrier
mailhandler
mailman
officer-in-charge
Official Personnel Folder
part-time flexible employees
part-time regular employees
periodic step increase
piece rate
pigeonhole
Postal Carrier Executive Service
postal clerk
postal director (military)
postal exams
postal inspector

Postal Service
Postal Service schedule
postal specialist (military)
postmaster
probationary period
quality assurance
quality (step) increase
register
7:01 rule
step increase
swing
swing time
trick
United States Postal Service
utility carrier

Power/Gas
customer service representative, utilities
electric power distributor and dispatcher
electric power generating plant operator
electrical powerline installer/repairer
engineer, stationary
gas plant operator
line installer and cable splicer
line installer and repairer (military)
load dispatcher
nuclear engineer
nuclear engineer (military)
Nuclear Regulatory Commission
nuclear technician
power dispatcher
power distributor
power generating plant operator
power plant electrician (military)
power plant operator (military)
power reactor operator
powerhouse mechanic (military)
powerline installer and repairer
switchboard operator
systems operator
utilities customer service representative
utilities meter reader
utilities operations manager
utility

Printing/Binding
bindery worker
blankbook binding worker
bookbinder
bookbinding worker
compositor
dot etcher
edition binding worker
job binding worker
library binding worker
lithographic and photoengraving worker
lithographic dot etcher
manifold binding worker
pamphlet binding worker
photoengraving worker
press operator, printing
print shop stenographer
printing press operator
printing specialist (military)
proofreader and copy marker
scanner operator, offset printing
typesetter

Prisons *See* **Law Enforcement/ Corrections/Regulators.**

Processing *See* **Manufacturing/ Production/Processing/Mining.**

Production *See* **Manufacturing/ Production/Processing/Mining.**

Professional Specialties
abstractor
aeronautical drafter
architect
architect, landscape
architectural drafter
archivist
certified arbitrator
certified public accountant (CPA)
choreologist
community planner
contract specialist
CPA
electronic drafter
engineering manager
geodetic surveyor
geophysical prospecting surveyor
land surveyor
landscape architect
landscape curator
maintenance data analyst (military)
map editor
mapping manager
mapping scientist

marine surveyor
mechanical drafter
operations research analyst
optometrist
optometrist (military)
orthotic specialist (military)
orthotist
photogrammetrist
regional planner
surveying and mapping manager (military)
surveyor
urban/regional planner

Publications *See* **Books/Publications.**

Qualities/Skills/Actions/General Terms

ability
accuracy
aesthetic
ambience
analyze
approval
aptitudes
assertiveness
assess
assets
assign
attitude
authority
authorize
consolidation
control
craft
decision making
delegate
delegating
dexterity
direct
empower
endorse
enhance
esthetic
estimate
ethical conduct
ethics
euphemism
evaluate
execute
expedite
forecasting
function
goal setting
goals
impartial
implement
inform
inhibition
initiate
inspect
instruct
intangible
intermittent
interpersonal skills
interpret
judgment
leadership skills
liaison
manage
manual dexterity
masculine career stereotypes
mechanical aptitude
mechanization
minorities
monitor
morale
motivated
motivating
nepotism
objective
obsolete
organization
outlook
patience
people skills
perform
performance
potential
practitioner
prerequisite
principle
productivity
profitability
promote
prototype
qualification requirements
qualifications
reasoning ability
recipient

chemical plant and system operator
clothing and fabric repairer (military)
coin machine servicer and repairer
commercial and industrial electronic equipment repairer
computer and office machine repairer
computer and peripheral equipment operator
computer equipment repairer (military)
computer operator (military)
computer service technician
construction equipment operator
construction equipment operator (military)
construction machinery operator
continuous mining machine operator
cooking machine operator and tender
customers' engineer
data processing equipment repairer
drywall installer
duplicating machine operator
electric meter installer/repairer
electric power generating plant operator
electrical/electronics technician
electrical inspector
electrical powerline installer/repairer
electrical products repairer (military)
electromedical equipment repairer
electronic home entertainment equipment repairer
electronic instrument repairer (military)
electronic weapons systems repairer (military)
electronics repairer, commercial and industrial equipment
elevator installer/repairer
elevator repairer
engine specialist
enrobing machine operator
environmental health specialist (military)
excavating and loading machine operator
extruding and forming machine operator and tender
extruding and forming machine setter and setup operator
field engineer
food service specialist (military)
furnace operator/tender
home appliance and power tool repairer
home entertainment electronic equipment repairer
industrial electronic equipment repairer
industrial machinery repairer
industrial truck and tractor operator
instrument repairer
inventory specialist (military)
kettle operator and tender
kiln operator and tender
leather repairer
log handling equipment operator
logging tractor operator
metalworking and plastics-working machine operator
metalworking machine operator
mining equipment repairer
mining machine operator
mixing and blending machine operator and tender
motor vehicle body repairer
motor vehicle repairer
musical instrument repairer and tuner
numerical-control machine-tool operator
office machine and cash register servicer
office machine repairer
oven operator/tender
packaging and filling machine operator
painting and coating machine operator
paving equipment operator (military)
paving, surfacing, and tamping equipment operator
peripheral equipment operator, electronic data processing
petroleum pump systems operator
petroleum supply specialist (military)
photographer and camera operator
photographic equipment repairer
photographic equipment repairer (military)
photoprocessing specialist (military)
physical therapy specialist (military)
plastic molding and casting machine operator
plastics-working machine operator
power tool repairer, home appliance
powerline installer and repairer
precision instrument repairer
precision instrument repairer (military)
printer operator
printing press operator
printing specialist (military)
radar and sonar equipment repairer (military)
radar and sonar operator (military)
radio equipment repairer (military)

radio intelligence operator (military)
radio operator (military)
railroad brake operator
recruiting specialist (military)
refractory repairer
religious program specialist (military)
repairman
roasting, baking, and drying machine
operator/tender
sales and stock specialist (military)
screen printing setter and setup operator
separating and still machine operator/tender
setter and setup operator, metalworking and
plastics-working machine
setter and setup operator, soldering and
brazing machine
setter and setup operator, textile machine
sewage treatment plant operator
sewer and sewing machine operator, apparel
Sheetrocker
shoe repairer
shoe sewing machine operator and tender
soldering and brazing machine operator/tender
soldering and brazing machine setter and setup
operator
sonar operator (military)
space systems specialist (military)
spray-machine operator
stock and inventory specialist (military)
streetcar operator
switchboard operator
systems operator
telegraph plant maintainer
telephone-answering-service operator
telephone line installer/repairer
telephone operator
telephone operator (military)
telephone repairer
teletype installer
teletype operator (military)
teletype repairer (military)
television camera operator
television service technician
tender, chemical
textile bleaching and dyeing machine
operator/tender
textile machine operator
textile machine setter/setup operator
tire building machine operator
tow truck operator
tower-crane operator
transportation specialist (military)
treatment plant operator, water and wastewater
TV repairer
VCR repairer
vending machine servicer and repairer
wastewater treatment plant operator
watchmaker
water and sewage treatment plant operator
(military)
water and wastewater treatment plant operator
welder, cutter, and welding machine operator
welding machine operator

Retirement *See* **Pension/Retirement/Social Security.**

S

Sales/Rental

account executive
agent, purchasing
agent, real estate
appraiser
broker, real estate
broker, securities and financial services
brokerage
brokers' floor representative
buyer, wholesale and retail trade
checker
cold calling
cold contact
driver-sales worker
equipment rental clerk
financial services sales representative
industrial buyer
industrial sales worker
insurance sales worker
jobber
life insurance agent
life underwriter
manufacturers' agent
manufacturers' representative
manufacturers' sales representative
marketing
marketing manager
multilevel selling/marketing
nonstore retailing
real estate agent
real estate appraiser

real estate broker
Realtor
registered representative, securities
retail buyer
retail sales worker
route driver
sales
sales and stock specialist (military)
sales associate
sales engineer
sales manager
sales representative
salesman
securities director
securities sales representative
securities trader
services sales representative
stock broker
stock specialist
store manager (military)
telemarketer
telemarketing
television selling
used car salesman
wholesale and retail buyer
wholesale bakery driver-sales worker
wholesale sales representative
wood machine operator

Scientists/Science-related

agricultural scientist
agronomist
analytical chemist
animal breeder
animal scientist
anthropologist
apiculturist
aquatic biologist
archaeologist
astronomer
biochemist
biological scientist
biologist
botanist
cartographer
chemist
chemist (military)
climatologist
clinical psychologist
cognitive psychologist
comparative psychologist
conservation scientist
consumer psychologist
counseling psychologist
dairy scientist
demographer
demographics
developmental psychologist
ecologist
economic geographer
economist
educational psychologist
engineering psychologist
entomologist
ergonomics
ergonomist
ethnobotanist
experimental psychologist
extractive metallurgist
forensic pathologist
forensic psychiatrist
forest and conservation worker
forester
geochemical oceanographer
geographer
geological oceanographer
geologist
geophysicist
gerontologist
health psychologist
herpetologist
historian
horticulturist
hydrologist
icthyologist
industrial psychologist
information scientist
life scientist (military)
limnologist
lupinologist
mammalogist
mapping scientist
marine biologist
marine geologist
mathematician
mechanical metallurgist
medical geographer
medical microbiologist
meteorologist

meteorologist (military)
microbiologist
mineralogist
oceanographer
oceanographer (military)
operational meteorologist
organic chemist
organizational psychologist
ornithologist
paleontologist
personality psychologist
physical chemist
physical geographer
physical metallurgist
physical meteorologist
physical oceanographer
physical science
physicist
physicist (military)
physiological psychologist
physiologist
plant breeder
political geographer
political scientist
poultry scientist
psychologist
psychologist (military)
range scientist
regional geographer
school psychologist
science manager
science technician
scientific illustrator
seismologist
social psychologist
social scientist
sociologist
soil conservationist
space science
statistician
stratigrapher
synoptic meteorologist
technical writer
technological change
transportation geographer
urban geographer
weather observer (military)
writer, technical
zoologist

Secretarial Services
administrative secretary
legal secretary
medical secretary
membership secretary
technical secretary

Servicer *See* **Repairer/Servicer/Installer/Operator/Specialist/Tender.**

Skills *See* **Qualities/Skills/Actions/General Terms.**

Slang *See* **Informal Terms.**

Social/Cultural/Geographic
baby boomers
behavior modification
consumer sector
consumerism
gender-blind companies
handicapped person
Hispanic worker
labor force trends
metropolitan area

Social Security *See* **Pension/Retirement/Social Security.**

Social Services *See* **Welfare/Human Services/Social Services.**

Specialist *See* **Repairer/Servicer/Installer/Operator/Specialist/Tender.**

Standards/Statistics/Evaluation
absenteeism rate
accreditation
admissions requirements
benchmark
business license
Career College Association
career goals
certification
certification requirements
Civil Service Commission Classification Standards
conflict of interest
consumer price index (CPI)
critical element

Statistics *See* **Standards/Statistics/Evaluation.**

T

Taxes

Technician/Technologist

engineering technician
euthanasia technician
field technician
food technologist
fuel and chemical laboratory technician (military)
histology technician
immunology technologist
industrial electronics technician
industrial engineering technician
laboratory animal technician
laboratory animal technologist
laboratory technician, dental
laboratory technician, film
legal technician (military)
library technician
maintenance technician
medical laboratory technician
medical laboratory technician (military)
medical records technician
medical records technician (military)
medical service technician (military)
medical technologist
mental health technician
metallographic technician
microbiology technologist
neurophysiologic technologist
noise pollution technician
nuclear medicine technologist
nuclear technician
nursing technician (military)
operating room technician
operating room technician (military)
ophthalmic laboratory technician
optometric technician (military)
orthodontic technician
orthopedic technician (military)
petroleum technician
pharmacy technician (military)
radiation therapy technologist
radio and television service technician
radiologic technician (military)
radiologic technologist
removable partial denture technician
science technician
service technician
social service technician
submarine cable equipment technician
surgical technician
surgical technologist
survey technician
surveying and mapping technician (military)
technician
technologist
telephone technician (military)
television service technician
ultrasound technologist
veterinary technician

Technologist *See* **Technician/Technologist.**

Technology *See* **Computer/Technology.**

Telephone Numbers *See* **Addresses/Phone Numbers.**

Television *See* **Media.**

Tender *See* **Repairer/Servicer/Installer/Operator/Specialist/Tender.**

Testing *See* **Education/Testing/Training.**

Therapist/Therapy
aromatherapist
corrective therapy assistant/aide
inhalation therapist
massage therapist
occupational therapist
occupational therapist (military)
occupational therapy
occupational therapy aide/assistant
occupational therapy specialist (military)
physical therapist
physical therapist (military)
physical therapy specialist (military)
recreational therapist
registered occupational therapist
respiratory therapist
respiratory therapist (military)
therapeutic recreational therapist

Time-related
administrative workweek
administratively uncontrolled overtime (AUO)
alternative patterns of work
annual leave
basic workweek

close of business
comp time
compensatory time off
cutoff time
daily tour of duty
downtime
fiscal year (FY)
flexitime
flextime
full-time work schedule
indefinite appointment/tenure
intermittent work schedule
job sharing
leave, annual
leave, court
leave, military
leave policy
leave, sick
leave with pay
leave without pay
maternity leave
medical leave
night-owl shift
night shift
off-the-clock
on-break
on-call employee
on-the-clock
overtime
overtime pay
part-time work schedule
punch in
punch out
service day
service obligation (military)
7:01 rule
shift
sick days
split shift
straight time
swing
swing time
time-after-competitive restriction
time-in-grade restriction
time management
timekeeping clerk
timeliness
tour of duty
trick
workweek

Trade Union *See* **Union.**

Training *See* **Education/Testing/Training.**

Transportation

aircraft technician
airline reservation and ticket agent
ambulance driver/attendant
brake operator
bus driver
bus mechanic
cargo specialist (military)
chauffeur
communications, transportation, and utilities operations manager
controller, air traffic
flight attendant
gate agent
helicopter pilot
helicopter pilot (military)
locomotive engineer
rail yard engineer
railroad brake operator
railroad conductor
railroad inspector
Railroad Retirement Board
road conductor
run
signal or track switch maintainer
sleeper run
steward/stewardess
streetcar operator
subway operator
switch operator
taxi driver
traffic controller, air
traffic inspector
transportation industry
transportation/maintenance manager (military)
transportation manager
transportation manager (military)
transportation specialist (military)
transportation ticket agent
truck driver
truck driver (military)
trucker
turnaround

yard clerk
yard conductor

Travel/Lodging

agent, reservation
lodging specialist (military)
reservation agent
reservationist
resorts
ticket agent
ticket clerk
ticket seller
tour conductor/guide
travel accommodations rater
travel agent
travel clerk

Trucking *See* Transportation.

U

Unions

American Federation of Labor and Congress of Industrial Organizations (AFL-CIO)
arbitration
arbitrator
bargaining agent
bargaining, collective
bargaining, industrywide
bargaining rights
bargaining unit
binding award
blue flu
business agent
closed shop
collective bargaining
collective bargaining agreement
collective bargaining unit
conciliation
conciliator
conciliator, labor relations
construction unions
consultation
contract
contracting out
craft union
dues
exclusive bargaining agent
exclusive bargaining representative
exclusive recognition
exclusive representative
Federal Labor Relations Authority
Federal Service Impasses Panel (FSIP)
grievance
grievance interview
grievance procedure
impasse procedures
industrial relations
intermediary
job action
labor-management relations
labor organization
labor relations
labor relations manager
lockout
mediation
mediator
National Labor Relations Board (NLRB)
negotiability
negotiated agreement
negotiated contract
negotiated grievance procedure
negotiations
nonunion contractors
permanent arbitrator
provision
quickie strike
representation
representation election
slowdown
Standards of Conduct for Labor Organizations
steward, union
strike
unfair labor practices
union
union apprenticeship programs
union hiring hall
union scale
union shop
United Auto Workers (UAW)
walkout
wildcat strike
work-to-rule

United States Postal Service *See* Postal Service.

Utilities

communications, transportation and utilities operations manager
customer service representative, utilities

powerline installer and repairer
utilities customer service representative
utilities meter reader
utilities operations manager
utility

V

Veterans *See* **Military/Coast Guard/Veterans.**

W

Welfare/Human Services/Social Services

case aides
caseworker
caseworker and counselor (military)
child welfare worker
community outreach worker
family service worker
human services worker
psychiatric social worker
school social worker
social service technician
social work assistant
social worker
social worker (military)
welfare eligibility worker and interviewer

If you liked this JIST book and would like to have input on terms to include in a future edition, please answer the questions on this page and return it to:

JIST Works, Inc. • Attn: Editor
720 North Park Avenue • Indianapolis, IN 46202-3431.

Name of book purchased:

Name ______________________________ Title ________________

Company ____

Address ____

City ________________________ State ____ Zip ________________

____

Phone (______) ________ - __________________ Ext. __________

Please check the appropriate answers to the following questions:

1. Where did you buy your JIST book?
   - ☐ Bookstore (name:) ______________________________________
   - ☐ Catalog (name:) ____
   - ☐ Direct from JIST ☐ Other: _______________________________
2. How many JIST books do you own? ☐ 1 ☐ 2-5 ☐ More than 5
3. What influenced your purchase of this JIST book?
   - ☐ Personal recommendation ☐ Advertisement ☐ Price
   - ☐ JIST catalog ☐ Other ________________________________
4. How would you rate the overall content of the book?
   - ☐ Very Good ☐ Good ☐ Satisfactory ☐ Poor
5. What do you like *best* about this JIST book? ____________________
6. What do you like *least* about this JIST book? ____________________
7. Please feel free to list any other comments you may have about this JIST book.

   ____

   ____
8. What are some terms that should be included in a future edition of this book?